A DECADE OF TECHNICAL INNOVATION

CHEVROLETS OF THE 1950s

David W. Temple

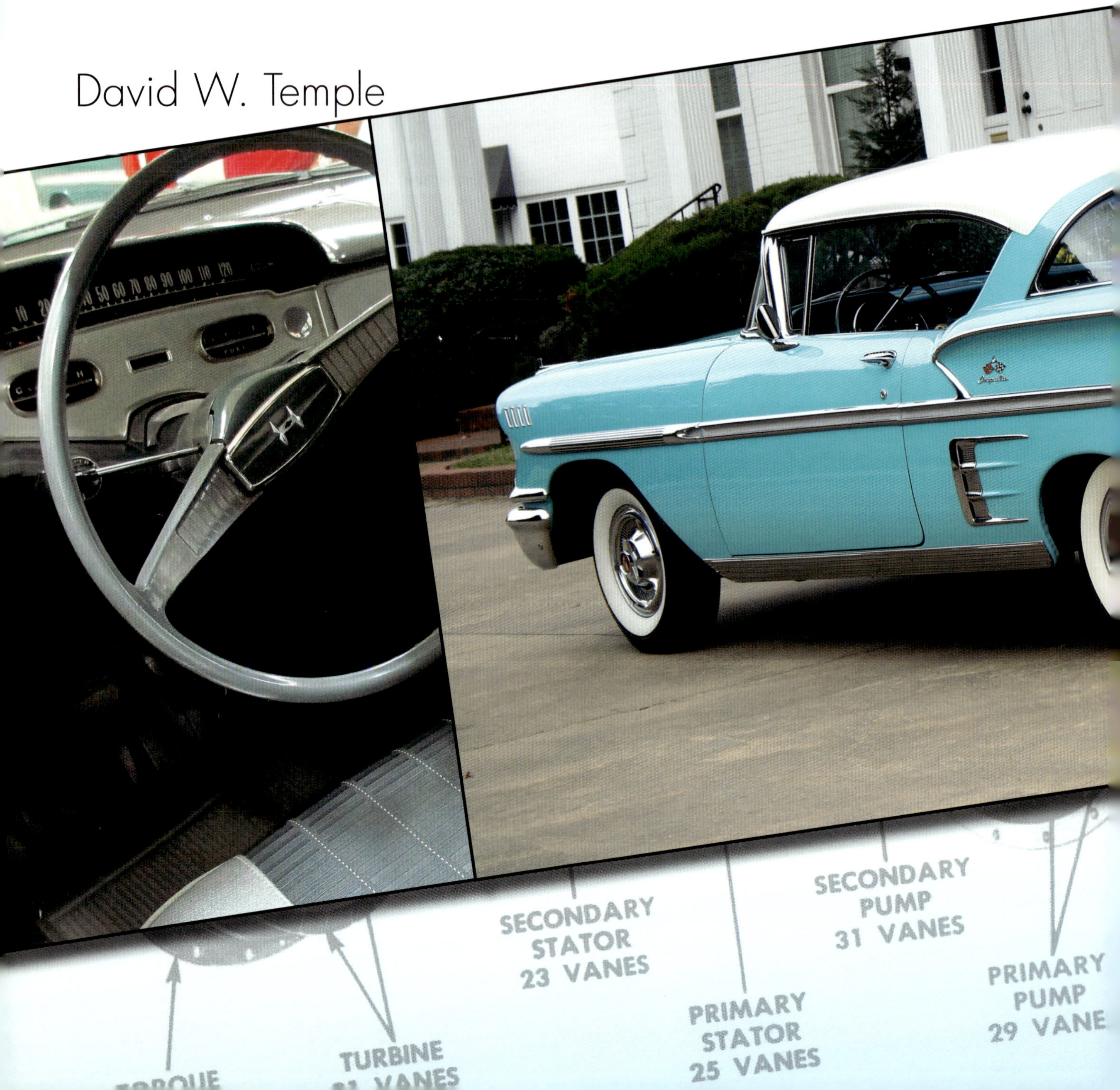

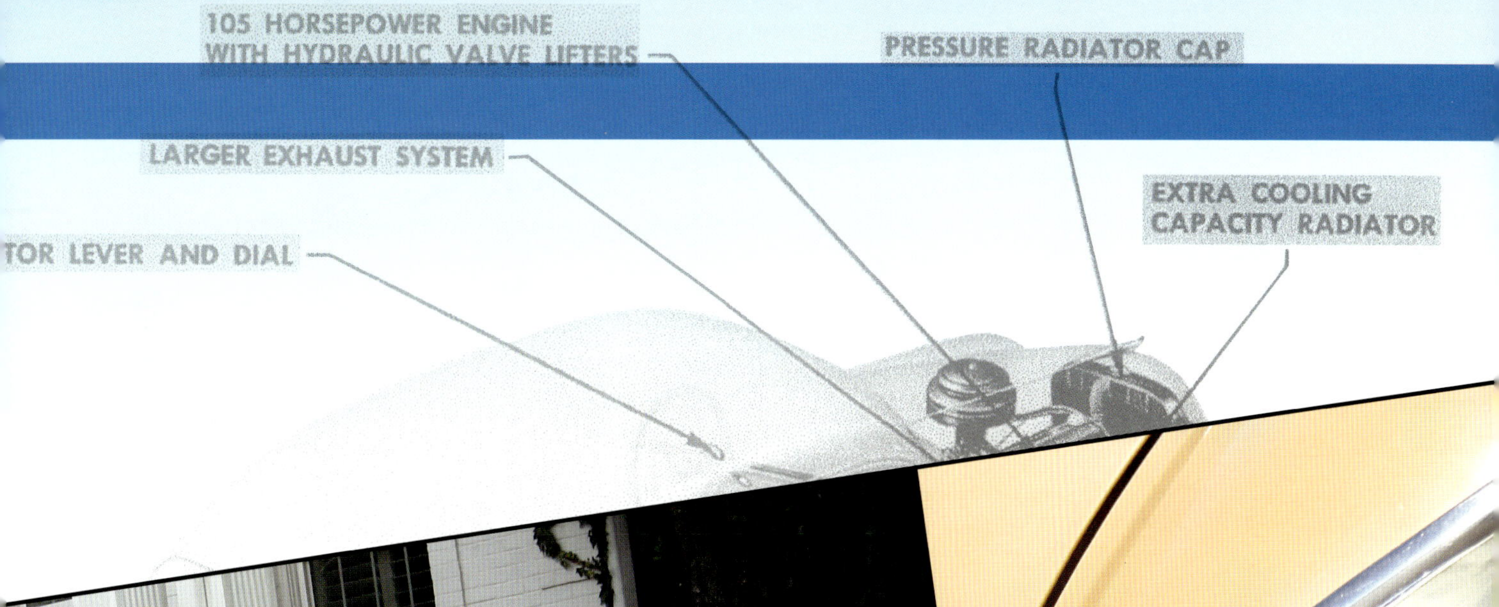
105 HORSEPOWER ENGINE
WITH HYDRAULIC VALVE LIFTERS
PRESSURE RADIATOR CAP
LARGER EXHAUST SYSTEM
EXTRA COOLING
CAPACITY RADIATOR
TOR LEVER AND DIAL

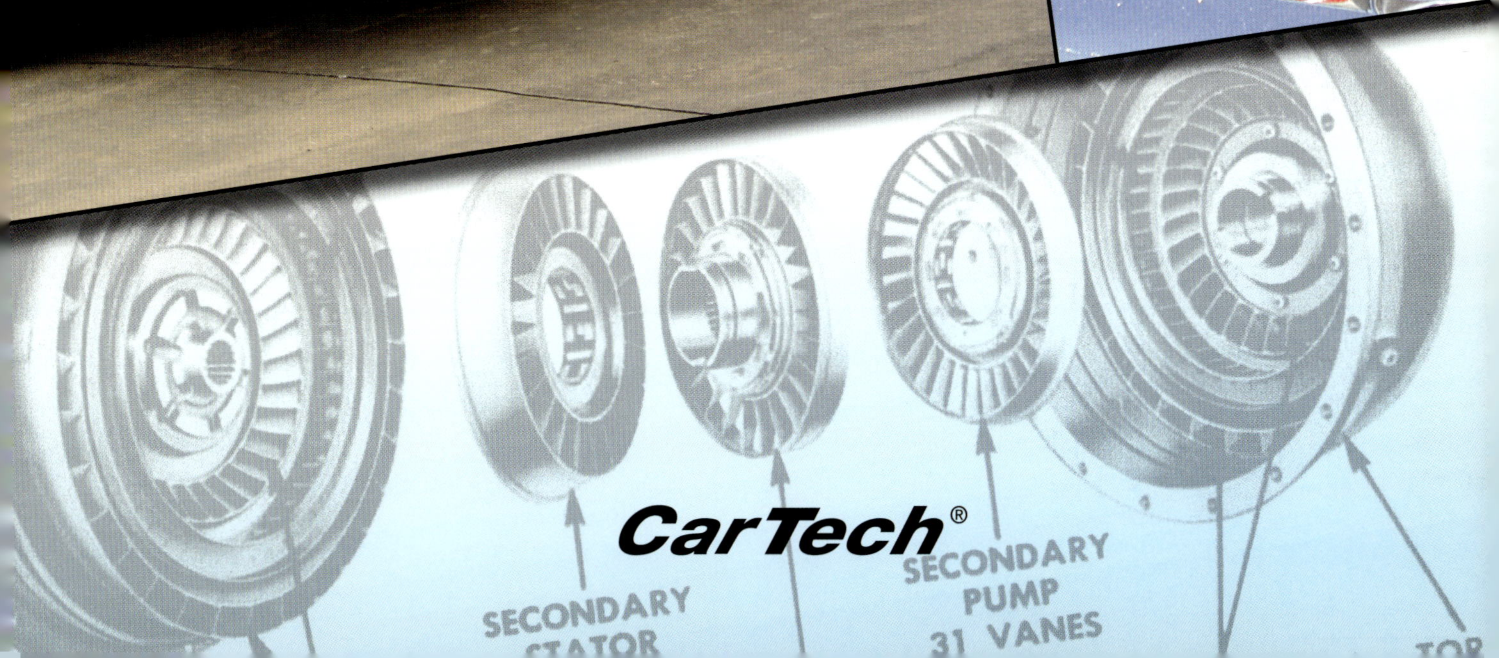
SECONDARY
STATOR
SECONDARY
PUMP
31 VANES
TOR

CarTech®

CarTech®

CarTech®, Inc.
838 Lake Street South
Forest Lake, MN 55025
Phone: 651-277-1200 or 800-551-4754
Fax: 651-277-1203
www.cartechbooks.com

Edit by Paul Johnson
Layout by Connie DeFlorin

ISBN 978-1-61325-374-8
Item No. CT608

Library of Congress Cataloging-in-Publication Data

Names: Temple, David W., author.
Title: Chevrolets of the 1950s / David W. Temple.
Description: Forest Lake, MN : CarTech Books, [2018] | Includes index.
Identifiers: LCCN 2017052032 | ISBN 9781613253748
Subjects: LCSH: Chevrolet automobile–History. | Automobiles–United States–History.
Classification: LCC TL215.C5 T46 2018 | DDC 629.222–dc23
LC record available at https://lccn.loc.gov/2017052032

Written, edited, and designed in the U.S.A.
Printed in China
10 9 8 7 6 5 4 3 2 1

DISTRIBUTION BY:

Europe
PGUK
63 Hatton Garden
London EC1N 8LE, England
Phone: 020 7061 1980 • Fax: 020 7242 3725
www.pguk.co.uk

Australia
Renniks Publications Ltd.
3/37-39 Green Street
Banksmeadow, NSW 2109, Australia
Phone: 2 9695 7055 • Fax: 2 9695 7355
www.renniks.com

Canada
Login Canada
300 Saulteaux Crescent
Winnipeg, MB, R3J 3T2 Canada
Phone: 800 665 1148 • Fax: 800 665 0103
www.lb.ca

CONTENTS

ACKNOWLEDGMENTS

I want to express many thanks to all those who contributed to this book. Without your cooperation, creating it would not have been possible. In recognition of this fact, I sincerely thank the following people for their assistance:

Phil Aubrey (Vintage Chevrolet Club of America, owner 1956 Bel Air Sport Coupe), Jimmy Blackburn (owner 1958 and 1959 Impalas), Angelo Van Bogart (*Old Cars Weekly*), Brad Brooks, Sam Cataldo (General Motors, retired), Tom Chinn (owner, 1954 and 1958 Corvette), Christo Danti (lead archivist, GM Media Archive), Brian Earnest (*Old Cars Weekly*), Tom Felton, Jim Hawes (owner 1955, 1956, 1957, 1958 Chevrolets), John Kyros (GM Media Archive), David McGee, D. J. Moore, Ken Pickering (General Motors, retired), Glen Rogers (director, Vintage Chevrolet Club of America\Lone Star Region), Gene Schneider (Vintage Chevrolet Club of America), Allen B. Simons, Joseph Trybulec (NCRS), and Ed Welburn (retired VP of GM Global Design, owner 1957 fuel-injected Corvette).

FOREWORD
BY SAM R. CATALDO

—Chief engineer of Chevrolet Impala/Monte Carlo & Buick Century/Regal, retired

I've been asked, "What was the essence of Chevrolet during the 'Fabulous Fifties'?" How did so many great products and innovations come to be? To address the questions, one must include at least two perspectives: What was the nature of the Chevrolet spirit, the brand, and the related products in the market and what was it like to work in the planning, design, engineering, manufacturing, and marketing of these products?

The Chevrolet spirit and brand was a reflection of the creative, innovative, energetic, youthful, trend-setting, growing, and rapidly evolving America in the postwar period. It offered an explosion of products to meet America's appetite with an outpouring of both passenger cars and trucks filled with new ideas, designs, and innovations. Reflect on this limited list of some of the ideas that came to be: a two-door, fiberglass body sports car named Corvette; the Chevrolet small-block and big-block V-8 engines with hydraulic lifters with a multitude of configurations, including fuel-injection; 2-barrel, 4-barrel, dual 4-barrel fuel systems with a series of head, manifold, and camshaft configurations providing a wide range of horsepower levels. Add to the engines the Powerglide, Turboglide, and 4-speed manual transmissions. In addition, there was the Level-Air suspension, the Nomad station wagon, the Bel Air's hardtop roof designs, and the legendary Impala nameplate to name a few. Further, the Chevrolet mainstream passenger car was provided in five major configurations during the 1950s, and this does not include the all-new Corvair that was in development during the late 1950s as well. These vehicles were not simply new models but became classics in their own right, especially the 1955–1957 Chevys. If you wanted to tour Woodward Avenue in style, and dominate from stoplight to stoplight, then you simply had to have a vehicle from this series with the "big engine," a 3- or 4-speed transmission, and a 3.56 or 4.11 rear axle. Of course, these pieces of art came in a wide array of models, colors, and interiors. Did it get any better than this for cruising with your best buddies or girlfriend while listening to Dinah Shore singing, "See the USA in Your Chevrolet"? Chevrolet was simply America's brand with approximately one-fourth of the market during the 1950s.

As a young engineer, working at the Chevrolet Engineering Center, this was simply the best place I could imagine. The group overflowed with ingenious, creative, and fun automotive workaholics. We simply loved what we were doing. It was a delicious blend of talents of World War II veterans, journeymen, young college graduates, and, of course, the likes of Zora Arkus-Duntov and Ed Cole to guide us. People have asked me if we knew that we were producing "classics" at the time. My response was this: "We didn't know we were producing classics; we were simply building what our customers wanted and what we wanted as fast as we could." Of course, our major objective, after pleasing our customers, was to beat Pontiac, Ford, Chrysler, and AMC, in that order, to the market with one exciting product after another. We were doing so well that the U.S. government actually considered breaking GM into two companies: Chevrolet and the rest of GM. Fortunately, wisdom prevailed and we were left to continue on our mission. The rest, as they say, is history. GM went on to dominate the market with its products by being leaders in styling, innovation, and engineering at a price that customers could afford. It wasn't just that Chevrolet was affordable; it provided a market-leading product year after year.

So what was it like to work at Chevrolet? It was fun, exciting, stimulating, and fulfilling working with a team of dedicated, talented, and mission-oriented people, "The Number One Team." It just doesn't get any better than that!

INTRODUCTION

Much has been written about the history of Chevrolet's automobiles, especially those of the 1950s, and justifiably so. This division of General Motors has a rich history and its cars of the past have stirred much interest among enthusiasts during the preceding decades. Styling has certainly played a large part in keeping Chevrolets of the 1950s among the most sought by collectors today. However, the story of these cars goes much further than skin deep. Chevrolet accounted for half the car market by the mid-1950s thanks in part to the leadership of Harley Earl, who oversaw a large team of stylists at GM Styling (renamed GM Design in 1956), but engineering also played a tremendously important role in the success.

This book traces the story of Chevrolet's innovations of the era, offering the reader a fresh look at what made Chevrolet the most successful producer of automobiles during the 1950s. Only twice from 1950 to 1959 did archrival Ford exceed the overall sales figures of Chevrolet, those being model years 1954 and 1957. Among the reasons for this are the Powerglide fully automatic transmission and the small-block V-8 released for 1955, as well as visually appealing features such as two-tone paint and richly appointed interiors. Optional equipment, such as air-conditioning, power brakes, and power steering, also played a vital role. However, nothing made by the hands of man is perfect, and not everything from Chevrolet was just right; air suspension, offered in 1958 and 1959, was largely a failure. Furthermore, its X-frame used in those same model years (and beyond) was questioned regarding its strength and safety. Still, there was much more right with Chevrolet than not. The sales figures of the era prove that.

Not every innovation appearing on a Chevrolet automobile originated with Chevrolet; indeed, some features trickled down to Chevrolet from as high up as the Cadillac Division of General Motors. That division often got the latest advancements before they filtered down to the other divisions. Still, by 1955, there was a little Cadillac in the cars produced by Chevrolet, which in itself was innovative.

Chevrolets of the 1950s will detail the story of this division of General Motors by focusing largely upon what was beneath the sheet metal of these cars, though the narrative would not be complete without some discussion of the matter of styling, as it, too, was innovative.

CHAPTER

1 A NEW DECADE DAWNS & CHEVROLET RISES

1950–1952

The strategic metals rationing of World War II resulted in the halting of civilian automobile production from early 1942 to the late summer/early fall of 1945. When production finally began with the 1946 model year, a car-hungry public did not mind purchasing what amounted to slightly altered 1942 models. Demand for new cars was so great that all-new designs were not needed for a while. However, the auto manufacturers knew they needed to seriously consider what was next. Despite the interruption of auto production during the war years, the public was still accustomed to ever-changing automobiles, and they would soon be expecting something better.

Chevrolet's prototype Bel Air (one of two built), was displayed at the GM Transportation Unlimited auto show held in New York City and Detroit. It was a forecast of Chevrolet's first hardtop model released the following year. (Photo Courtesy GM Media Archive)

The wraparound rear windshield was a novel feature for 1950. Forming it in three pieces was a far easier process than attempting an expensive one-piece wraparound glass. However, Libbey-Owens-Ford found a means to mass produce a one-piece unit for GM and the one-piece wraparound, or Panoramic, windshield became commonplace by the mid-1950s. Note the extra-cost guard atop the bumper guards on this 1950 Bel Air.

For Chevrolet, the "something better" came along with the start of the division's 1949 model year. It was a much-altered car from what had been essentially a warmed-over 1942 model. Among its styling attributes of the 1949s were flush-fitting fenders, a much lower overall height, and concealed trunk hinges. Thus, the new postwar Chevrolets appeared to be much more advanced than their predecessors. Except for the powertrain, they were virtually all-new underneath the body, too.

1950

At GM's first postwar auto show, dubbed "Transportation Unlimited," onlookers got a preview of what was in store for 1950. The hardtop body style was introduced at the show; Chevrolet's version was a prototype labeled "Bel Air." The idea probably seemed new to just about everyone. However, the concept first appeared in the teens when several automobile companies offered two-door models with front windows that would slide down; removable rear windows; and a center, or "B-pillar," that could be folded down or detached. Once all that was accomplished, the closed body style models resembled touring cars. Chrysler built seven prototypes of a 1946 Town & Country two-door hardtop, too, but it was not put into production, creating a missed opportunity to beat General Motors to the hardtop craze.

Other advancements for the duration of the 1950s included ever lower, longer, and wider cars with high-performance V-8s, automatic transmissions, and advanced styling features inspired by modern aircraft, such as wraparound windshields and fins, bright colors, two-tone paint options, and others. Not every innovation worked as planned, but failures were few. Sales of Chevrolets soared throughout the decade as a result.

The Chevrolet division of General Motors benefited from GM's innovative offering of installment purchasing during the postwar years, allowing up to 36 months to pay for a new automobile. This enabled millions of families to purchase automobiles, especially Chevrolets, which accounted for as much as 23 percent of the market during the 1950s.

Sales of the redesigned 1949 models soared past 947,000 units, though archrival Ford sold roughly 200,000 more cars. However, Ford launched its new car in June 1948 while Chevrolet did not launch its until six months later on January 7. Ford was in a desperate situation financially after years of poor management and had to get its 1949 models released as soon as possible. As a result of the rush, the new Fords were plagued with defects such as door latches that failed to keep the doors closed while driving. Chevrolet was not without its own problems with its 1949 models, but they weren't as extensive as Ford's and were remedied during the model year.

Chevrolet's new cars offered fully integrated front fenders and rounded rear decks on Styleline models and a new instrument panel consisting of clustered, circular pods over the steering column. The new design was carried forward for 1950 with few cosmetic changes.

Chevrolet's advertising boasted "the highest vote of owner loyalty," the 105-hp engine with Powerglide, and the economy of owning a 1950 Chevrolet. Owner loyalty fell sharply four years later, though, with Ford getting the benefit. That trend was extremely brief.

This very pleased driver is evidently happy to be driving a car that is "first in styling and stamina among all cars in its field," "finest in all-around performance and economy," and all "at lowest cost," as claimed by Chevrolet's advertising. The model shown is a Deluxe Fleetline four-door sedan, one of 57,693 built for 1950. The so-called torpedo shape, or fastback, was at the time an aging design and falling out of favor with the public. (Photo Courtesy GM Media Archive)

A freshly built 1950 Chevrolet Special Styleline four-door sedan leaves its assembly line in this photo taken by GM Photographic Services. The Special was the economy model and the series also included the Fleetline, a fast-back body style in two- and four-door sedan versions. Four choices were available in the Styleline series. Other than the sole four-door type shown here were three, two-door offerings: the Business Coupe, Sport Coupe, and the Sedan. (Photo Courtesy GM Media Archive)

Chevrolet continued using the general 1949 body design through the 1952 model year, though with distinctive aesthetic updates and typically introducing some form of innovation, both major and minor.

The Bel Air Hardtop

While few styling updates differentiated the 1950-model Chevrolets from the previous model year, one very notable body style was released, a two-door hardtop dubbed "Bel Air." The style was originally referred to as a "hardtop convertible" because the design gave the look of a convertible with its top raised and windows lowered. To create the hardtop, the B-pillar (middle post on non–station wagon bodies) of the hardtop was terminated at the windowsills and did not continue all the way up to the roof. Indeed, the lower body, windshield, and side glass of the convertible was used in the design of the hardtop.

Truncating the B-pillar, though, made the body more flexible. To make up for the reduced rigidity, the hat-section box girder frame for the Bel Air was strengthened by welding a reinforcement the entire length of each frame side member. Each reinforcement was divided into three pieces and welded to the top of the side member. The body was attached at 20 points where frame stiffness was greatest and thin rubber shims at these locations insulated the body from noise and vibration. Late in 1949, each side frame member was made more rigid by increasing the bottom plate thickness by 1/32 inch to 1/8 inch. Chevrolet proclaimed that they sold the only cars in the low-priced field with double-drop construction with hat-section box girders extending the entire length of the frame.

Chevrolet's *1950 Engineering Features* 96-page manual boasted: "The Bel Air is grouped with the De Luxe Styleline models, combining features of both the convertible and the regular Sport Coupe. This ingenious design, with its vigorous, youthful lines, has previously been available in much more expensive automobiles." In fact, Cadillac and Buick offered the hardtop body style during the 1949 model year, so the latter statement was exactly right. Standard features included a two-toned combination of leather and gray, striped-cord cloth upholstery, chrome-plated door and quarter window frames, stainless steel drip molding, stainless steel garnish moldings, stem-wind 39-hour clock, two interior lights in back with a manual on-off switch in the left quarter trim panel, dome light

This unrestored 1950 Bel Air is painted in one of the four extra-cost two-toned paint schemes offered for the hardtop model, Moonlight Cream and Falcon Gray Poly (polychromatic or metallic). Two-tone paint emphasized the hardtop body style. The sole standard color offered for 1950 was Mayland Black, but single-color selections were expanded by the following model year. All Deluxe models, including the Bel Air, were equipped with fender skirts, stainless steel moldings on the front fenders and doors, and a 39-hour wind-up clock. The Bel Air was a popular new model that accounted for 74,634 of Chevrolet's sales for the 1950 model year.

The Bel Air returned for 1951 and faced competition from archrival Ford with its Victoria two-door hardtop by about the midpoint of the model year. Chrysler Corporation also responded with models in this body style. Ford was far and away the most popular, but Chevrolet won the sales race for the model year. Four two-tone interior combinations were offered for the Bel Air for 1951. (Photo Courtesy GM Media Archive)

The name "Bel Air" did not actually appear anywhere on the car until the 1953 model year. Until then, the name "Deluxe" was placed on the body. The Bel Air was grouped with the Deluxe Styleline series.

A fancier interior was included as standard issue for the 1950 Bel Air. Two-toning and bright bows across the headliner were part of the allure. The instrument panel was, of course, shared among all models, though the radio was an extra-cost option regardless of model. Note the vertical layout of the radio dial.

with manual on-off switch, chromed headliner bows, and an exclusive wraparound rear windshield, though a three-piece affair. Strangely, this top-of-the-line model did not have any identifying script other than "DELUXE"; the name "Bel Air" did not appear on the outside or the inside of the car.

The public, evidently, heartily approved of Chevrolet's new hardtop with a total of 74,634 built. Its success could not have gone unnoticed by the competition. Chrysler Corporation built a mere 700 of its Town & Country Newport; its body, like the Town & Country convertible, was made with a considerable amount of wood. Chrysler's New Yorker Newport and Windsor Newport hardtops accounted for only about 5,000 combined sales. More significant was Ford's offering released for the 1951 model year, the Victoria, which outsold the Bel Air by approximately 7,000 units at just a bit under 110,400.

Powerglide: Chevrolet's First Automatic Transmission

The foreword of Chevrolet's *1950 Engineering Features* manual began, "One year ago, we brought out the widely accepted car that established the basic 'postwar' Chevrolet. The 1950 car that you will meet on these pages goes a full step ahead, combining beauty and utility in good measure that the buying public has come to expect from us. In the Chevrolet cars described in past 'yearbooks' were many features whose contributions to better driving have been memorable, but never, we think, has Chevrolet, or any other car in its price class, offered the great step forward in simplified driving that is represented by this new torque converter transmission."

Its new transmission was named "Powerglide" and was available as a $159 option for any model in the Deluxe series. Upon its release, it was the only automatic transmission offered in the low-price class of cars and was one of only a few in the entire industry with a hydraulic torque converter. (Ford released its Ford-O-Matic designed by BorgWarner the following year.) Chevrolet's achievement is particularly impressive when one considers the relatively high cost of tooling and production of the transmission's key component, the torque converter. Cars equipped with this option were noted with chromed block letters on the decklid above the combination emblem and handle.

Included with the automatic transmission was an "EconoMISER" rear axle with a slightly lower rear axle ratio, 3.55:1 versus 4.11:1, to improve economy and performance as well as larger four-ply tires, 7.10 x 15 inch versus 6.70 x 15 inch.

The Powerglide was similar in concept to Buick's Dynaflow transmission, utilizing a five-element, multiphase hydraulic torque converter along with a planetary gear set. In normal forward motion, only the torque converter was in operation; the planetary gears were needed for reverse and for low-gear, emergency power. The gear selector was mounted on the

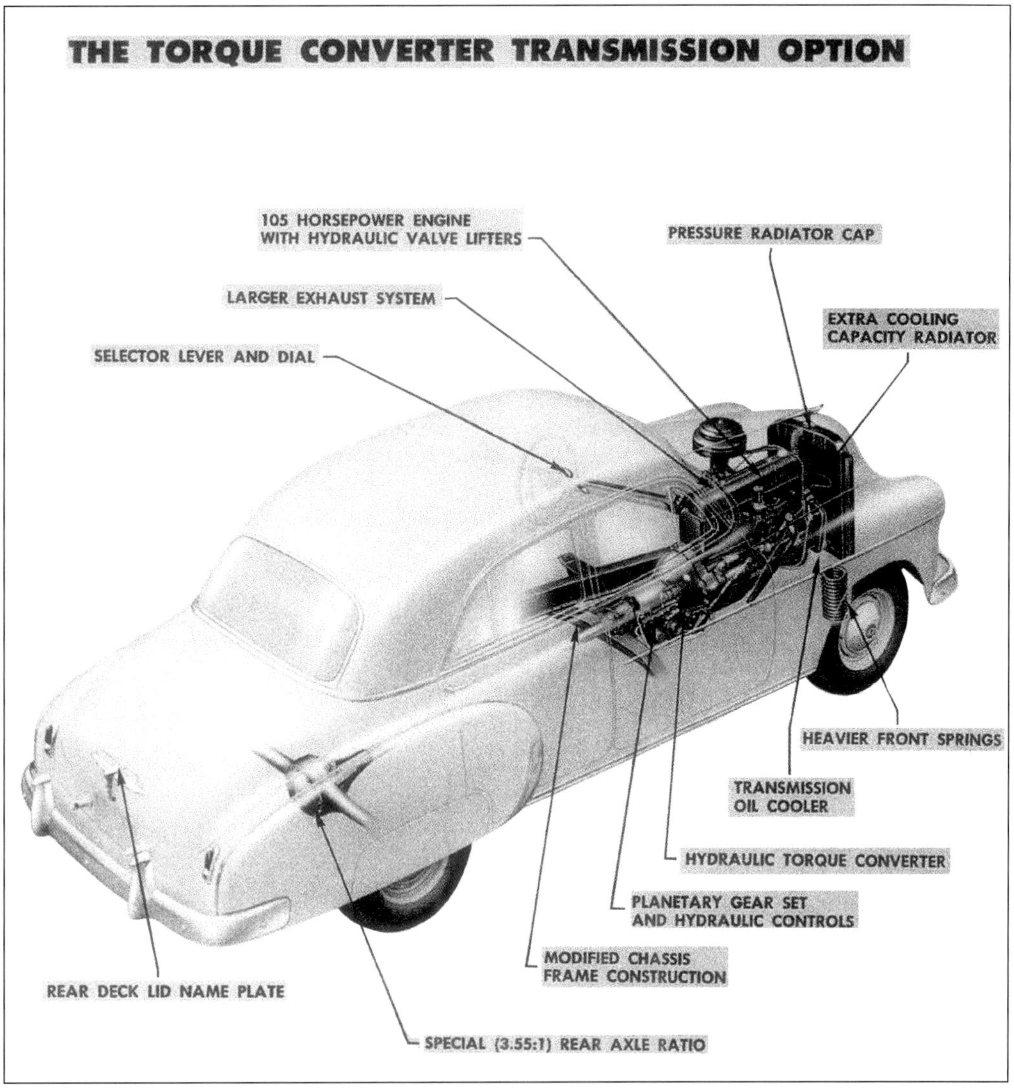

This diagram shows the various features included with the optional Powerglide transmission. Included with it was a more powerful 105-hp engine, extra-capacity radiator, heavier front springs, transmission oil cooler, 3.55:1 rear axle ratio, and "Powerglide" in block letters mounted on the decklid.

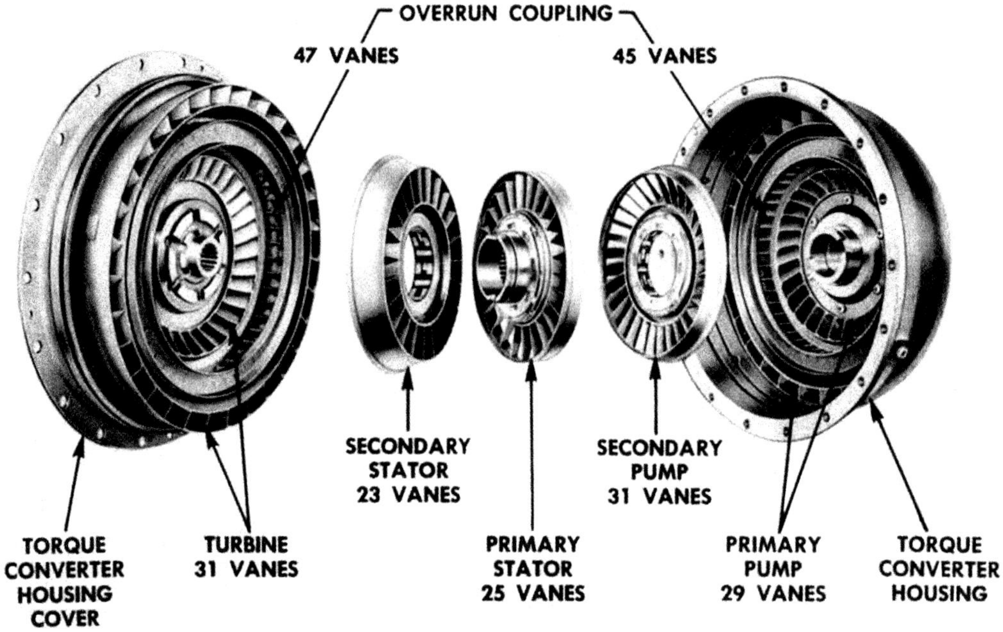

The Powerglide was an automatic similar in concept to Buick's Dynaflow transmission, utilizing a five-element, multiphase hydraulic torque converter along with a planetary gear set. In normal forward motion, only the torque converter was in operation; the planetary gears were needed for reverse and for low-gear, emergency power.

steering column and gear positions of PARK, N, D, L, and R were placed on a clear plastic dial atop the steering column. An electrical switch integrated into the mechanical linkage kept the car from starting in any gear except park or neutral. A simple mechanical linkage engaged the parking lock, while a hydraulic slide valve was repositioned with the movement of the gear selector to any of the other selections. Use of the engine as a brake was retained through the torque converter drive since the fluid coupling between the engine and rear wheels was maintained regardless of the position of the accelerator. (Some automatic transmissions of the era allowed the car to coast when the accelerator pedal was released, a feature dubbed "free-wheeling.") Engine braking helped reduce the need for applying the brakes in some situations, thus decreasing wear on the brake system.

As with the manual transmission, the push-start feature was also included with the Powerglide. If the vehicle failed to start conventionally, placing the gear selector into neutral and pushing the vehicle up to a speed of about 15 mph then moving the selector lever to low would get the engine running. Low gear could be engaged manually for better acceleration up a grade, or for faster takeoffs up to a maximum of 40 mph. However, such shifting could be brutal on the Powerglide; for 1953 the transmission was improved with automatic shifting from first to second gear. Though officially a 2-speed automatic, the early version of the Powerglide was essentially a 1-speed transmission unless the driver selected "low" range manually. Relocation of the second front crossmember to a place 2⁵/₈ inches rearward was necessary to provide support for the Powerglide. The entire package added 130 pounds to the total weight of a 1950 Chevrolet Deluxe model.

The torque converter, which took the place of a mechanical clutch, was not particularly an innovation at the time. It was originally developed in Germany prior to World War I for use in ships and was later developed for automotive use. GM's experience with torque converters began in the late-1930s with the development of automatic hydraulic drives for buses. For 1940, General Motors released the first fully automatic transmission for a car, dubbed "Hydra-Matic" (though it used a torus rather than a torque converter), followed in 1948 by Buick's "Dynaflow," which used a torque converter. Research into adapting the torque converter for U.S. Army tanks began at General Motors in 1938. These vehicles were cumbersome to operate via a series of control levers. Tank drivers had to frequently remove their hands from one set of levers to move others, making shifting gears awkward at best, especially in combat. This research later led to Buick's Dynaflow. A heavy-duty version of the Hydra-Matic emerged during the war years.

A torque converter is a fluid coupling that transfers rotating power from an engine (or electric motor) to a driven load. In concept, the design is simple, but much research over a four-year period was necessary to create a practical and reliable automatic transmission simple enough to be profitable in a low-priced automobile. The Powerglide's hydraulic torque converter was comprised of five major elements: primary pump, secondary pump, turbine, primary stator, and secondary stator. All were essentially a vaned wheel constructed of many spot-welded, cooper-brazed steel stampings. (A stator consists of airfoil-shaped blades set at a fixed angle within a rotating structure providing torque multiplication.) Typically, these were intricate castings; Chevrolet's approach allowed for high-volume production. The product was a simple and compact design that stayed in production throughout the next decade when it was reworked into a heavy-duty type with a lightweight aluminum case that could be used behind a 340-hp variant of the 409, an engine that emerged from the 348 developed in the 1950s.

The Powerglide, though a significant advancement, was

not particularly efficient; slippage was serious enough for some to criticize Chevrolet's new automatic with such verbiage as "power slide, power slip," and "slip and slide with Powerglide." With only modest torque multiplication from the torque converter in the drive range, acceleration was relatively slow. (Starting in low and shifting to drive improved acceleration.) The slippage resulted in higher engine revolutions, so the engineers chose hydraulic lifters to reduce engine noise. Slippage was also the motive behind the higher-output engine.

Despite the slippage, Powerglide offered the purchaser advantages beyond convenience. A road test report published in the July 1952 issue of *Motor Trend* compared the differences in performance in a Chevrolet with Powerglide and another equipped with what the writer, Walt Woron, termed a "conventional" (synchromesh 3-speed) transmission. In the end, each had its advantages, and the choice was simply a matter of preference. Acceleration from 0–60 mph was 20.1 seconds for the car with Powerglide versus 20.46 seconds for the one with the synchromesh transmission; using "low" and "drive" for the test reduced the Powerglide car's 0–60 time to 19.35 seconds. Top speed with the automatic transmission in the fastest one-way run was 87.38 mph versus 82.95 mph in the car with the manual transmission. The net result was nearly the same in the average of four runs. Fuel economy was reported to be better with the Powerglide; at a steady 60 mph the Powerglide-equipped test car got 15.2 mpg while the other got nearly 1 mpg less at 14.3 mpg. The synchromesh provided a slight advantage in economy at a steady 45 mph, but was bested by the Powerglide again at a steady 30 mph. Regardless of performance and economy matters, the Powerglide offered easier driving and excellent reliability.

The 1-millionth Powerglide was installed in a Chevrolet in October 1952. Clearly it was a popular option for reasons that included 80-percent reduced effort of gear manipulation compared to the manual transmission, elimination of jerky starts, quieter operation, smoother acceleration, and smoother ride. The latter was credited to the fluid coupling of the torque converter, which mitigated road shocks transmitted through the driveline. Cars equipped with the manual transmission had a continuous mechanical connection through which vibrations, such as those of the rear wheels over a bump, could be transmitted more easily to the car and passengers. Rough roads were more common during the early 1950s and any improvement in ride qualities was much appreciated by the public.

Powerglide maintenance was not burdensome; oil changes were recommended every 15,000 miles (later increased to 25,000 miles), and, since high pressure was confined to the interior of the transmission, oil leaks were not common. Furthermore, there was no mechanical clutch to replace periodically. A running change made to the Powerglide during the 1950 model year was a switch from two drain plugs (one higher than the other) to just one. The lower one was for draining the fluid from the torque converter while the upper drain plug provided the required air vent, which allowed the fluid to flow out. Deleting the lubrication check valve, proven not to be needed, allowed venting through the lubrication oil passage into the case.

Another running change was made to the assembly process of the planetary gear set. The new method allowed for disassembly for servicing rather than having to replace the entire gear set in the event of a problem with the setup. Four other upgrades included substituting rolled bronze for sintered bronze in the low sun gear thrust washer, addition of a spring steel thrust washer between the hub and flange of the drive range clutch to prevent possible scuffing of these parts, a more rigid control shaft lever, and a change from a hex-head to a T-head bolt to clamp the control shaft lever onto the control shaft to provide more clearance and facilitate assembly.

Larger, Improved 6-Cylinder with Powerglide

Powerglide-equipped Chevrolets received a modified truck engine tailored for Powerglide that generated a peak horsepower output of 105 hp at 3,600 rpm, 13 more than the 6-cylinder used for cars with the 3-speed manual transmission. Torque increased by 17 ft-lbs to 193 ft-lbs at 1,110 to 2,200 rpm. The 235.5-ci "Stovebolt" six, which had its origins in the late-1920s, was quickly becoming outdated despite major modifications over the years, being made obsolete by much more advanced, overhead valve (ohv) V-8 engines. However, the ohv V-8s were still relatively new and available only in higher priced cars; in GM's case a V-8 was standard for Cadillac models and an option for Oldsmobiles. (Ford retained its old flathead used since 1932 through the 1953 model year.) Chevrolet had a V-8 program under way, but the first attempt did not result in a particularly advanced engine. (The small-block V-8 story is detailed in chapter 3.) Until the end of the 1954 model year, Chevrolet buyers would have to accept 6-cylinder power as their only choice of engine. Several upgrades were made to the 6-cylinder for the 1950 model year: a larger bore and stroke resulting in 19 additional cubic inches of displacement, a new carburetor with automatic choke, new intake manifold, larger intake and exhaust valves, higher compression (6.7:1 versus 6.6:1), larger coolant passages in the head, plus repositioned oil galleries resulting in more space (up to about 1 inch versus 3/16 inch) between them and the water jackets, thus providing a stronger engine casting and eliminating any porosity between them.

GM's Rochester Division developed an all-new carburetor. The new design of the single-barrel carb gave a more constant fuel level in the main nozzle passages, greater protection against vapor lock, continuous fuel flow from idle

Along with the new, optional Powerglide automatic transmission was a modified version of the 6-cylinder truck engine. The changes included hydraulic valve lifters, higher compression ratio, an improved carburetor, and different intake and exhaust manifolds. The Powerglide had a five-element, multiphase hydraulic torque converter along with a planetary gear set. This option cost $159. (Photo Courtesy GM Media Archive)

to higher speeds, more uniform air distribution within the carburetor throat, a smoother and faster response to acceleration input, a fully enclosed accelerator pump, a vacuum-operated fuel enrichment valve, ball-type valves throughout, and twin floats. Plus, it was easier to service. More important, though, was the relocation of the float bowl from ahead of the carburetor throat to a concentric arrangement around it. The previous design would allow the main fuel passages to flood on steeply inclined roads or cause fuel starvation during sudden braking and on a steep downgrade. Later in the model year, a throttle return check, or dashpot, was added to retard the closing of the throttle and prevent stalling of the engine when the driver suddenly released the accelerator during low-speed operations.

Intake valve size increased by 19/64 inch to $1^{15}/_{16}$ inches while the exhaust valves received a 1/32-inch increase in head diameter to $1^{1}/_{2}$ inches and the exhaust valve seat angle was changed from 30 to 45 degrees to increase valve strength. The exhaust pipes and tailpipes were enlarged by 1/8 inch as well.

With the 105-hp engine and Powerglide combination came the need for a radiator that dissipated heat faster as well as a means to cool the transmission fluid. An oil cooler for the transmission was placed between the radiator outlet and the water pump; the engine's coolant passed through it before flowing into the engine block. Hot transmission fluid passed from the transmission to the cooler via a spring-loaded ball check bypass valve opened and closed via a bi-metal thermostat. It was connected to the cooler by hot and cold pipelines running along the right side of the engine. When the fluid reached its operating temperature of about 240 degrees, the thermostat closed.

Other Changes for 1950

Outwardly, the 1950 Chevrolets were distinguishable from the 1949s through minor styling alterations, such as a reduced number of vertical bars in the grille, addition of decorative posts below the park lamps, the addition of CHEVROLET lettering stamped and highlighted in blue enamel into the upper grille, a license plate guard separate from the bumper guards, revised hood ornament, and more prominent park lamps. In back (on non–station wagon models) were revised taillights, decklid hardware, and taller bumper guards front and rear.

Taller bumper guards were said to decrease the likelihood of bumpers being locked in a minor collision. The altered taillights, which extended farther out from the body, were more prominent as a result. Front suspension saddles, which were parts of the front suspension crossmember, were made thicker to increase their strength and rigidity. The redesigned fuel filler decreased the chance of gasoline being spilled onto the painted surface underneath the filler access. Spilled gasoline could drain directly to the ground. In addition, a whistle was installed on the lower end of the fuel tank vent pipe that extended into the fuel tank; as the fuel level reached the

The prism-shaped taillights were redesigned for 1950 to provide much greater nighttime side-view visibility for other drivers, making driving a little safer.

lower end of the vent pipe the whistle ceased to be audible, thus preventing an overflow. At this point, there was 1 gallon of capacity more, which was enough to allow for expansion of the gasoline in hot weather. Other improvements included key locks covered with spring-loaded doors rather than sliding shutters. The change, which provided better sealing of the keyholes, was said to make the opening of the locks easier when coated by ice.

Raising the convertible top was simplified and could be done completely from the front seat thanks to extending the sides of the convertible top downward into the quarter panels where they attached to the body above the wheelhouses. Sponge rubber pads were enclosed in the top material in those areas to provide a weathertight seal between the sides of the top and the upper edges of the quarter panels. The top frame in this area pressed firmly against these pads, giving a tight seal. Previously, the sides of the convertible top extended only to the belt moldings on the outside of the quarter panels and had to be fastened by hand to a metal flange after the top was raised.

Wind noise was reduced by reshaping the outer surfaces of the ventipane uprights from flat into a V-shape. The revision placed the vertical bars farther into the airstream. Self-canceling turn signal was added and dual backup lights were available to replace the single unit at extra cost. Signal indicators were available at extra cost as well. At mid–model year, the steering ratio was

The only station wagon offered for 1950 was in the Deluxe series, a six-passenger model with a steel body sporting wood appliqués. Chevrolet discontinued the wood-bodied version with the end of the 1949 model year. The Deluxe station wagon was the highest priced model in the lineup at $1,194. (Photo Courtesy GM Media Archive)

increased from 17.4:1 to 19.4:1 to reduce low-speed maneuvering and parking effort.

Decorative hardware received attention, too, with painted highlights. The park lamp bases each had three recesses painted blue, as did the Chevrolet bowtie trademark on the wheel covers and rear emblem. The latter were set against a gold-painted background. Pinstriping was applied to the wheels; color (such as Argent Silver, French White, Maryland Black, etc.) depended upon the body color and model of the car. Careful attention was given to color harmony for the interior as well. These styling innovations were the product of Harley Earl's styling department.

Chevrolet was a pioneer in the use of two-tone paint beginning in the late 1920s. It was used effectively on the notchback Styleline models in which the roof and lower body were separate colors when the optional scheme was ordered by the buyer. This year, five of the nine basic shades of paint offered were new. One of the new shades was a deep-luster metallic Windsor Blue. (Deep-luster metallic paint, however, was carried forward from 1949.) Colors were said to be carefully selected each year to complement the new styling and appeal to current customer preferences. Unfortunately, metallic paints were not as durable as non-metallic types and would remain that way for many years to come. Chevrolet and other automotive divisions of General Motors from about the mid-1920s well into the 1950s used pyroxylin lacquer, also known as nitrocellulose lacquer, a product of DuPont. This single-stage type of paint had the advantage of drying quickly, though it required much hand rubbing to bring it to a high luster and it was brittle. It was finally superseded by another DuPont innovation, acrylic lacquer, for the 1959 model year.

Last, Chevrolet cut the price of the Styleline Deluxe station wagon by $250, a significant percentage, thus dropping the price to $1,880.

1951: Better Brakes and Minor Updates

Outwardly, there were only a few changes for the 1951 Chevrolets; revised grille, hood ornament, taillights, a new Powerglide emblem, and quarter panels were among the most instantly recognizable. (Station wagons, however, retained the 1950-style rear fenders.) Side trim for the front fenders and doors of the Deluxe series cars was redesigned and relocated to a lower height for a more effective lengthening highlight. Furthermore, the placement of the park lamps more outboard helped give the illusion of greater width to go along with the appearance of greater length. However, the most significant update to the exterior was the smooth blending of the rear fenders into the body; no longer was it a bolt-on panel with a welt between it and the body. The rear fenders were also longer and higher in back than those of 1950.

The goal of the mild sheet metal and trim alterations was to create a proportionately longer, lower-appearing car, which was one of the major objectives of GM Styling Chief Harley Earl. "My main purpose . . . has been to lengthen and lower the American automobile, at times in reality and always at least in appearance. Why? Because my sense of proportion tells me that oblongs are more attractive than squares just as a ranch house is more attractive than a square three-story flat-roofed house or a greyhound is more graceful than an English bulldog," wrote Earl for a 1954 article in the *Saturday Evening Post*. His philosophy regarding styling contributed greatly to GM's rise to the top of the auto industry during his three-decade career there. Of course, GM's Chevrolet Division benefited from his innovative methods, such as the use of full-scale clay modeling, and a team of dedicated stylists to develop aesthetically appealing automobiles. (For a detailed account of how Harley Earl led General Motors to the pinnacle of success from the 1930s through the 1950s purchase, *The Cars of Harley Earl*, published by CarTech Books.) Another Earl method was the highly effective annual model-year change in which new models were altered so that cars of the previous model year seemed at least a little or even very outdated.

In addition to external updates, 1951 Chevrolets received a new "Safety Sight" instrument panel with instruments grouped into two circular clusters ahead of the driver, a full horn ring for deluxe models, as well as changes in interior fabrics and colors. Even control knobs were redesigned. More significant

The 1951 model year for Chevrolet began on December 9, 1950. Outwardly, there were only a few changes. Inside, the 1951 Chevrolets received a new "Safety Sight" instrument panel and new interior fabrics and colors. Brakes were slightly wider. (Jim Hawes collection)

The Deluxe Styleline four-door sedan was the most popular model in Chevrolet's lineup with 380,270 sold. All Deluxe models were distinguished outwardly with a stainless steel molding starting above the front wheel openings and extending onto the doors with a "Deluxe" nameplate on the front fenders, fender skirts, and chromed gravel shields on the rear fenders. (Photo Courtesy GM Media Archive)

The 1951 Chevrolet Deluxe convertible was priced $106 higher than the Bel Air two-door hardtop. The convertible accounted for well under half as many sales as the hardtop with 32,810 units produced. All Deluxe models received foam rubber seat cushion pads, etched aluminum step plates, as well as additional bright moldings, and a wider variety of interior color choices compared to the Special series. (Photo Courtesy GM Media Archive)

This idea for exhaust-through-the-bumper was rejected for the 1950 Chevrolet. It was likely inspired by a very similar feature on the not-yet-completed 1951 GM LeSabre concept car. (Photo Courtesy GM Media Archive)

Cutaway car displays offered a look at the construction and mechanical details. Such displays had long been used by Chevrolet at auto shows. Shown is a 1951 Styleline Deluxe four-door sedan. (Photo Courtesy GM Media Archive)

A new "Safety Sight" instrument panel was one of the few updates offered for the 1951 Chevrolet. The instruments were lighted indirectly against a subdued black background with the pointers, graduations, and figures glowing in a soft green hue from reflected light off the bright green walls of the instrument cases. (Photo Courtesy GM Media Archive)

were the completely new braking system, chassis improvements providing a better ride, and better instrumentation lighting for night driving. The pointer for the gear selection of the Powerglide was increased 1/4 inch in length to make for easier reading by the driver. Two types of optional radios were again offered, but the dial was changed from vertical to horizontal. Heater controls were also redesigned.

As before, Chevrolets were equipped with "Jumbo Drum" hydraulic brakes with 11-inch drums. However, the drums were increased in width by 1/4 inch to 2 inches in front and had redesigned webs along the outer surface of the drum rim to reduce contamination by dirt and mud. They were also more effective at dissipating heat. The overall design was changed to reduce braking effort by as much as 25 percent, provide better self-energizing effect and a longer brake shoe life, simplify maintenance, give better sealing against contaminants, and be less prone to grabbing and surging. Chevrolet said the redesign was needed to deal with trends of increasing highway cruising speeds and growing in-town traffic congestion.

Instruments were lighted indirectly against a subdued black background. The pointers, graduations, and figures glowed soft green from reflected light off the bright green walls of the instrument cases. Turning the light switch knob could brighten or dim the illumination.

Additional improvements included revisions to the carburetor for improved hot-idle operation and hot starting, a simplified and more secure latching mechanism for the hood, an ignition switch with a more rigid mounting, redesigned exhaust system mounts that transmitted less vibration to the car, and rear seat springs in sedans and coupes constructed like those of the front seat with flat, continuous S-shaped springs. Expanded manufacturing facilities made possible the wider application of this more modern construction method.

Public approval of the 1951 Chevrolets was high. Well-known automotive journalist of the day Floyd Clymer, writing for *Mechanix Illustrated*, found that 90 percent of owners rated their Chevrolet as excellent or good while only 1 percent rated their car as poor and only 2 percent said they would not buy another Chevrolet. The most liked features included styling (99 percent), larger brakes (96 percent), visibility (93 percent), and ride quality (92 percent).

1952

Only a few new engineering updates were made for the 1952 models, but they were significant. The fourth iteration of the original 1949 design had been refined almost as much as was practical to that point, and a redesigned Chevrolet was coming for 1953.

Full-size clay modeling was introduced to GM by Harley Earl when he was hired by company president Alfred Sloan to establish a styling department. While Earl agreed with the adage that a picture is worth a thousand words, he believed a clay model "was worth a thousand pictures." Shown is a styling proposal for the 1952 Chevrolet Styleline four-door sedan. Note the grille and stone shield on the lower rear fender that did not make production. (Photo Courtesy GM Media Archive)

The use of optional two-toning for the exterior of the Bel Air highlighted its hardtop styling. In this case, the combination is Cherry and Beach White, 1 of 14 two-tone combinations offered. Single-tone colors numbered 4. (Photo Courtesy GM Media Archive)

The magazine advertisement for the 1952 Chevrolets touted the advantages of ownership, which included the car's styling; the 26 single and two-tone color combinations available; color-matched two-toned blues, greens, or grays for Deluxe interiors; "Centerpoise" Power; and the newly available optional "E-Z-Eye" shaded windshield.

"Centerpoise Power" was the marketing lingo chosen to describe the new three-point powertrain mounting arrangement. Two mounts, one per side, were placed high alongside the 6-cylinder engine and the other at the rear was under the transmission. The new setup suspended the engine, and as a result, transmitted less vibration to the car and passengers. Previously, the engine sat directly upon the engine mounts.

"Centre-Point Steering" referred to the new steering geometry in which "control is centered between the front wheels," making a "Chevrolet surprisingly easy to steer, maneuver, and park."

"Shade-Lite" tinted glass was another innovation for Chevrolets this model year. It was optional on all models.

A side roof-rail mechanical sealing strip was added to the Bel Air two-door hardtop. This chrome-plated "flipper" sealing strip was attached by screws to the lower face of the side roof rail directly above the doors to provide an adequate weather seal for this area. Slotted attaching screw holes allowed for adjustment to achieve a proper fit. It had a spring-tensioned outer hinged section actuated mechanically by contact with the upper section of the door ventilator frame when the door was opened and closed. When the door was closed, the hinged outer section of the sealing strip under spring tension flipped downward to form a conventional

The Deluxe Styleline two-door sedan was the second most popular model Chevrolet offered for 1952, finishing behind the Deluxe Styleline four-door sedan. Deluxe models generally outsold those of the lower-cost Special lineup by a large margin. (Photo Courtesy GM Media Archive)

The fastback body style, perceived by many as old-fashioned, was fading in popularity by 1951. It was dropped during the following model year as sales fell off sharply. It was offered in both the lower-cost Special and the upper-level Deluxe series. Shown is the Deluxe four-door sedan version. Incidentally, the Ambassador Bridge connecting Detroit with Canada appears in the background. (Photo Courtesy GM Media Archive)

Starting with the 1950 model year, all Chevrolet station wagons utilized a steel body. The wood insert was simulated with Di-Noc decals. Shown is the 1952 Deluxe version seating up to eight. (Photo Courtesy GM Media Archive)

channel that compressed against the chrome channel along the top of the door ventilator and window, forming a tight weather seal. When the door was opened, the outer section of the sealing strip flipped upward out of the way to provide clearance for the door glass and ventilator frame.

The usual revisions, such as a revised grille, hood ornamentation, side trim, larger selection of exterior single-tone and two-tone paint schemes, etc., were made as well, along with more color and pattern choices for the two-toned interior of the Bel Air. Dropped by about the middle of the model year were the Fleetline fastbacks due to ever-decreasing sales of the body style. Times were changing. The fastback design was becoming dated in the eyes of the growing youth market.

By the time the basic 1949 design came to an end, it had brought approximately 4.5 million sales to Chevrolet during its four-year run.

The Fleetline fastback body style was quickly dropping in popularity, so it was dropped during the 1952 model year. Fastback, or torpedo, body styles dated back well before World War II and were viewed as old-fashioned by the early 1950s. In fact, only a two-door sedan Fleetline was offered and only in the Deluxe series. Previously both the Special and the Deluxe offered two- and four-door sedans in the Fleetline body style. (Photo Courtesy GM Media Archive)

NEW MODELS & TECHNOLOGY FOR THE FABULOUS FIFTIES

CHAPTER 2

1953–1954

Though the 1953 models had some resemblance to the 1952s, they were indeed completely different on the outside with what was labeled the "Fashion-First Body by Fisher." New sheet metal wrapped around the 1949–1952 inner body structure along with single-piece front and rear windshields on all models provided a fresh appearance to the older body shell. A new grille, bumper, bumper guards, and park lamps appeared up front, while reshaped taillights and a new bumper along with revised bumper guards were in back. Side trim was also completely new, and finally, the name "Bel Air" actually appeared on the model. Overall height was reduced by as much as 1/2 inch on many body styles. The slightly lower height combined with "dynamic body lines," as expressed in the *1953 Chevrolet Engineering Features* guidebook, helped to add the illusion of greater overall length when, in fact, the 1953s were 2 inches shorter. (Wheelbase remained unaltered at 115 inches; the reduced length was from wheel center to bumper ends.) Keeping proportions looking balanced was the wide grille and smooth blending of the hood and fenders to give the appearance of greater width.

A Bel Air four-door sedan was one of several GM cars brought out on stage at the 1953 GM Motorama. This all-GM automobile show with lavish stage shows and decor was GM's first cross-country Motorama to promote the company's products. These shows continued through 1956, and then were held two more times for 1959 and 1961. This touring auto show was an innovative way to promote Chevrolet and all other divisions of General Motors until television became more popular and a more affordable promotion tool. (Photo Courtesy GM Media Archive)

This prototype from 1952 shows some of the styling features chosen for the 1953 Chevrolet passenger cars. The grille layout was similar to the production version, but the side trim and stone shield designs were not. (Photo Courtesy GM Media Archive)

Bright metal double moldings with series name and crest on the rear fenders helped differentiate the new 1953 Bel Air from lower-level series cars. Bel Air was now a separate series promoted by Chevrolet as a "luxury line" rather than a part of the Deluxe line. Furthermore, the two-door hardtop body style was no longer exclusive to the Bel Air, but was also offered in the Deluxe Series Two-Ten line. (Photo Courtesy GM Media Archive)

Chevrolet's four-door sedans remained the most produced body style for 1953. This Bel Air four-door sedan is shown nearing completion on one of the division's 11 assembly plants in the United States. It was the third most built model for the model year. A Bel Air two-door hardtop was next in line. All Bel Air models were distinguished by their body side trim with the painted insert and model name and by the standard fender skirts. (Photo Courtesy GM Media Archive)

This 1953 Bel Air convertible, one of 24,047 built for the model year, is on display at an auto show. It was fitted with the dealer-installed accessory grille and fender guards. Wide white sidewall tires were an extra-cost option. Base price was $2,175. (Photo Courtesy GM Media Archive)

Additional body styles were added to the Bel Air series, which in its previous two model years consisted of only a two-door hardtop and convertible; two- and four-door sedans were now included in the lineup. Bright metal double moldings with series name and crest on the rear fenders helped to differentiate the Bel Air from lower-level series cars. Of note is that the Bel Air was now a separate series (promoted by Chevrolet as a "luxury line") rather than a member of the Deluxe line. However, the Bel Air was not the only two-door hardtop offered; the body style, now dubbed Sport Coupe, was also offered in the Deluxe line. With the fastback no longer offered, the Fleetline sub-series was dropped, eliminating the need for the Styleline sub-series identification for the notchback-bodied cars. In the process, naming of trim levels was altered with the three-series lineup consisting of the base Special 150 (aka Series 1500), midlevel Deluxe 210 (aka Series 2100), and the Bel Air 240 (aka Series 2400). The labels 150, 210, and 240 corresponded to the first three digits in the series number, which in turn was based upon the model style number. For instance, the series 1500 cars consisted of five model styles: 1502 (two-door sedan), 1503 (four-door sedan), 1504 (two-door Business Coupe, which lacked a back seat), 1509

The Townsman station wagon was offered as a six-passenger version in both the Special One-Fifty and Deluxe Two-Ten lines. An eight-passenger model was also available in the latter series. Shown is the Two-Ten Townsman, which was among the highest priced models behind only the Bel Air convertible. A total of 18,258 of the six-passenger type were built, while only 7,988 of the eight-passenger model found buyers. The Two-Ten Townsman was dropped during the following model year. (Photo Courtesy GM Media Archive)

For many years, Chevrolet offered the Business Coupe, later called the Utility Sedan, a model without a back seat. It was often purchased by traveling salesmen or for business fleets. The rear compartment offered additional storage to carry inventory or inventory samples of many types and offered easy accessibility. This 1954 One-Fifty Business Coupe has traveled just 38,000 miles; its original tires were installed for this photo shoot of the car. It is mostly original, though its suspension has been lowered 1 inch.

The rear compartment of the One-Fifty Business Coupe, in this case a 1954 model, was typically used to carry inventory or inventory samples of many types. Its rear floor, like the front, was covered with a rubber mat, and a heavy cardboard panel separated the interior from the trunk.

The circumstances behind this photo are unknown, but this 1953 Bel Air convertible has the combination spotlight/outside rearview mirror and a radio. (Photo Courtesy GM Media Archive)

(four-door station wagon), and 1524 (two-door club coupe). In all, the midlevel 210 comprised seven styles, while the 240 had just four styles.

Furthermore, an entirely new model, a sports car with a fiberglass body, was introduced late in the model year, the Corvette. This specialty model and the challenges it offered Chevrolet are the subject of chapter four.

During the 1953–1954 model years, comfort and convenience items were added to the list of extra-cost equipment, including power steering, power brakes, power windows, and a power front seat.

1953

Although major sheet metal and trim changes provided a new appearance, more room for occupants, increased luggage compartment space, and greater body strength, the new cars had relatively few mechanical changes underneath the new skin. However, the availability of power steering (a $178 option) added a fresh touch of luxury to Chevrolet. (Ford caught up late in the model year by also introducing power steering as an option.) The Chevrolet Blue Flame 6-cylinder got additional horsepower and the Powerglide was upgraded.

Chevrolet's first sports car, the Corvette, went into production at the end of June 1953 as a 1953 model. This publicity photo shows serial number 1 leaving the Flint assembly line. Though debuting with much fanfare, the Corvette soon faced an uphill battle for survival, finding favor with neither the "boulevard cruiser" nor the true sports car fan. (Photo Courtesy GM Media Archive)

This advertisement for the 1953 Chevrolets promoted the cars' "entirely" new features, including styling, more powerful 6-cylinder engine, the optional power steering, and upgraded optional Powerglide transmission. (Photo Courtesy GM Media Archive)

Power Steering Gets a Boost

As the automobile evolved during the post–World War II years, the passenger compartment was relocated farther forward and low-pressure tires of larger cross section were used to improve ride qualities. This, however, resulted in a larger tire area in contact with the pavement, and thus more steering resistance. Steering gears and linkage were designed to reduce friction and offer higher mechanical efficiency. The ratio of steering wheel rotation to angular deflection of the wheels was increased to ease steering effort for the driver. Employing a large steering wheel also helped to overcome steering resistance. At this point, the only way to significantly reduce steering effort was to make power steering available.

The March 1953 issue of *Motor Trend*, in the regular column "Spotlight on Detroit," referred to power steering as "the most important single engineering development introduced to the public since the end of the war." The writer also wrote in bold type, "Power-assisted steering is here to stay!" Another prediction was that power steering "most likely will become standard equipment in the not-too-distant future." Both statements proved to be accurate, of course. At that time, only seven makes of cars did not have a power steering option.

For 1953, Chevrolet became the first in the *low-price class* to offer optional power steering. Power boost came into effect at 3 pounds of steering effort; no more than 8 pounds of force was needed at any time to engage the power steering system, providing the driver up to 80 percent steering assistance. Chevrolet said the option offered "fingertip ease" for steering and parking. The booster also reduced the ability of road-induced shocks to deflect the wheels and transmit forces to the steering wheel, and it improved steering control in the event of a tire blowout.

Despite the improved control and comfort hydraulic automotive power steering provided, automotive product engineers expressed disdain for it when Francis Davis first patented the design in 1926. He installed a prototype system on a 1926 Pierce-Arrow to demonstrate the benefits of power steering. Product engineers thought paying royalties to the patent holder was a waste of money since they saw no need for the new invention. At the time, mostly men drove cars and they had the arm strength required to turn a steering wheel in even the most difficult situations. The few women drivers simply had to endure the ordeal of parallel parking.

Only after Davis's patent rights expired did power steering begin to find acceptance. A Bendix system based upon Davis's patents was used during the war on Chevrolet armored cars, earth-moving equipment, and track-laying vehicles. Engineers for Chrysler began to see the positive aspects of power steering. It became standard issue for the 1951 Crown Imperial and optional on other Chrysler V-8s. The Chrysler system, though, did not provide adequate road feel, thus it was redesigned for the following year. According to the June 26, 1996, issue of *Automotive News*, Frank Winchell, a retired engineer for General Motors, thought power steering was "superfluous." Many other engineers of the time agreed. On a 1951 road trip from Detroit to Colorado with Ed Cole, who was then chief engineer at Cadillac, Winchell experienced firsthand what power steering could do, but still he was not convinced of any great benefit. (The two may have been using a GM model fitted with an advanced prototype system.) To him, "the steering felt mushy" and road feel was poor. However, Ed Cole believed the public would enthusiastically accept it.

General Motors introduced power steering as an option for the Oldsmobile, Buick, and Cadillac divisions for the 1952 model year. For 1953, it was made available for Chevrolet and Pontiac. The setup, designed and built by the Saginaw Division of General Motors, used valve plungers and spring sets to create a sense of road feel for the driver. Other components included a hydraulic booster added to a recirculating-ball-type steering gear; the booster system consisted of a hydraulic pump, oil reservoir, double-acting cylinder, and a control valve. The hydraulic pump was driven by the crankshaft pulley and wedge-type belt and was mounted on the cylinder block. It was connected to the control valve through a pair of high-pressure hoses. Up to 750 pounds per square inch could be created by the pump. A pump bypass valve allowed for mechanical steering in the event of a failure in the power boost system.

Several modifications to the engine and chassis were required to install the power steering system. Among them

Additional luxury was introduced into Chevrolet passenger cars when optional power steering was offered.* Motor Trend *magazine editors pronounced power steering to be "the most important single engineering development introduced to the public since the end of the war." Chevrolet became the first in the low-price class to offer optional power steering, though Ford soon followed.

was replacement of the regular crankshaft pulley with a double sheave pulley, and the left engine-mount frame bracket had to be reshaped to allow for clearance of the pitman arm. A flexible air duct directing outside air into the interior replaced the metal one on the driver's side and was routed higher over the inner fender to provide clearance for the steering gear.

Power steering allowed for a lower steering gear ratio, which in turn allowed for as much as a 3-inch decrease in steering wheel diameter. As cars got larger during the 1950s, power steering became increasingly important. Trying to parallel park a 1959 Cadillac, for example, without power steering would have been extraordinarily difficult and an unacceptable characteristic, especially in a luxury model. When Chrysler introduced it in 1951, showroom traffic increased significantly, and power steering became a necessary offering for other auto manufacturers. The development of power steering allowed further refinements to the front suspension, resulting in better handling qualities and eliminating the need for a heavy steering shaft, which in succeeding years allowed for tilting steering wheels and collapsible steering columns. Ironically, the conditions that led to the availability of power steering began to fade not long afterward. Parallel parking on city streets diminished as suburban parking lots became more common, and cars eventually got smaller and lighter, reducing the need for power steering.

A lot of testing was performed to refine GM's automobiles. This photo shows the engine compartment of proving grounds car #7566, a 1953 Chevrolet Two-Ten Sedan. GM's proving grounds test facility was (and still is) located in Milford, Michigan. It was the industry's first dedicated automobile testing facility when it opened in 1924. The nature of the testing that resulted in this photograph is not known. (Photo Courtesy GM Media Archive)

More Horsepower and a Better Powerglide

The 235.5 ci received stronger connecting rods with inserted bearings, aluminum pistons, additional crankcase ribbing, a more rigid crankshaft with increased counterweighting to reduce loading on the four main bearings, improved ignition system, and fully pressurized lubrication. In addition, a boost in its compression ratio increased output to 115 hp at 3,600 rpm and torque to 204 ft-lbs at 2,000 rpm when combined with the Powerglide; coupled to the 3-speed manual it was rated at 108 hp at the same revs per minute, though the official torque rating was said to be identical. The larger engine, previously available only

Chevrolet continually upgraded its inline 6-cylinder, first introduced in 1929. It was revised into a second-generation version starting in 1937 and continued to be used in this form into 1964. Model year 1953 was the next-to-last year Chevrolet relied solely upon it to power its cars. It was dubbed the "Blue Flame" for 1953 when coupled with the optional Powerglide. In this guise, it developed a maximum of 115 hp (though 150 in the Corvette). Chevrolet's inline-6 was not phased out in North America until 1990, though it continued to be used in Brazil with fuel injection until 1998. Chevrolet, incidentally, did not offer another inline-6 until 2002.

with the Powerglide, was now available as an option without having to get the automatic transmission. Standard issue with the 108-hp engine was a 3.7:1 axle ratio while the smaller 216-ci 6-cylinder maintained the 4.11:1 ratio. The 3.55:1 axle ratio was retained with the Powerglide.

"Blue Flame Six" was the name of the 235.5 engine when coupled to the Powerglide and was visually differentiated now with blue enamel paint rather than gray. Furthermore, the letters spelling out "Blue Flame Six" were painted atop the valve rocker arm cover in white with red speed lines overlaying them. Less immediately noticeable was the addition of three cylinder head bolts. "Thrifty King" was the label applied to the inline-6 when coupled to the synchromesh transmission. Compression was raised to 7.5:1 from 7.1:1 for this engine. A new automatic carburetor choke was standard equipment on all Chevrolet passenger car models for 1953. A Rochester BC 1-barrel or Carter 2101S was used by the Blue Flame engine while the Thrifty King got a Rochester B or the Carter 2101S 1-barrel.

The price of the Powerglide climbed $178 and was available for not only the Bel Air, but also the 210 series. For the extra expense, the buyer got a Powerglide with a new automatic shift mechanism offering drive with a low and cruising range. Pressed metal was used for the new pump and turbine assemblies. Vanes with tabs fit into slots in the inside and outside shells; the tabs were spun flat to hold the assembly together. Airfoil-shaped vanes of the aluminum stator assembly were integrally cast with its center hub and a wide concave ring was

The 1953 Powerglide Low and Cruising Range

A larger, more efficient three-element torque converter replaced the five-element type originally used. All the components of the earlier torque converter assembly were fabricated from pressed metal and brazed together. Also, moving the selector lever to low or drive adjusted the valve, which controlled the flow of oil pressure. With the new design, the selection of drive directed oil pressure to an automatic shift valve, the relative position of which was controlled by opposing hydraulic pressures. To accomplish this, the new shift valve had a piston in a cylinder applying speed-sensitive pressure at one end and load sensitive pressure at the other end. The transmission rear pump created speed-sensitive hydraulic pressure, and a governor-controlled valve regulated it. Upon initial vehicle motion, the rear pump developed the oil pressure, and the pressure passed to the shift valve piston controlled by a governor driven by the transmission mainshaft.

When extra power was needed after initial motion of the vehicle, such as sudden acceleration just after a start or for passing in traffic, the higher power sought as pressure was being passed by the governor to the shift valve piston was achieved via a load-sensitive hydraulic pressure added to the force of the shift valve piston spring. This allowed low range to be used to obtain the transmission gear multiplication for the higher power demands. Application of the accelerator pedal regulated pressure from the main hydraulic line in the transmission supplying the additional force opposing the governor pressure. Linkage to the accelerator pedal controlled the throttle valve, passing increased main line pressure to the shift valve piston as the pedal was depressed. The main line pressure passed via the throttle valve to the shift valve piston was regulated by a plunger in the shift valve body. Rather than a piston operating in a separate cylinder for controlling the shift valve position, the piston was machined onto the end of the valve spool. Governor pressure was channeled to the end of the shift valve spool to increase the valve area against which it acted. The throttle valve spring regulator slid in a spring-loaded valve detent.

A forced downshift could be made at speeds up to about 40 mph by pressing the accelerator pedal to maximum travel. As the pedal approached its full travel, the shaft of the spring regulator for the throttle valve became flush with the detent valve in which it moved by sliding action. Further pressure compressed the detent valve spring, and a groove in the valve opened the main line pressure directly to the shift valve piston head. The larger area against which the main line pressure acted increased the forces opposing the governor pressure and moved the shift valve to the low range. A high clutch-low servo valve was added to cushion a low-throttle downshift, such as occurs when a car is being brought to a stop. The valve lifted off its seat to allow a more rapid downshift at higher speeds. When the selector was placed in low (or reverse), the governor pressure cut-off valve was forced against its spring and cut off the governor pressure to the cavity at the end of the pressure regulator valve. The converter pressure regulator valve protected the new torque converter from being supplied with excessively high hydraulic pressure. The pressure regulator valve performed the same regulation of the main hydraulic system oil pressure as in the previous Powerglide. However, the governor pressure was now supplied by the cavity at the inner end of the valve.

On June 9, 1953, the 29-millionth Chevrolet, a Bel Air two-door hardtop, was built at Chevrolet's assembly plant in Kansas City, Missouri. This plant was one of 11 in the United States. Chevrolet was the leader in car sales throughout much of the 1930s, 1940s, and 1950s. (Photo Courtesy GM Media Archive)

The Bel Air four-door sedan was again the leading seller in the Chevrolet lineup for 1954. Introduced for the 1950 model year as a two-door hardtop in the Deluxe series, the Bel Air had become its own line by 1953, comprised of four body styles that also included a two-door sedan and convertible. Two-tone paint was optional on all except the convertible. (Photo Courtesy GM Media Archive)

Perhaps the smile on the lovely sunbather's face is because her friend's 1954 Bel Air convertible offers the convenience of power brakes, power front seat, and power windows, all of which were options available for the Bel Air as well as the Two-Ten lines. The Bel Air convertible, with a base price of $2,185, generated 19,383 sales for Chevrolet for this model year. (Photo Courtesy GM Media Archive)

The Townsman station wagon was moved up to the Bel Air line and offered only as an eight-passenger model for 1954. Faux wood returned to the Townsman this year. Its base price of $2,283 made it the most expensive passenger car Chevrolet offered. The rear two seats of the Bel Air Townsman could be removed for extra cargo capacity. Only 8,156 were built before the model was terminated. (Photo Courtesy GM Media Archive)

Shoreline Beige and Pueblo Tan was among the 18 two-tone exterior paint combinations offered for the Bel Air two-door sedan for 1954. Chevrolet was a pioneer in the use of two-tone paint beginning in the late 1920s. Nitrocellulose lacquer, a product of DuPont, was used by Chevrolet and other automotive divisions of GM from about the mid-1920s well into the 1950s. This single-stage paint had the advantage of drying quickly, though it required much hand rubbing to bring to a high luster and was brittle.

Five combinations of leather-grain vinyl and nylon-faced pattern-cloth were offered for the Bel Air two-door sedan. The two-tone interior was standard issue for the series. Interior design was an important part of GM's Styling Section.

This colorful diagram consisting of overlays in the 1954 Chevrolet dealer's showroom album provided a detailed look at inner workings of the "Oil-Smooth Power Flow" Powerglide transmission. The Powerglide was now an option for all series of Chevrolet passenger cars.

Power and economy were promoted with this magazine ad for the 1954 Chevrolet lineup. The "Blue Flame" inline-6 with Powerglide gained 10 additional horsepower through the "highest compression ratio in any leading low-priced car." The ad explained the relationship between more power and improved economy through higher compression. Powerglide was now available for all models.

These colorfully illustrated pages from the 1954 Chevrolet dealer's showroom album explained all the benefits offered by the improved "Blue Flame" inline 6-cylinder with Powerglide and "Economizer" rear axle. Among the boasts is, "With this great 125-hp Automatic Power Team, smooth, silent, economical power takes command on the highway–you'll discover a new and thrilling driving experience." The engine used with the Powerglide transmission had its power increased via a higher-lift camshaft. Aluminum pistons replaced the cast-iron type used since the earliest days of the engine.

welded onto the outside ends of the vanes. Better acceleration from a stopped position as well as at traffic speeds and more power for hill climbing and poor surface conditions (e.g., mud, sand, and snow) were benefits of the revisions. The higher price of the Powerglide was eventually offset by the improved fuel economy of the upgraded six. The extra power added to the 6-cylinder helped propel a Two-Ten sedan equipped with Powerglide to a first-place finish in the Light Stock Class of the Mexican Road Race that year.

Other Improvements

Two types of optional heaters remained available; the recirculating type heater and defroster was retained, but the airflow type was replaced with a new system providing greater operating flexibility and better warm weather ventilation. It allowed outside air from the ventilator duct or air within the passenger compartment to be fed through the heater. If excessive fumes from traffic got into the car, the outside air could be shut off and the temperature maintained by recirculating inside the passenger compartment through the heater. The heater core was relocated from the right-hand ventilator duct to behind the instrument panel.

The electrical system got some attention, too. Either of two optional generators of 45- and 50-amp capacity could be had with a low cut-in speed unit that allowed the generator to charge at very low driving speeds. Increased starting reliability in damp weather was achieved with a revised static-free ignition system comprised of a new distributor, new spark plugs, and new spark plug caps more resistant to moisture.

An automatic headlight dimmer, dubbed the "Autronic Eye," was made available at extra cost for Chevrolet (as well as Pontiac and Buick) this year. It made its debut the previous model year as an option for Oldsmobile and Cadillac. The final chapter of this book provides details on how the system functioned.

Turn signal indicators, front compartment courtesy lamp, remote control outside rearview mirror, and an anti-icing windshield wiper blade assembly were also added to the list of optional equipment this year. The latter had a flexible hood covering all but the rubber blade and its metal support. Its flexible hood was meant to flake off ice as it moved along the curvature of the windshield.

A completely redesigned fuel tank with a one-piece filler neck did away with the vent tube and filler signal (whistle sound) feature. It was no longer needed since the filler neck had a continuous slope to the tank and a larger diameter providing a high rate of fuel flow and air discharge.

Further upgrades included crank-operated vent windows, softer springs for improved ride quality, and optional white sidewall tires that were better protected against curb scuffing simply by no longer extending the white sidewall rubber outward to the chafing rib.

Sales

Sales of the 1953 Chevrolet passenger cars exceeded 1.35 million units. On June 9, 1953, Chevrolet's Kansas City, Missouri, assembly plant built the 29-millionth Chevrolet, a figure reached within six months of Chevrolet's 28-millionth car being built. The total figure was well ahead of that for rival Ford Motor Company; however, the 1954 model year would not be nearly as successful.

1954: More Power and More Luxury

The 1954 Chevrolet sales catalog boasted, "The new 1954 Chevrolet is brimming with beauty, on the outside and in. Its sparkling new styling reflects the sparkling new performance you'll discover when you take the wheel. New interiors are smartly tailored in fashionable, durable fabrics and vinyls. Exteriors are more sleek and sweeping than ever, with fresh new styling details that tastefully accent Chevrolet's long, low Fisher Body beauty. Colors, too, are new!"

Despite the ad writer's boastfulness, the 1954 models were not that different from the 1953s; a revised grille, a bumper that wrapped farther around the fenders, altered side trim, and wheel covers were among the exterior changes. Choices for the exterior colors were also updated and included so-called "Glamour colors" that were metallic shades. The interiors for 1954 were enhanced with two-toned schemes in vinyl and nylon-faced cloth.

In June 1953, Chevrolet built its 29-millionth car. Within one year, Chevrolet had built another 2 million cars. Shown is the 31-millionth Chevrolet, a 1954 Bel Air convertible. In the end, Ford won the model year sales race, though just barely. The release of the small-block V-8 and all-new styling the next model year would again give Chevrolet a comfortable margin over Ford. (Photo Courtesy GM Media Archive)

More important were the additions of power brakes, power front seat, and power windows to the list of optional equipment for the Bel Air and Two-Ten lines and the availability of Powerglide for the One-Fifty series. Furthermore, the output of the Blue Flame Six and Powerglide combination was upped to 125 hp and the compression ratio was standardized at 7.5:1 regardless of the transmission choice, though the horsepower rating for the six coupled to the standard transmission was lower at 115. The 6-cylinder engine used with the Powerglide transmission had its power increased via a higher-lift camshaft. Aluminum pistons replaced the cast-iron type used since the earliest days of the engine. A muffler of greater length and with a deeper tone and more sound-deadening was yet another new feature for 1954.

To get the optional power brakes, the buyer also had to purchase the Powerglide transmission. (This restriction was lifted for 1955.) The power brake unit incorporated a hydraulic cylinder and reservoir, a vacuum power cylinder, and a control valve assembly utilizing engine intake manifold vacuum and atmospheric pressure for its operation. It was mounted to the engine side of the firewall and was connected to a vacuum reserve tank placed on the back of the driver's-side wheel splash pan. Compared to conventional brakes, the power system reduced pedal travel by 50 percent. The reduced pedal travel brought the height of the pedal down to about the same as that of the accelerator pedal, permitting the driver to apply pressure to the brake pedal without lifting his or her heel from the floor; a simple pivot of the foot was all that was needed.

The low cut-in generator, optional for 1953, was now standard for all series Chevrolet passenger cars.

Concluding Remarks

Sales of the 1954 models exceeded 1.151 million, which was more than 200,000 units less than the output for the previous model year. Change was needed to keep pace with the marketplace. The 1954 Chevrolets marked the end of an era at Chevrolet in a sense. Its image was due for a change with the advent of a more youthful marketplace. A new V-8 was coming along with thoroughly different styling. The venerable 6-cylinder was retained as a standard feature of the car, but the powerful V-8 would sell in high numbers. The new car with the new engine arrived just in time, as 1955 was a year of great change for all the major automobile manufacturers and the competition was fierce!

CHAPTER

3 SMALL-BLOCK REVOLUTION & BOLD INNOVATION

1955–1957

From 1949 to 1954 Chevrolet built approximately 7.5 million cars; Ford trailed them by as much as 40 percent in calendar year production through 1951, at which point the sales gap had narrowed to about a 25 percent difference. By 1954, Chevrolet's margin advantage over Ford was gone. In plain numbers, Ford bested Chevrolet in model year production by a little more than 15,000 cars.

The 1957 Bel Air convertible proved to be the most popular of all the so-called "tri-five" years with 47,562 built. Shown in this promotional photo is a Matador Red example. It was clearly aimed at the youth market, which was growing at the time. (Photo Courtesy GM Media Archive)

This promotional photo of a 1955 Bel Air convertible not only shows the car's all-new styling, but suggests it sits three side-by-side comfortably. It also clearly shows the two-tone paint scheme, Gypsy Red and India Ivory, one of many possible two-tone possibilities offered for the Bel Air. Note the "V" emblem under each taillight; this indicated the car was equipped with one of the optional small-block V-8s. (Photo Courtesy GM Media Archive)

Ford had also beaten Chevrolet in the matter of the V-8 engine. Ford offered its Y-block overhead valve engine in passenger cars starting with the 1954 model year. Even Studebaker was offering a V-8. Demand for a V-8 engine had grown from 26 percent of the new car market in 1950 to 33 percent in 1952 and to 50 percent by 1954, leaving no doubt that the V-8 was a major consideration for those buying a new car. Within General Motors, only Chevrolet and Pontiac were without one. Fortunately for General Motors, Chevrolet had already acted to reverse the trend of losing market share to Ford with planning for all-new and exciting 1955 models that began in late 1951 with serious body development commencing by the

The Chevrolet Engineering Center was still being constructed when the 1955 Chevrolets first went on sale. This 638,000 square-foot facility in Warren, Michigan, north of Detroit, was built alongside the GM Tech Center. As originally built, the facility contained a fully equipped experimental shop approximating a self-contained automobile factory, a machine shop, 18 dynamometer rooms, and enough equipment to put automobile hardware through as many as 3,600 tests, some running for weeks at a time. (Photo Courtesy GM Media Archive)

Chevrolet's innovative styling was born in the Chevrolet Studio of GM Styling with designers such as Clare "Mac" MacKichan (standing in foreground) who became chief of the Chevrolet Studio in 1951, a position he held for 11 years. He was deeply involved in the designs of the first-generation Corvettes, the Corvette-based dream cars for the 1954 GM Motorama, and the 1955–1957 Chevrolets. All styling studios were under the command of the vice president of the styling section, Harley J. Earl. (Photo Courtesy GM Media Archive)

middle of the following year. General Motors purchased new plants, including facilities in Flint, Michigan, for production of the new V-8, as part of a major expansion program labeled by the press, "GM's Billion Dollar Gamble."

Chevrolet's 235-ci 6-cylinder was not a help to sales as the early portion of the 1950s ticked away. Those with performance in mind either had to swap engines or take the advice given in contemporary automotive publications such the May 1953 issue of *Hot Rod* magazine on how to double the horsepower of the "Stovebolt Six."

Well before the author wrote that *Hot Rod* article, though, Chevrolet's engineers had been at work developing the new V-8, a small-block engine that had far more potential than initially recognized. Chevrolet engineer Zora Arkus-Duntov agreed with an interviewer in the mid-1970s that the 283 would "go down in history as the most efficient V-8 in the history of automotive 8-cylinder engine building," adding that it was capable of "660 hp at 8,500 rpm in dragsters." That small-block was not only important to the success of the all-new Chevrolet released in 1955, it was also vital to the Corvette's survival.

The V-8 was not all that was in development during the early 1950s. An all-new Chevrolet body design was in the works as well as an air-conditioning system fully contained within the engine compartment. Three years were expended in the 1955 Chevrolet design, and it was a major achievement in automotive history owing to all the features included in what was classed as a low-priced car. The introduction to the Fingertip *Facts for the 1955 Chevrolet* (an informative book for dealers) said of the new car: "It's a completely new concept of low-cost motoring—without parallel in automotive history. Starting with a clean slate, Chevrolet first found out, through exhaustive research, exactly what people want in a car of lowest cost; then developed—in one compact design—values that exceeded people's greatest expectations of a car of Chevrolet's class . . . As a result . . . Chevrolet is by far the most beautiful, most enjoyable, and finest performing Chevrolet ever built." Those were bold words, but many buyers of cars in the low-price class evidently believed Chevrolet was offering them a very good automobile for their money.

1955

In the December 1954 issue of *Motor Trend*, Walt Woron detailed the new 1955 models. His introductory comments regarding the 1955 Chevrolet revealed the stark contrast between the 1950 to 1954 models and the new car:

"Seldom has there been a car that year in and year out has been described in the same monotonous style:

'Not a car of high performance'

'Continues to provide good, economical transportation'

'A car that won't set the connoisseurs aflame with desire'

Ed Cole posed with the new 1955 Bel Air in this photo taken prior to the opening of that year's GM Motorama at the Waldorf-Astoria.* Motor Trend *magazine editor Walt Woron wrote in the December 1954 issue about the new car: "The Engineering Dept. headed up by Ed Cole has come out with a machine that's not only going to give fits to the other members of the Low-Priced Three, but is going to keep the other divisions of General Motors hopping to stay out of the Chevy's way." He was right. (Photo Courtesy GM Media Archive)

"Who said this about what car? We did, about the Chevrolets of model years 1950 through 1954, and justly so. Now, there could be no one happier to announce that we can junk all these old phrases."

Woron attributed the change to "mostly a new philosophy in thinking about their product and its relation to the competition. The Engineering Deptartment, headed up by Ed Cole, has come out with a machine that's not only going to give fits to the other members of the Low-Priced Three, but is going to keep the other divisions of General Motors hopping to stay out of the Chevy's way."

The Chevrolets of 1956 and 1957 that followed were, of course, built upon the foundation of the 1955 model. Under the fresh, modern styling of all these models were multiple and popular innovative features (albeit a number of them were optional at extra cost) all of which were offered for a low-priced automobile. Ultimately, the combination of styling and performance offered by the 1955–1957 models, especially with the Bel Air series, led to one of the most successful and important Chevrolets in automotive history. While General Motors had about half the automobile market in 1955, the Chevrolet Division of General Motors alone accounted for half of the company's sales. Today, the 1955–1957 Bel Air two-door hardtops and convertibles are at least as captivating as they were six decades ago, thus they are among the most sought automobiles among collectors.

The New Small-Block

Under the stylish sheet metal of the brand-new 1955 Chevrolets was an all-new optional small-block V-8 displacing 265 ci. It offered performance previously unknown in a Chevrolet, and it served the division in various displacements (up to 400 ci) and revisions throughout the 1950s and into the early 21st century.

By the time the 1952 models were in showrooms, Thomas Keating, Chevrolet's general manager at the time, was well aware that the division he was charged to oversee was facing stiff competition from Ford. Chevrolet had become dated in the eyes of many potential buyers. Ford released a virtually all-new design for 1952 with a more modern look with flush quarters that was lower and wider than the 1949–1951 models. It had a new chassis as well with a longer wheelbase of 115 inches, equaling that of the Chevrolet. The 1952 Chevrolet looked like a near clone of the 1951 model and still had only a straight-6 to power it while Ford had a V-8, albeit the old flathead dating back to the early 1930s.

Keating warned GM's Engineering Policy Committee that Chevrolet was "too 6-cylinder minded." His arguments were evidently convincing because in December 1951 the committee agreed a modern V-8 was needed.

The small-block program was begun under Edward Kelley, who had developed Chevrolet's Stovebolt Six, introduced with the 1929 models. A second-generation version was introduced for 1937. While Kelley was a respected engineer, those around him reportedly felt he seemed to be stuck in the past. The engine under way at that time was a scaled down version of Cadillac's 331, which debuted for the 1949 model year. It had a displacement of 231 ci. Kelley's V-8 was essentially complete when engineer Edward N. Cole was tapped to take over the project. Cole could see that the Cadillac-based engine had little potential for growth, was relatively heavy, and had unacceptably high production costs, according to *Chevrolet: A History from 1911* by Beverly Rae Kimes and Robert C. Ackerson. Indeed, the Kelley engine would have added about $100 to the base price of a Chevrolet had it been put into production. Though an insignificant amount of money today, the extra cost would have amounted to adding roughly 5 percent to the base price of a Bel Air with the V-8.

In May 1952, Ed Cole was appointed to the position of chief engineer for Chevrolet; at the suggestion of Cole, Kelley was moved to head the manufacturing side of the upcoming V-8. Chevrolet's new engine finally went from drawing board to the first prototype in 15 weeks. Less than two years after the first prototype engine was built, the new small-block was in production.

In all, about 2,900 people were responsible for engineering the 1955 Chevrolet. One of them included Assistant Chief Engineer Harry Barr, with whom Cole worked when designing the Cadillac ohv V-8. Barr not only participated in the V-8 program but was also placed in charge of engineering the new chassis. Russell Sanders, a mechanical engineer, was also a member of the chassis development team. Additional appointments made by Cole included Ellis Premo to take charge of body development and Maurice Olley as director of research and development. Olley was recognized as one of the most knowledgeable of suspension engineers; he came to General Motors from Rolls Royce in 1930. Working under Olley, starting about mid-1953, was Zora Arkus-Duntov, who soon made his mark in automotive history through his work on the Corvette. Others included Al Kolbe and Don McPherson, an assistant to Kolbe. Years earlier, Kolbe had worked on Packard's so-called "Twin-Six" V-12. McPherson began his career as a draftsman and later played roles in the development of the Chevy II and Camaro, was director of engineering for Cadillac before becoming the head of the Buick Motor Division, and was later named president of General Motors of Canada.

With the release of its new V-8, Chevrolet proudly stated, and truthfully so, that its "Turbo-Fire" 265 was "a milestone in automotive history." At the time, no one could foresee just how significant the engine would become in later years as the small-block design served as the basis of much larger displacement versions up to 400 ci. Revisions of the design kept it in use into the 21st century. For 1955, the base 265 V-8 offered 162 hp at 4,400 rpm and added $99 to the base price of a Chevrolet. (Photo Courtesy GM Media Archive)

At the time of his appointment to Chevrolet's chief engineer position, Ed Cole was managing GM's Cleveland Tank Plant where he had been since 1950, working on the M41 light tank for the U.S. Army. He began his career at General Motors after receiving a grant from Cadillac to attend the GM Institute in Flint. He went to work for Cadillac even before graduating

Ed Cole, chief engineer for Chevrolet, headed the design of Chevrolet's modern overhead valve small-block V-8. Cole believed new manufacturing methods were necessary to significantly reduce the cost of mass-producing the V-8. Cost was as critical a factor as any engineering specification. His thinking proved to be correct. In the end, the small-block weighed less than Chevrolet's inline 6-cylinder and was ultimately found to be adaptable to much larger displacements. The small-block V-8 served into the early 21st century! It also helped save the Corvette from cancellation. (Photo Courtesy GM Media Archive)

from the school. In 1946, he became Cadillac's chief engineer. These experiences made him the right man in the right place at the right time when he took over Chevrolet's V-8 program.

In May 1952, however, Cole was asked to become the manufacturing manager for Chevrolet, not its chief engineer. He felt that Chevrolet was not exciting enough to take on that job, but said he would accept the position of chief engineer, to which General Motors agreed. Thus, Kelley took on the job initially offered to Cole. In the book *Chevrolet 1955: Creating the Original*, author Michael Lamm quoted Ed Cole as saying, "Ed Kelley's background was heavily oriented toward manufacturing. Anybody who's been in manufacturing has a tendency to design what the manufacturing people feel they need. [And an engineer with that background wouldn't] stretch them out perhaps as much as they could be. For example, when we talked about 5/32nd crankcase walls, and the casting for the new block, the manufacturing people said, 'Well, you just made a mistake. We don't make anything less than 5/16th.' Ed Cole 'stretched' them in order to produce the right engine."

Alex C. Mair, executive engineer in charge of 1955 Chevrolet truck bodies, noticed the immediate impact Ed Cole had on the 1955 Chevrolet design effort. Mair was assigned to an aircraft engine project (General Motors had the Allison Division at that time) in Tonawanda, New York, when he received a call from Ed Kelley. Kelley told him to come back to Detroit. Mair, who was interviewed by Lamm, said, "So I had one day's notice that Chevrolet Engineering was going to be reorganized, and I must tell you that in all my life's work—in all the time I worked at General Motors—it was never so obvious that a new person was in charge . . . almost, I would say, one day after Cole got there, Chevrolet Engineering had a whole new feel. It was a vibrant feel, exciting, and you knew Ed Cole was there. Boy, I'll tell you: What a change!"

Mair also explained how General Motors got on a path to the new Chevrolet V-8: "Chevrolet had become so powerful and was so far ahead, outselling everybody . . . because almost everything Chevrolet did sold well. As a result, some of the top people at GM began to notice, and the sharpest ones realized that Chevrolet was standing on its laurels. The division wasn't leading the way as it had in the past; the new 6-cylinder engine for 1929, all-steel roof for 1934, independent front suspension in the lowest-priced cars for 1935, automatic transmission and hardtop convertible for 1950; that sort of thing . . . they figured they needed somebody who would come in there and just knock the place apart. And Ed Cole did that, because as you know, Chevrolet sold 1.83 million cars that first year of the V-8, 1955, plus 393,000 trucks."

With the release of its new V-8, Chevrolet proudly stated, and truthfully so, that its "Turbo-Fire" 265 was "a milestone in automotive history." At the time, no one could foresee just how significant the engine would become in later years. An interesting aside is that Ford was initially planning to discontinue offering a V-8 for 1955 (though it would have continued to be used by the Mercury and Lincoln divisions)! The out-of-touch upper management was convinced the cost of the V-8 versus the 6-cylinder was too high and that Ford buyers would accept the inline 6-cylinder. Fortunately for Ford, a recently hired manager was able to persuade them otherwise. If that had not happened, Chevrolet would not have had Ford as a perennial archrival for many years to come.

A Different Approach and Teamwork

Cole believed new manufacturing methods were necessary to significantly reduce the cost of mass-producing the V-8. Cost was as critical a factor as any engineering specification. In *Chevrolet 1955: Creating the Original*, Lamm quoted Ed

Cole, regarding the Cadillac-inspired engine developed under Kelley, as saying: "Chevrolet had been working on a V-8 for some time. And when you do that, you lay down a design and you start making just little changes on an existing design without starting with a clean sheet of paper. What we did was to start with a clean-sheet approach. We did that with the entire car." His clean-sheet approach included a different way to cast the engine block.

> I felt there were other ways to make that engine; make it better, more precise, and less costly . . . we decided to make the precision cylinder block, which became the heart of the engine. [We did this] by using an entirely different casting technique. We used the green-sand core for the valley between the bores, the 90-degree V-angle in the center. We used a green-sand core to eliminate [most of] the dry-sand cores [used previously]. Getting rid of the dry-sand cores let us cast the block upside down. That allowed the plate that held the bore cores to be accurately located, so the wall thickness could be controlled. And we could cast down to 5/32-inch jacket walls. That was the technique we used. And then we went to the stamped rocker arms and the hollow push rods for a different oiling system.

The green-sand technique, according to Cole's interview, "was a combination of ideas" and he credited John Dolza, of the GM Engineering staff, as having "as much to do with that as anybody." Dolza had used the concept of the green-sand technique while working on a V-6 for Pontiac. (See sidebar "The Canceled Chevrolet V-6" on page 43.) The new block-casting technique delivered much higher precision cylinder bores. It also represented a breakthrough in thin-wall castings. Dolza, incidentally, had earned two master's degrees, one in electrical engineering and the other in mechanical engineering from Polytechnic Institute in Turin, Italy. In 1927, he began working for Buick as a draftsman; by 1946, he had been transferred to the GM Engineering staff as head of power development.

The weight of the small-block is often quoted as having been only 488 pounds, about 40 less than Chevrolet's 6-cylinder. However, the book *The Hot One—Chevrolet: 1955–1957* by Pat Chappell gives the total weight as 531 pounds, 147 of which was in the cylinder block and 47 in the crankshaft versus 163 pounds and 79 pounds, respectively, for the 6-cylinder. A side-by-side breakdown of the weight of the components for both engines, though, does reveal the small-block V-8 weighed 41 pounds less than the six.

Dubbed the Turbo-Fire V-8, it was a compact oversquare (larger bore size than stroke) type featuring hollow pushrods, independent stamped-metal rocker arms, an intake manifold that also served as the valley pan, interchangeable heads, a superior heat rejection rate compared to the straight-6, fully water-jacketed ports, aluminum pistons, a relatively high compression ratio, wedge-shaped combustion chamber, and a pressed forged-steel crankshaft rather than alloy iron.

Displacement at first was figured at 245 ci, but soon a displacement of 260 to 265 ci was selected because it would not materially add to the weight of the engine and the additional size was needed to keep pace with the trend toward ever-increasing displacement. For a 260 ci, bore size was then established at 3.75 inches, resulting in a 2.93-inch-long stroke, but this was soon changed to an even 3 inches that finally led to a 265-ci V-8. Bore centers were firmly established at 4.4 inches, which in turn determined the length of the crankshaft and other parameters, leading to a compact cylinder block 21.75 inches long.

According to the *1955 Chevrolet Engineering Features* manual, the 265 V-8 had one of the best stroke-to-bore ratios (0.8:1) attained up to that time in an oversquare design. Its advantages were listed as less piston travel per mile of vehicle travel, lower reciprocating loads for smooth operation, and materially less wear on the pistons, rings, and cylinder bores. Its compression ratio of 8.0:1 helped to optimize fuel economy and power. The compact size (cylinder block length of less than 22 inches) resulted in high structural rigidity and allowed ample installation clearance within the engine compartment for easy serviceability.

Hollow pushrods allowed for splash lubrication to the rockers and valve stems, thus eliminating the need for separate oil lines, as well as the typical oil passages in the heads. The idea was not at all new, though. Hollow pushrods had been in use for about a half century by this point. Still, other issues regarding the rocker arm mechanism required innovation. *Chevrolet 1955: Creating the Original* contains the transcript of an interview with Harry Barr who said:

> There were problems with the hemispherical ball; the mating surface of the rocker arms. Also in the amount of the oil that came up through the hydraulic lifters. One of our engineers, [Bob] Papenguth was his name . . . came up with a little wafer, a method of metering that oil in the lifter . . . a little logjam that was essentially overcome. Then there was the mating surface between the rocker ball and the arm to be sure that contact was broken. That contact was heavier at the lower surface. In other words, [we needed] some mismatch of contact [in order for the oil to get between the two surfaces]. And then [we had to have] the right amount of [oil] metering and distribution.

That matter was still not exactly right when the engine went into production. Early rocker arms squeaked at the rocker balls along with other problems that had to be fixed. Three holes were drilled horizontally into the block: one main and two tappet oil galleries. A drilled hole from the high-pressure main oil gallery aligned with a hole in the camshaft rear bearing shell to maintain steady oil flow under high pressure and through another hole to each of the tappet galleries.

The stamped sheet metal rocker arm originated at Pontiac and is credited to engineer Clayton Leach, who was working on the division's V-8 in 1947. (Pontiac's V-8 program experienced delays; it was originally intended for release in 1953, then 1954, before finally arriving for 1955.) At the same time Chevrolet was crafting its V-8, Pontiac was working on its version, also scheduled for release for the 1955 model year. Chevrolet's engineers consulted with the manufacturing group, and personnel soon determined the stamped rocker arm could be made without any machining being necessary. It was a significant determination during the development of the small-block because it allowed for the assembly of a lightweight valvetrain that could safely rev up to about 5,500 to 6,000 rpm.

Michael Lamm interviewed Leach for his book on the development of the 1955 Chevrolet. Leach said:

> So Chevy, in order to prevent too much oil from flying around, going down the exhaust valves into the combustion chamber . . . decided to save some money by not drilling the passages to the main ball pivots which carry, of course, the main load. And when they did that, they had to get some lubrication on that, so they had to drill a small hole in the pushrod socket in the rocker arm . . . Now later, Pontiac did the same thing, sometime in 1965. They dropped that pressure lubrication to that main ball, which in my opinion was a big mistake. It caused a lot of problems. They went back and did what Chevrolet did. . . .

As an aside, the rocker arm covers were designed with aesthetics in mind. Ed Cole believed they should be made to have as nice a look to them as cost considerations would allow; hence, the stylish Chevrolet script across the top.

By having the intake manifold also serve as the valley pan, production costs (as well as a bit of weight) were reduced. The use of interchangeable heads also helped cut costs, eliminating the need to produce left and right versions.

Heat dissipation was improved over that of the 6-cylinder to the point that a lighter radiator could be used, which again reduced cost and weight. The V-8's water pump had a 3.5-inch diameter rotor to push coolant throughout the cooling system; the rotor's blades were curved at the entrance then straightened to a 90-degree exit angle. The pump pulley was driven at 95 percent of crankshaft speed.

Turbo-Fire's fully water-jacketed ports and aluminum pistons provided an improved heat dissipation rate. The "autothermic" slipper-type piston with three rings had a circumferential expander for the single oil ring that provided axial and radial force to control the burning of oil. Piston pins were pressed in place, which eliminated the need to slit the rod and add a locking bolt. The short stroke naturally kept the rod length relatively short. This, in combination with the use of aluminum for the pistons, reduced the overall reciprocating mass.

New forging techniques made a rather short crankshaft possible and reduced torsional vibration. Testing showed the vibration levels to have very low peaks without sharp peaks throughout much of the rpm range; a harmonic balancer canceled the remaining vibration. New technological and process-

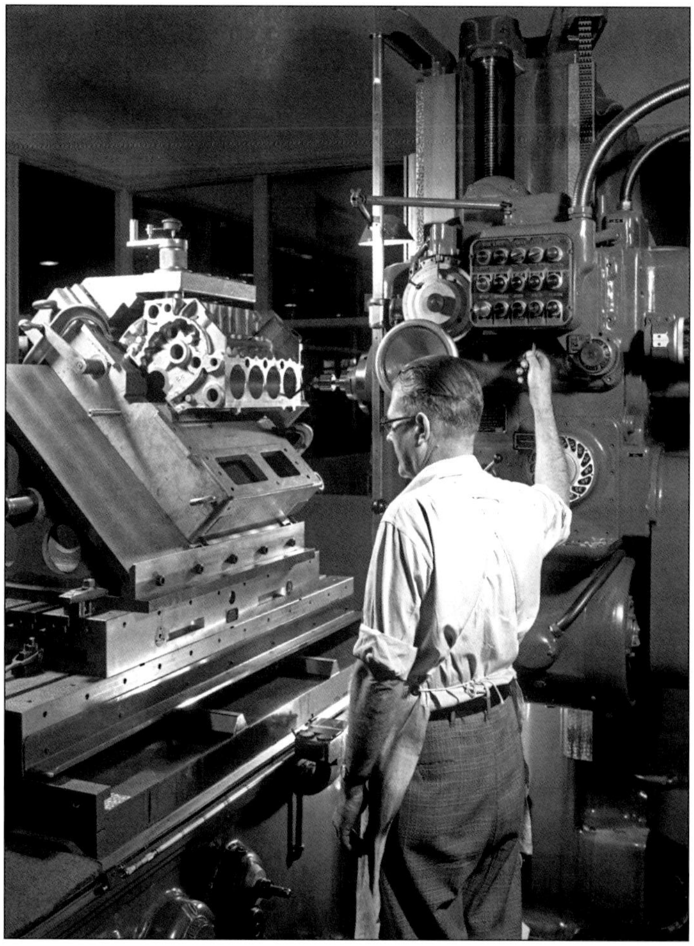

New methods of manufacturing had to be developed to produce the new small-block V-8. The green-sand core eliminated most of the dry-sand cores previously used, which allowed casting the block upside down. This, in turn, allowed the plate that held the bore cores to be accurately located so that wall thickness, down to 5/32 inch, could be controlled. In the past, wall thickness was limited to twice that dimension. (Photo Courtesy GM Media Archive)

ing developments had to be adopted to balance the engine. Its crankshaft was partially balanced on a new machine with electronically controlled indicators. Final balancing of the assembled engine (minus the oil pan) was accomplished on another new device that could stop the rotation at the point it went out-of-balance and drill the front and rear crankshaft counterweights the required amount to achieve balance.

Also important in regard to damping engine vibration was the dynamically balanced four-point "Poised-Power" engine mount setup for the V-8 (as well as the 6-cylinder). The four mounting points were located and inclined so that the resulting roll axis produced only minor reactions to the frame and body from torque produced by the engine. In front were two strut-type mounts; each consisted of four circular rubber biscuits on a metal spacing stud secured to a bracket on the front lower corner of the cylinder block and perpendicular to a seat on the frame front crossmember. A set of the rubber biscuits was placed on either side of the bracket and likewise on either side of the crossmember. Two shear-type mounts were in back and replaced the single compression-type mount used in the past. They attached to the lower rear edges of the clutch housing and the engine mounting brackets welded to the frame side members. The mounts consisted of two brackets separated by bonded rubber. The rubber acted in shear upon engine roll and in both shear and compression for engine support.

The engine's wedge-shaped combustion chamber had, according to the *1955 Chevrolet Engineering Features* manual, "a large quench area for control of detonation. This flat quench area also acts as a squish surface when the piston compresses the intake mixture. As the piston rises, the mixture is forced away from the squish area, imparting turbulence to the fuel-air mixture and assuring fast and complete combustion. The cylinder head design places the spark plug in the hottest area of the combustion pocket. When ignition occurs, the flame spreads evenly and rapidly throughout the combustion chamber for a smooth pressure rise and freedom from detonation. A portion of the cylinder head forms a lip which overhangs the cylinder bore and protects the spark plugs from oil which may be scraped off the cylinder walls by the piston rings, thus ensuring reliable ignition."

As compression ratios increased during this era, consideration had to be given to preventing detonation, or premature combustion of the fuel-air mixture, which can impart destructive forces upon the pistons. Higher compression was a key component to increasing power, as well as economy, from engines and was made possible by tetraethyl lead, a fuel additive. At the time, a compression ratio as high as about 12:1 was envisioned by engine designers. Any ratio much beyond that was determined to be of little benefit.

A newly designed pulsator fuel pump moved fuel from the fuel tank to the carburetor. It did away with the glass bowl and filter screen used in the earlier type, eliminating the need for periodic cleaning. During its pumping stroke, air from the dome over the diaphragm was compressed by the incoming fuel and then expanded as the fuel was released into the carburetor. The pump valves were increased in size to help prevent vapor lock.

The 265-ci Turbo-Fire was offered in two versions for most of the model year. Both came bolted to one of three transmissions offered: the standard 3-speed transmission, the optional 3-speed with overdrive, or the optional Powerglide. The respective standard axle ratios for each of these three were 3.7:1, 4.11:1, and 3.55:1. Regardless of the transmission attached, the 265 with a Rochester 2-barrel was rated at 162 hp at 4,400 rpm and had a torque rating of 257 ft-lbs at 2,200 rpm. It added $99 to the base price of any model. The one topped with the so-called "Power-Pack" Carter 4-barrel carburetor became available shortly after the start of the 1955 model year. It was rated at 180 hp at 4,600 rpm and torque was advertised as 260 ft-lbs at 2,800 rpm.

Carburetor linkage for the Power-Pack (described as "two dual carburetors contained in one assembly") was designed so that the secondary throttle plate opened when the accelerator was pressed to about 50 percent of its maximum travel. The secondary throttle plate would not open regardless of accelerator position, though, until the engine temperature was high enough to open the automatic choke. A special air cleaner and dual exhaust (except in station wagon models, which had a fuel tank shape preventing the use of a second exhaust pipe) were included with the Power-Pack. The 180-hp engine had the same 8.0:1 compression ratio as the 162-hp type. To get the Power-Pack option, the buyer had to pay an additional $59.20 above the $99 base price of the V-8, for a total cost of $158.20. A 154-hp version with 7.5:1 compression was an option for pickup trucks, which were also new for 1955. (Trucks are detailed in chapter 5.) Very late in the model year, a Super Turbo-Fire version packing 195 hp became available (see the sidebar "Racing Raises Chevrolet's Image" on page 65). Compared to a 1950 Chevrolet, the 1955s offered a much higher level of performance. A 1954 Bel Air with Powerglide required about 18.1 seconds to accelerate from 0–60 mph.

A 1955 Chevrolet powered by the 180-hp engine, however, cut that time by almost half. *Motor Trend* editor Walt Woron, who ventured to the GM Proving Grounds in Milford for the press showing to test-drive 1955 Chevrolets with both versions of the V-8 and Powerglide, wrote in the December 1954 issue of the magazine that the time for 0–60 mph was reached "around 6 seconds *less time* than it took the '54 Chevy to reach the same speed. At passing speeds (30 to 50), it'll lop off over 2 seconds, and takes around *13 seconds* less to reach 80 from 50 mph. These speeds are awfully close to what the hottest cars of '54 could do—and this is only the 162-hp version!"

Reporting on the 180-hp car he stated, "From 0 to 60 . . . we knocked off from $1^1/_2$ to 2 seconds *more* than the 162-hp job. And from 50 to 80, we knocked off another 4 seconds, making the '55 Chevy faster in this speed range *than all '54 cars tested!*" *Motor Trend* also tested a 6-cylinder with stick-shift, and, not surprisingly, it was quicker than the heavier 1954 model; 0–60 mph was accomplished in 15.3 seconds and 19.9 seconds was required for the quarter-mile.

This was just the beginning of a lengthy high-performance era based upon Chevrolet's small-block.

Early Engine Problems

As revolutionary as the small-block was for the day, it was not perfect when it was released. High oil consumption proved to be a problem with the early 265s. Writing for *Popular Mechanix*, Floyd Clymer reported that an Ohio shipping clerk complained of his car using 3 quarts of oil every 10 days, but after driving it 1,000 miles the oil consumption dropped to 2 quarts then later to 1 quart. Clymer personally experienced 1 quart of oil consumption in 400 miles of driving. As it turned out, 22 percent of owners were complaining of the problem. The trouble was traced to two flaws: too fine a honing of the cylinder walls and a greater oil supply to the valve operating mechanism than was intended. Some dealers had a unique fix for the fine honing of the cylinder walls; it was pouring the cleaning abrasive "Bon Ami" into the carburetor to scuff the cylinder walls. It appeared to work, but was not (and is not) a recommended procedure because of the high risk of cylinder wall damage.

Another early problem with some engines was failure of the stamped rocker arm assembly. Solid lifters were installed on cars with the manual-shift transmission, and the failures were confined only to these engines. The problem was traced to over-revving by high-spirited owners. However, those engines were more prone to this failure because of an error on the engine assembly line. According to Michael Lamm's interview with executive engineer Alex C. Mair for the book *Chevrolet 1955—Creating the Original*:

> There were three items on the engine that they had trouble with. One had to do with the machine [on the engine assembly line] that pressed in the rocker studs. They had an automatic system in the plant which, if the studs were pressed in too high, the engine would be rejected. And if they were pressed in too low, the engine would also be rejected . . . somebody apparently loosened up that automatic system in the plant and didn't tell anyone. It was not rejecting the low end of the force being pushed in. Quite a few of those engines, when the driver would over-rev them—and the engine was so lively that people weren't used to that—they would run up to the valve-float speed, and the valves would touch the pistons when they stayed open too long. When they did that, the force would push the stud out of the head a little ways. And, of course, then when it came down, the valve wouldn't open all the way up. It was also extremely loud because of the big clearance, the valves would clatter. So, we had a series of those all happening in the first two or three days. But they fixed that in the plant right away.

By November 1955, all 265s were equipped with hydraulic lifters.

These early problems had only a negligible impact at most on demand for the V-8. Once the engine became available, keeping up with demand for it became something of a challenge for Chevrolet. The new engine plant built in Flint had to work at maximum capacity and even that was not enough; some production had to be performed at the Tonawanda plant. The V-8 was chosen by 43 percent of the people who purchased a new 1955 Chevrolet. Some sales were lost because customers simply did not want to wait for their new car.

The Chevrolet bowtie and "V" combination emblem was attached beneath the taillights of 1955 Chevrolet passenger cars equipped with one of the optional V-8 engines.

The Chassis

With the new body came a new chassis giving what was dubbed "Quadra-Poise Ride" through a "Glide-Ride Front Suspension" along with an "Outrigger Rear Suspension" and wide-base wheels and tires. *Fingertip Facts for the 1955 Chevrolet* conveyed the concept this way: "From the new

Glide-Ride Front Suspension to the location and construction of the seats . . . from the softer-riding tubeless tires, to the new Outrigger Rear Suspension, new designs and features have been incorporated . . . to assure better riding comfort, better roadability, and even greater stability. Its lower center of gravity, well-distributed weight, and wider tread combine to give a safer, road-hugging ride."

Everything was designed with weight as an important consideration, though function and reliability were, of course, foremost. Ed Cole noted, "The whole concept of the car was built around lighter components. We started, in other words, to get away from the heavier torque-tube drive and went to the Hotchkiss type. We went to a Salisbury-type axle instead of the banjo-type. And then we went to a ball joint front suspension for weight savings and to a tubular frame." It all added up to the best chassis design to date for Chevrolet.

The frame side rails were a square-tube type with uniform wall thickness and increased cross-sectional area, which provided increased resistance to twisting. Relative strength of the frame was increased 18 percent over the previous design. Convertibles had a slightly different frame with an added X-member fabricated from I-beams. While the side members

The Canceled Chevrolet V-6

From road to roof, much was new in the 1955 Chevrolet passenger cars. Even so, another revolutionary change almost came about for the model year: a V-6! In an age when the V-8 was highly desired by many, a V-6 may seem quite out of fashion for the times. The V-6, though, was intended to replace the inline 6-cylinder engine, and therefore would have been fitting for the times. Chevrolet was all set to release its V-6, but at the last moment decided against it despite seven years of research and development. Instead, the engine appeared in public in only conceptual form in two nondivisional dream cars displayed at the 1955 GM Motorama show tour and other venues, the GM LaSalle II roadster and sedan.

Chevrolet almost introduced what would have been a revolutionary change in the automobile industry in 1955: a V-6! At the last moment, however, management decided against it despite the seven years expended on its development because they felt there was quite enough that was new in the 1955 line.

The 60-degree V-6 engines for the LaSalle concept cars were nonfunctional castings without provisions for internal components, but represented all-aluminum, fuel-injected, double-overhead cam (DOHC) powerplants expected to produce a maximum horsepower of 150 in finished form. Phillip Frances Jr. was one of the engineers assigned to the V-6 project by GM Engineering Power Development Manager John Dolza. Previously, Dolza had designed a 60-degree V-6 for Oldsmobile prior to joining Ed Cole on the Chevrolet V-8 program. Frances had previously worked on a 120-degree V-6 for Pontiac, though it was a completely different design. He believed Charles Chayne initiated the concept for the 6-cylinder program and that the motivation for it was its more compact size. According to him, this engine was not originally intended to be a fuel-injected aluminum DOHC design, but had a conventional cast-iron block and heads with a single cam; the more advanced aspects were seen as prospects for the future, though.

As work progressed, the LaSalle II project began concurrently and Dolza asked Frances to change the design into a DOHC type. However, that task could not be completed in time to use real engines in the LaSalles. Work continued on the V-6 until it was ready for production as a Chevrolet engine, but GM managers evidently reconsidered the idea of releasing it due to production cost considerations as well as the fact the division had just authorized the release of its new V-8 and a virtually all-new Chevrolet. Managers felt Chevrolet simply had enough new ideas debuting for 1955 and that one more might be tempting fate.

for closed models were square tubing made from flat steel stock that was rolled and welded, those of the convertible were made from stamped channels (one slightly narrower than the other) joined by overlapping them slightly, then welded together to form a rigid unit. Both the convertible and the hardtop bodies had extra body mounts. Rather than a crossmember for rear engine support, an engine support bracket was welded to each inner surface of the side rails.

Adding rigidity to the frame assembly was the integration of the front crossmember into the frame structure. The previous design had the front crossmember as an assembly with the front suspension and attached with eight bolts per side to the bottom flanges of the frame side members. Structurally integrating the frame-to-front crossmember allowed the frame side member to form part of the coil spring tower and made the provision for the mounting of the rebound control bumper.

The *1955 Chevrolet Engineering Features* manual describes the front suspension as: "Chevrolet's Knee-Action suspension, time-tested by millions of owners, incorporates important new design features for 1955 and an innovation exclusive to Chevrolet—braking dive control." The new front suspension retained the short- and long-arm parallel link principle of independent suspension, but all of its components were newly designed. Among the innovative components were lightweight spherical joints with nonmetallic (phenolic impregnated fabric laminations) concave bearing surfaces, rubber-mounted control arms that required no lubrication and reduced the transmission of road shocks and vibrations, and diagonally mounted coil springs and shock absorbers. The nonmetallic concave bearing surfaces were an adaptation of those made for use in steel rolling mills. Their advantages included improved durability, increased longevity in conditions of infrequent lubrication compared to metal-to-metal bearings, and decreased sensitivity to foreign matter. Mounting the coil springs and shocks diagonally positioned them nearly tangent to the lower control arm arc of travel, thus minimizing distortion of the springs and providing a nearly constant deflection rate for the suspension. The new front suspension was said to offer greater durability, improved ride and stability, and simplified maintenance. Furthermore, the spherical joints in combination with the front suspension geometry reduced braking dive by 45 percent.

The Outrigger Rear Suspension allowed for a lower vehicle profile as well as improved handling, ride quality, and smoother drivetrain reactions to torque and braking application. Its leaf springs were 9 inches longer and 1/4 inch wider than in 1954, which reduced their deflection rate and increased their durability; they were spaced farther apart by 3/4 inch and mounted outboard of the frame, too, improving roll stability. Sedans and coupes had four leaves while station wagon models received five. Hotchkiss, or open drive, was employed rather than torque tube drive. (With torque tube drive the driveshaft is enclosed in a tube filled with oil and utilizes only one U-joint, which is mounted at the transmission end.) The setup gave greater durability and higher torque capacity while eliminating the oil seal assembly problems associated with torque tube drive. More rigid pinion shaft supports, cast Armasteel differential housing, higher capacity differential bearings, heavier axle shafts, integral bearings and wheel seals, and a more rigid axle housing were included in the design.

Tubeless tires were now standard equipment on all models; a new tread design provided a quieter ride. Because of the use of tubeless tires, extra quality control for the wheels was necessary, but other than having four stamped lugs on the outer horizontal portion of the rim for more secure attachment of the wheel covers, the wheels were unchanged.

In the aforementioned December 1954 *Motor Trend* article, test driver Walt Woron had high praise

Shown is test car 5203 (note the stencil on the rear frame crossmember), which was thoroughly photographed inside the GM Proving Grounds garage prior to the car's 25,000-mile run. (Photo Courtesy GM Media Archive)

for the new chassis: "The way it performed around the winding, twisting, asphalt handling road at GM Proving Grounds, I wouldn't be afraid to stack it up against many of the so-called sports cars. The long, outrigger rear springs, lowered center of gravity, and good weight distribution all add up to a car that *stays where you put it in corners*. If you take it too fast, it'll break, as it should. But, all you need do is to punch the throttle and you're out of trouble."

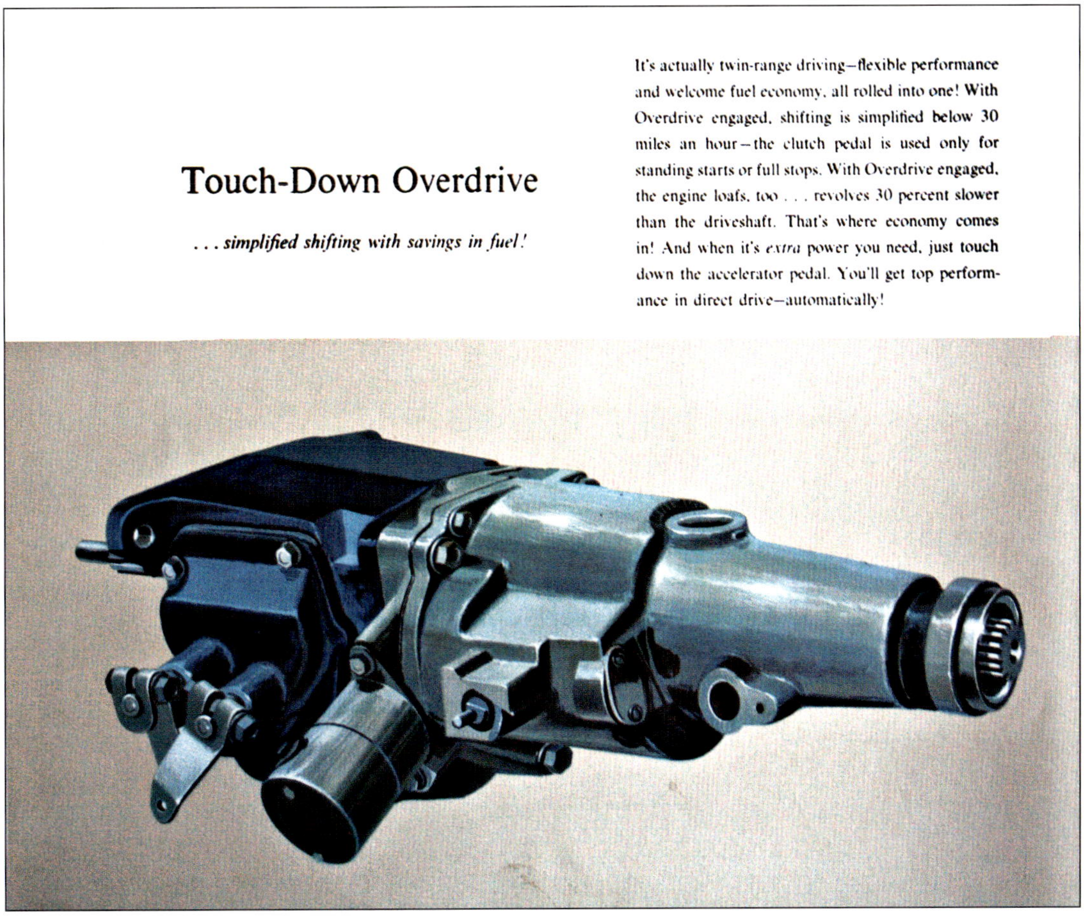

The optional "Touch-Down" overdrive transmission greatly reduced engine speed, thus improving economy of operation. For 1957, it received various upgrades to improve "shift feel" and dependability.

Additional Mechanical Features

Chevrolet (as did Pontiac) switched to a 12-volt electrical system for 1955, making all passenger car divisions uniform in this respect. The 12-V system provided improved starting capability for the V-8, more efficient generator output, and allowance for smaller-gauge wiring and cabling.

Although many resources were dedicated to the V-8 project, Chevrolet's engineers did not ignore the 6-cylinder engine. It received a new, side-mounted air cleaner to fit under the new, lower hood contour, an improved water pump with a larger impeller, a larger cooling fan, a redesigned oil pump with a floating-type pickup, and grooveless main bearings. An oil pan baffle was added to reduce oil surging upon hard stops. Furthermore, several design changes reduced its overall dimensions to adapt it for installation in the new chassis. Output was now rated at 136 hp at 4,200 rpm with Powerglide and 123 hp at 3,800 rpm with the 3-speed manual transmission.

Both the V-8 and the inline-6 when coupled to the manual transmission could also be had with the newly optional overdrive unit made by BorgWarner. The "Touch Down" overdrive option cost an extra $108. It had a 0.7:1 ratio, cut in at about 31 mph, and reduced engine speed by 22 percent.

The 3-speed manual transmission was modified to provide increased torque transmitting capacity and greater durability. Improvements consisted of a larger-diameter mainshaft, more intensive surface treatment of the gears, a sliding spline with a better fit, and wide-spread mounting centers for a more rigid attachment to the clutch housing. Another improvement associated with the manual transmission was both cosmetic and mechanical: the concentric gearshift control. It gave a new look to the steering column and reduced rattles associated with the old design.

The Powerglide transmission was extensively redesigned for 1955 to give smoother operation, increased durability, and easier servicing. A greatly simplified hydraulic system featuring a double-wrap low band was the greatest change. The double-wrap low brake band was composed of three circular segments, which provided greater holding power and faster and more positive disengagement of the band. Since it had up to four times more holding power than the previous single-strap band, it could be operated with lower main line pressure. The vacuum modulator, the primary and secondary clutch valves, and high-clutch low servo valve were no longer required with the lower pressures. Other changes were made to adapt the Powerglide to the Hotchkiss drive and the new, optional V-8.

Power steering, a $91.50 option, was redesigned to give

Chevrolet's innovative Powerglide received improvements for 1955. Among them were double-wrap low-band and modified hydraulic pressures to create a smoother shift. Since its release for the 1950 model year, more than 2 million Chevrolets equipped with the Powerglide automatic transmission had been sold.

more efficient operation and greater driving comfort. Key components were relocated to increase their effectiveness, and a longer pitman arm reduced the overall steering ratio to 23.1:1 from 25.7:1. A vane-type hydraulic pressure supply pump similar to the one used for 1954 was used, but the pump was mounted on the rear of a special generator and was driven by a splined extension of the armature shaft. A hydraulic fluid reservoir was placed in a concentric arrangement around the pump. Also, the non–power steering system incorporated the recirculating ball and nut principle formerly only available with power steering. The recirculating ball and nut steering gear transferred rotating force into a linear force through many free rolling balls that performed much like threads of a bolt act against a nut. Because a ball rolls with little friction, the recirculating ball and nut steering gear provided efficient, smooth operation.

Also improved was the power brake system, which was now available on all Chevrolet models. It added $37.70 to the base price of any model. The pedal mechanical ratio was changed to 1.55:1 from 1:1. This change was said to reduce pedal effort under power-off conditions by one-third. Pedal travel was increased due to the change in the car body design; however, the low brake pedal position was maintained so that the driver could move between brake and accelerator pedals with a mere pivot of the heel, as had been the case when power brakes were introduced the previous model year.

New rotary door latches allowed doors to close more easily and quietly and held them securely shut. Even if the door was not fully closed, it would not accidentally open because of the teeth in the rotary latch acting as a safety catch.

At midyear, revised optics to the headlight lens increased low-beam visibility by as much as 80 feet.

A Youthful Look

Chevrolet advertising for the 1955 models made many claims: "For the young in spirit" and "Here's Chevrolet's new show car styling at its beautiful best . . . New look! New life! New everything!" Some promotional material featured the slogan "Motoramic Chevrolet," which, along with the phrase "new show car styling," was a reference to the dream cars shown at the GM Motorama, the traveling exhibition General Motors sponsored. The best known today of all the catchphrases is "The Hot One." All these boasts had merit. The wraparound, or "Sweep-Sight," windshield, planned from the start of the styling process for the 1955 models, was a styling touch lifted from the GM LeSabre and Buick XP-300 concept cars, both completed in 1951 and included in the 1953 GM Motorama show circuit. The wraparound windshield went into use for three production models starting with the 1953 model year; all the cars with the innovative windshield were limited-production models: the Cadillac Eldorado, the Oldsmobile Fiesta, and the Chevrolet Corvette. By 1955, all of GM's new models, including its trucks, had the wraparound windshield.

While the wraparound windshield was planned from the start, other aspects of the car's innovative styling underwent some changes. For instance, the early design process positioned the hoodline low between the front fenders with the fender line continuing into the front door where it would subtly dip at the A-pillar (windshield post). From there, the body line continued straight back. As the engine design progressed, it simply became too high to fit under the low hood, leading, of course, to a higher hoodline, which in turn caused the fender height to be raised to maintain the recessed hood. This forced the dip to be much greater than in its previous form, creating an awkward

An early Fisher sample body is shown here inside the Argonaut Building's 11th-floor auditorium. Early bodies were mounted on a chassis for testing at GM's Milford, Michigan, proving grounds. Deliveries of early bodies began in February 1954. (Photo Courtesy GM Media Archive)

The new features of the 1955 Chevrolet passenger car body were detailed in this diagram for the dealer's showroom album, now a rare and collectible piece of literature for enthusiasts. Of note is the "high-level ventilation" in the cowl that allowed air to flow into the engine compartment. This was at a time when air-conditioning in an automobile was still uncommon and an expensive option. Chevrolet introduced air-conditioning for 1955, though its high price resulted in few orders.

appearance. The changed height of the hood and fenders also altered the proportions of the car, giving it a tall, narrow look. Finally, the recessed hood concept was abandoned and was essentially raised to fender height. (As it was, an air cleaner for the 6-cylinder had to be designed to fit underneath the hood, which necessitated a small revision to the carburetor main metering jet to compensate for the slight increase in restriction caused by the side-mounted air cleaner.) The fender line continued almost through the door then dipped near the C-pillar just as on other GM passenger cars, except for station wagon models, which had a straight line from pillar post to pillar post.

This Fisher-built convertible was used for testing at GM's Milford, Michigan, proving grounds. Early cars like this one were not fully trimmed but had all major hardware installed. Note that the parking lamp openings were covered with plates. (Photo Courtesy GM Media Archive)

The Ferrari-inspired grille arrived late in the process. Earlier proposals for the grille carried forward the general look of those for 1953 and 1954, none of which suited the vice president of GM Styling, Harley Earl. He found what he wanted during his annual trip to the European auto shows in the fall of 1953, where the egg crate grille of the Ferrari gave him inspiration. Earl decided an adaptation of the Ferrari grille was exactly the look the new Chevrolet needed. When the new Chevrolets were introduced in October 1954, though, the grille design appeared to have been a major mistake. Dealers did not like it (which is reminiscent of how

This unrestored 1955 Bel Air Sport Coupe with 70,000 actual miles still wears its original India Ivory paint. It is equipped with the 162-hp engine coupled to the optional Powerglide transmission. Production of the Bel Air Sport Coupe for 1955 (185,562) was exceeded only by the Bel Air and Two-Ten four-door sedans and the Two-Ten two-door sedan. The lower cost of those models does not explain their higher production. The Two-Ten Sport Coupe was also lower priced than the Bel Air Sport Coupe, but only 11,675 of those were sold. The economy was strong at the time and people could afford the more luxurious Bel Air.

dealers reacted to Harley Earl's tail fin on the 1948 Cadillacs) and the public resisted it as well. People were used to seeing a full-width grille and for a time, by all appearances, Harley Earl seemed to have violated his own principle of not going too far too fast with change; in other words, presenting more change than the public could and would accept at one time. However, soon the public warmed up to, or at least learned to live with, the Ferrari-style grille and sales took off.

The 1955 Chevrolets' styling made them *appear* to be lower, longer, and wider. The look was partly an illusion; the car was indeed lower (about 6 inches for wagons and more than 2 inches for other models), but was around 1 inch *shorter* and 1 inch *narrower*. The lower height in combination with a hood line nearly flush with the top of the front fenders helped obtain the desired effect.

Other styling highlights included flush rear fenders, a vast number of two-tone paint schemes for the 1955 Bel Air and Two-Ten lines, and a twin-cowl dash and instrument panel very similar to that of the Corvette, a car that first appeared in prototype form at the 1953 GM Motorama. A decorative panel along the instrument panel of Bel Air models had 987 "Chevy bowties," the official logo for the division, cut into it. The idea for this feature was probably inspired by an external panel, also with the logo cut into it, placed at the rear of the 1954 Chevrolet Corvair shown during that year's GM Motorama and other venues. Those flush rear fenders were a first for Chevrolet; the bulging rear fenders used through 1954 dated back to the 1940s. The overall look of the car gave cause for some to think of it as a "baby Cadillac."

The matter of styling was not limited to the car's exterior. The so-called "Coloramic interior" was offered in 30 distinct arrangements of color-coordinated, two-tone patterns consisting of fabric and vinyl. The seats for the Bel Air and Two-Ten models were decorated with chromed moldings

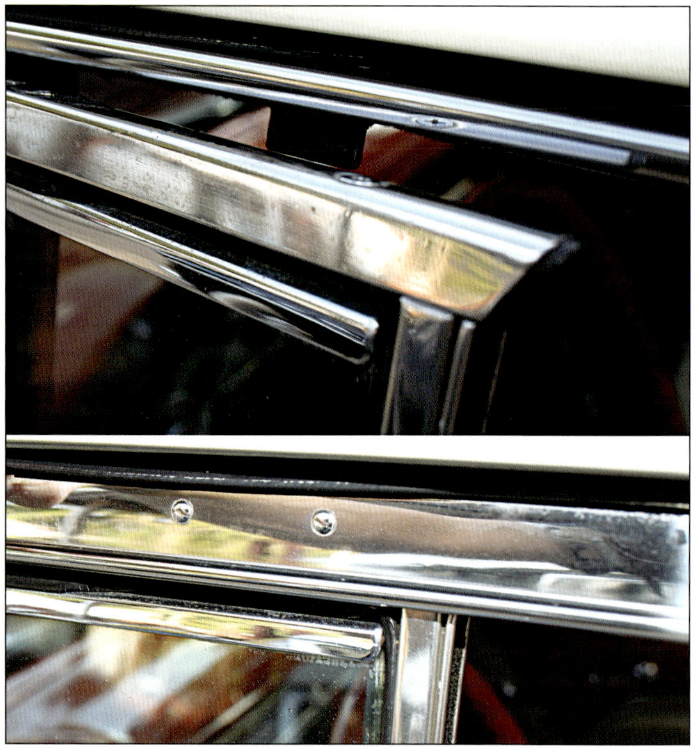

The "flipper" along the roof rail, which first appeared on the 1952 Chevrolet Bel Air two-door hardtop, was continued with the 1955 two-door hardtop. It closed over the door glass window frame to provide better sealing against wind noise.

along the front seat end panels. Furthermore, these two lines of cars had as standard equipment automatic interior lamps that lit when any door was opened. The One-Fifty line had its own distinctive upholstery pattern, including the Delray introduced later in the model year. The Delray offered a more attractive interior than other members of the One-Fifty series.

Harley Earl's innovative use of lines, curves, trim, and

This molding served as the dividing line for the special two-tone paint in which the roof, rear deck, and upper quarters contrasted with the rest of the body. The conventional two-tone paint option resulted in the roof and lower body being painted contrasting colors. Note the black-out paint on the vertical piece to simulate air intakes. In addition to 21 two-tone schemes offered were 14 single-tone color choices such as the India Ivory seen here.

This aircraft-inspired hood ornament was standard for all 1955 Chevrolet passenger car models. It was a one-model-year-only design, though the 1956 version was similar.

New fabric and vinyl upholstery patterns were among the many new features of the 1955 Chevrolets. The Bel Air received two-tone upholstery as standard issue, except for the convertible, which had a two-tone all-vinyl interior. Straw-pattern cloth and red vinyl is shown here. This Bel Air Sport Coupe is equipped with the accessory parking brake reminder light, deluxe push-button radio, and the accessory accelerator pedal cover that included a rubber heal disc to protect the flooring.

The two-toned door panel featured a built-in armrest and a flattened V bright metal molding, all standard features of the Bel Air. Built-in armrests were on all doors of Bel Air models, except those of the station wagon.

The V theme of the main instrument panel was continued on the passenger's side of the dash. The "Bel Air" name appeared over the black mesh in an anodized gold finish. Note the Chevrolet bowtie emblems cut into the bright molding running across the full width of the dash.

These five standard upholstery color combinations were offered for the 1955 Bel Air Sport Coupe. Four of them combined straw-pattern cloth with vinyl while the other was gray pattern-cloth with vinyl.

The Delray Club Coupe was introduced later in the 1955 model year. This version of the Two-Ten two-door sedan had all-vinyl upholstery and heavy-pile carpeting as well as the other standard features of the Two-Ten line. Black and ivory was the standard color combination for the interior, though two alternate choices, dark green with ivory and dark turquoise with ivory, were available.

color greatly contributed to another major success for General Motors. Chevrolet sales, which were the best ever, easily exceeded those of archrival Ford, which also had new styling for 1955 (though it retained its 1952 inner structure) and also had its best sales year ever. The Chevrolet Division accounted for about half of GM's passenger car sales while GM had half of the overall car market.

Leadership and Cooperation Lead to Success

Cole certainly had the right people working under him as well as the right philosophy to achieve success. He believed in efficiency and was very much against unnecessary weight in an automobile. (He was something of a maverick in this regard because at the time heavy weight in a car was perceived as somehow better.) His philosophy was passed along to those he appointed to take charge of the various components making up the new Chevrolet. In the end, 151 pounds were shaved off the previous Chevrolet, 99 from the chassis. Greater interchangeability of major body panels between Chevrolet and Pontiac further reduced tooling and manufacturing costs.

In the introduction to the *1955 Chevrolet Engineering Features* manual Ed Cole wrote, "The 1955 Chevrolet is a tribute not only to the technical skill, but also to the vision, ingenuity, and the enthusiasm of those responsible for its conception and ultimate design." In his interview for *Chevrolet 1955: Creating the Original* Cole noted that today [1974] "if

The Innovative Harley Earl

Harley J. Earl directed the styling of all the so-called "Tri-Five" Chevrolets. Earl was hired in 1927 by then–GM president Alfred P. Sloan to set up a styling department for the company. Up to that time, styling had not been a priority, but Sloan had wondered for some time why the matter of styling had not played a major role in the development of mass-produced automobiles. Thanks to a confluence of events that led to Harley Earl meeting Frederick Fisher, one of the founders of Fisher Body, which by then was a division of General Motors, styling was ultimately elevated to as much a priority as engineering. This meeting in the early 1920s put Earl on a course for a three-decade-long career with General Motors. Under his leadership, sales of GM cars rose from a 12 percent market share in the 1920s to 52 percent by 1956. Styling was a major reason for that tremendous growth.

Harley Earl was born on November 22, 1893, in Los Angeles and grew up in Hollywood before the advent of the movie industry. He was the second of five children born to Jacob and Abbie Earl and the only one to follow in his father's footsteps. Jacob, who had experience as a woodworker and lumberjack, established the Earl Carriage Works in 1889 in Los Angeles, where he repaired and built horse-drawn wagons and carriages. With the automobile gaining in popularity, Jacob began constructing car bodies, and in 1908 he renamed his company to Earl Automobile Works. The clientele of Earl Automobile Works also flourished during this period thanks to the successful new movie industry in Hollywood. Film producers, such as Cecil B. DeMille (who lived only a short distance from the Earls), along with movie stars, such as Roscoe "Fatty" Arbuckle, Douglas Fairbanks, Tom Mix, and Mary Pickford, became customers. Earl later sold his company to Don Lee, a Cadillac distributor and owner of nearly four dozen dealerships throughout the state of California. He continued to build custom cars during his employment with Don Lee Coach & Body Works.

In 1926, Harley Earl was given a contract to design the LaSalle, a car meant to fill the price void between Buick and Cadillac. The success of the 1927 LaSalle convinced Sloan that Earl was the man to set up a studio to direct the styling of GM's automobiles. Harley Earl had used full-scale clay models at Earl Automobile Works to

Harley Earl began his designing career while working at his father's Earl Carriage Works, where he helped build horse-drawn carriages. With the advent of the automobile it soon evolved into a custom-car business. Earl took over his father's business and developed styling techniques, such as the full-scale clay model, he later brought with him to General Motors where he was hired in 1927 to establish the company's styling department. (Photo Courtesy GM Media Archive)

THE INNOVATIVE HARLEY EARL CONTINUED

show his customers the custom styling touches he would add to their cars. Earl was quoted as saying, "A picture is worth a thousand words, but a model is worth a thousand pictures." In an article he wrote in 1954 for the *Saturday Evening Post* he said, "My primary purpose for 28 years has been to lengthen and lower the American automobile, at times in reality and always at least in appearance. Why? Because my sense of proportion tells me that oblongs are more attractive than squares just as a ranch house is more attractive than a square, three-story, flat-roofed house or a greyhound is more graceful than an English bulldog." His approach was highly successful.

An article published in the October 1955 issue of *Industrial Design* magazine said, "Harley J. Earl, a large man who directs design for the world's largest manufacturer of consumer goods, has in the past 30 years left his personal mark on some 40 million General Motors cars. To some extent he has left his mark on the cars of all GM's competitors too. Fiercely addicted to his product . . . and inspired by an uncanny instinct for the likes of the masses, he has developed a unique and rigid esthetic that has influenced American car design beyond calculation. Often this influence has been direct and personal—the majority of the top designers in Detroit have worked for Earl at one time or another, and to many of them he has been the sole master from whom the trade was learned."

The article explained that Earl's "domain" consisted of 5 auto studios and 12 special studios and shops with each having a studio head reporting directly to him. At that time, the combined number of people working under Harley Earl totaled about 850 with 150 being designers, 100 working as clay modelers, 100 as engineers and shop workers, and about 500 working as administrators. The story noted that "the presence of such an imposing body of skilled personnel has helped to establish styling as a solid and respectable branch of business activity. Harley Earl rules his business-within-a-business like an exemplary executive, multiplying his authority by delegating it. He seldom lifts a pencil. The studios in which the pencils lifted are organized so efficiently to harness talent and channel authority that if you try to unearth one genius behind any GM design you have but one choice . . . Earl's unique ability to channel ideas of hundreds of minds into one product has been one of the major factors in the growth of the Styling Section at General Motors, and in the development of the character of the American car."

you wanted to take the same risk [with so many new components for one car design], you'd promptly be fired."

One other important point about Ed Cole's leadership in the creation of the 1955 Chevrolets was his friendly relationship with styling chief Harley Earl. Earl and engineers many times did not see eye-to-eye, so this was an unusual and productive situation. Cole firmly believed the new car had to perform well *and* look great, an attitude that served General Motors very well. As noted in *The Hot One: Chevrolet 1955–1957*, "the 1955 Chevrolet was a styling sensation as well as an engineering tour de force, and it benefited in this respect from the talents of a man equally as gifted in his field as Ed Cole was in his—Harley Earl. GM's Styling Section readied an all-new body to go with the new engineering of the '55 Chevy, one appropriate to the advances Cole's team had made."

The Nomad

The 1955 season began with Chevrolet offering 14 models, but in February the sporty two-door Nomad wagon was added to the line. It was another rationale for the "Motoramic Chevrolet" ad slogan. A Corvette-based, fiberglass bodied two-door station wagon named "Nomad" was on display at the 1954 GM Motorama. Its debut at the Waldorf-Astoria in January was met with great approval, so much so that the Nomad was given the official go-ahead for production but with the Nomad concept car's greenhouse grafted to a Bel Air body. Incidentally, the same was done at Pontiac to create the Safari.

The Nomad was not expected to sell in large numbers, but instead was intended to create publicity for Chevrolet. This publicity would cause the public to go to dealerships to see the new model and, more often than not, buy a different Chevrolet automobile.

Lifted from the Nomad concept car and adapted to the Bel Air were a roof featuring transverse grooves across its rear half, forward-leaning B-pillars, and the seven vertically mounted bright metal trim pieces on the tailgate. It also had the Corvette-like open rear wheelwells as seen on the Nomad concept. This particular feature, though, was unique to the 1955 version.

The Nomad was positioned as a part of the Bel Air line and as such had high-grade two-tone upholstery and other appointments of the Bel Air series.

Sales of the first-year Nomad totaled 8,386 units, the highest output the model would generate. Modest sales volume was a consequence of the sporty design featuring only

The Panoramic Windshield

The wraparound, or Panoramic, windshield was the idea of Harley Earl. Earl had tried to have glass bent into a wraparound shape around 1918, but the experiments always ended with the glass cracking. He did not quit on his idea. Finally, Libbey-Owens-Ford was able to develop methods of mass producing wraparound windshields for Harley Earl. It was showcased on his concept cars, the LeSabre and XP-300, in 1951, then spread to production cars, even to competitors. Shown is a 1956 Chevrolet Bel Air Sport Sedan with wraparound glass front and rear. (Photo Courtesy GM Media Archive)

Along with fins, the wraparound windshield is a well-recognized hallmark of automobiles of the 1950s. GM's styling chief, Harley Earl, introduced the idea to the motoring public first with two concept cars, the GM LeSabre and the Buick XP-300. For 1953, the wraparound (General Motors labeled it the Panoramic Windshield) went into production with the release of the limited-production Oldsmobile Fiesta, Cadillac Eldorado, and the Chevrolet Corvette. The former two were luxury cars while the Corvette was a sports car, which in itself became another of Chevrolet's innovations and is a story told in the next chapter of this book. Even GM's all-new pickup trucks got the new style of windshield during 1955, scoring another first in the industry.

The wraparound windshield moved the corner post blind spot from the driver's vision. It also added significantly more glass area (more than 18 percent for 1955) for greater all-around visibility. It was visually appealing to car buyers and was soon copied by GM's competitors. Ford even included it on the F-100 pickup by 1956. Unfortunately, the sharply curved areas caused some distortion, though drivers learned to live with it. The wraparound windshield could be had as a tinted version at extra cost. Iron-oxide added to the glass produced a blue or blue-green tint to alleviate tiring glare for drivers.

The path to making the wraparound windshield practical to mass produce was not an easy one. At least as far back as 1918, Harley Earl had tried to have glass bent to form such a windshield, but his manufacturer could never find a process to keep the glass from ultimately breaking. The closest Earl could get to the idea was a multipiece arrangement with angled-back end panels. (An example of a car he designed with this arrangement while working for coachbuilder Don Lee is a custom-built 1920 Cadillac in the collection of the GM Heritage Center.) In the late 1940s, Earl contacted Libby-Owens-Ford to ask them to try to develop the means to manufacture the wraparound windshield. Harley Earl's persistence was rewarded when L-O-F discovered how to bend laminated glass. He further specified a tint for the LeSabre and XP-300 versions.

The 1955 Nomad combined the most important styling elements of the 1954 Corvette-based Nomad concept car with the Bel Air body: forward-swept B-pillar posts, rounded rear wheel openings, transverse grooves in the rear portion of the roof, and chrome-trimmed tailgate. This sporty two-door station wagon was added to the Chevrolet line in March 1955. At $2,472 with the inline-6 and $2,571 with the base V-8, it was the most expensive model offered. Not surprisingly, it was the least produced with only 6,103 made. However, high-volume production was not its purpose; its purpose instead was to entice people to visit their local Chevrolet dealer. (Photo Courtesy GM Media Archive)

The Beauville, which seated up to six, was the top-of-the-line station wagon model with all the amenities of the Bel Air and advanced features introduced by Chevrolet for 1955. Styling, of course, shared the design of the rest of the passenger car line except for the beltline dip. Instead, the beltline followed a straight line. The same was true of all wagon models. A total of 24,313 Beauvilles were built. (Photo Courtesy GM Media Archive)

The Nomad had a unique upholstery pattern of waffle-pattern cloth and vinyl. That waffle pattern was transferred to vinyl for the 1956–1957 Corvette's upholstery. Chevrolet's designers were constantly looking for innovative styling ideas not only for the exterior of their automobiles but also the interior.

The 1956 Nomad was a little less distinctive than the original version. Its quarter panel wheel opening shape was the same as the rest of the passenger car line rather than rounded as it was for 1955. Upholstery, too, more closely matched that of the Bel Air.

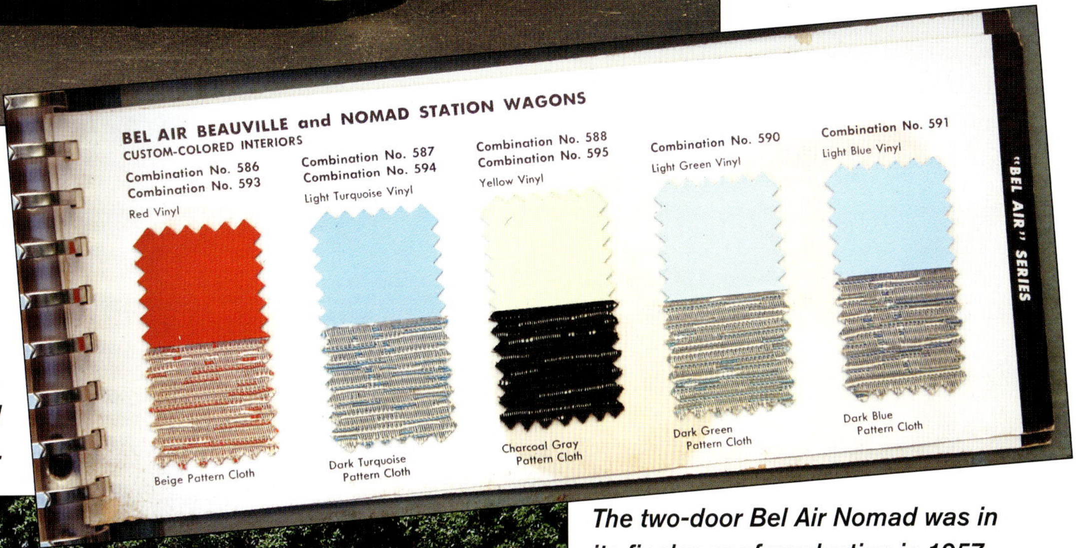

These five vinyl and cloth upholstery color combinations were offered for the 1956 Beauville and Nomad station wagons. Upholstery of the latter was not as distinctive as it was for the 1955 Nomad, which had a waffle-pattern cloth.

The two-door Bel Air Nomad was in its final year of production in 1957. Many of them were modified in the 1960s for drag racing and many are customized today, leaving factory stock examples like this Dusk Pearl and India Ivory version quite uncommon today. This Nomad, one of 6,103 built, is well-equipped with air-conditioning, power windows, power seat, electric windshield wipers, backup lights, 220-hp 283, Powerglide, and wheel covers with simulated knock-offs.

As on previous renditions of the Nomad, the 1957 model featured chromed vertical strips on its tailgate. Note the use of anodized gold for the model identification scripts. Also clearly visible is the bumper guard and taillight combination with the upper crescent-shaped portion housing the tail, stop, and directional signal lights while the lower section served as the bumper guard as well as the housing for the optional backup lights, which this Nomad has. When the backup light option was not ordered, decorative plates covered the opening.

The Nomad seated six. However, the rear seat could be folded down to make room for additional cargo. Bright metal bows graced the headliner of this model. Interior dimensions changed a bit for 1957 with small losses in headroom (front and back), legroom (front and back), and shoulder room (front only).

The rear seat of the Beauville folded down to give additional cargo capacity. Its backrest was split about 80/20, so that either side or both could be folded down, though most likely the larger portion would have been folded down, allowing one person to sit in back while space was made for extra cargo.

two doors instead of the four needed by most station wagon owners and the relatively high base price of $ 2,571, the highest for any model in the Chevrolet lineup. A four-door Beauville station wagon, a member of the Bel Air series, could be had for more than $200 less. For 1958, the Nomad became a four-door model selling in far higher numbers.

The Bel Air

While the more economical Two-Ten series accounted for more of Chevrolet's overall sales from 1955 to 1957, the Bel Air Sport Coupe two-door hardtop far and away outsold the Two-Ten Sport Coupe for all three model years. As for the Bel Air series, it was the only one to offer a convertible. The latter accounted for 41,292 sales for 1955, a nearly identical total for 1956 of 41,268, and 47,562 sales for 1957, the highest figure of the three model years.

The Bel Air, also available as a two-door sedan, four-door sedan, and a four-door hardtop dubbed Sport Sedan, offered a rather high degree of luxury. In fact, Harley Earl once said there was "a little Cadillac" in these cars. Standard features included extra side trim, anodized gold nameplates, a bright metal cove insert along the dash, full-circle horn ring, electric clock, armrests of greater length than those of other series, higher-grade upholstery, unique door panel design, and full carpeting.

For 1955, the Bel Air upholstery consisted of a "new selection of the latest fabrics and new textures in the coated fabrics, vinyl, and Elascofab, all used in striking color combinations." The bright metal insert ran the full width of the dash and featured hundreds of cut in Chevrolet bowtie trademark emblems. Bright metal headliner bows, standard for the Bel Air Sport Coupe, were unique to the 1955 model year.

The midlevel Two-Ten Sport Sedan of 1957 accounted for 16,178 sales. Far more popular was the higher priced Bel Air version of this body style with more than eight times as many sales. The Two-Ten could easily be distinguished from the Bel Air because it lacked the trio of simulated vents on the forward portion of the front fenders and the aluminum insert on the quarter panels. (Photo Courtesy GM Media Archive)

The Sport Coupe was the second-most produced model in the Bel Air line and the third-most overall, even exceeding the lower priced two-door sedan in the Two-Ten line. A total of 166,426 were built. (Photo Courtesy GM Media Archive)

As on a two-door hardtop, the four-door hardtop's B-pillar was truncated at the beltline, and in the case of the latter, served as the hinge post for the rear doors. The use of twin models served to draw attention to the openness of the design. Note that this sport sedan was equipped with the power-adjustable front seat. (Photo Courtesy GM Media Archive)

Chevrolet's advertising drew a connection between the GM Motorama concept cars and the styling of its all-new 1955 model with the phrase "Motoramic Chevrolet." It also noted the special styling attributes seen on the earlier concept cars, such as the "Panoramic windshield" and dipped beltline. Last, the ad claimed more people bought a Chevrolet than any other car in 1954, but it did not note calendar year sales, rather than model year sales were the basis for the claim. However, Chevrolet regained the lead in model year sales for 1955. Though Ford had a new-looking car, it was a cleverly reskinned version of the 1952–1954 body. The 1955 model year was a big one for the Big Three auto producers, but with GM, and especially Chevrolet, coming in first place.

Upholstery for the 1956 and 1957 Bel Airs was a combination of Jacquard weave cloth and vinyl.

The level of luxury and sportiness when combined with a high-performance small-block made the Bel Airs of 1955 and 1956 the most successful passenger cars in the low-price field of the era while the 1957 faltered a bit, allowing Ford to catch up that year. Today, all three model years, collectively known as the "Tri-Fives," are among the most treasured of the decade of the 1950s.

Optional Equipment

The list of optional equipment and dealer-installed accessories was extensive. Other than the choices of V-8, overdrive, and Powerglide were tinted glass, 6-ply white sidewall tires, directional signal, push-button AM radio, Signal Seeker radio, the automatic headlight

General Motors celebrated a special milestone with the production of the company's 50-millionth car, a 1955 Bel Air Sport Coupe painted gold with hundreds of gold-plated components, such as the bumpers, grille, park lamp bezels, and ornaments. Even the shock absorbers were gold-plated! The car was displayed at many venues, including that year's GM Motorama, as seen here. (Photo Courtesy GM Media Archive)

These all-vinyl interior schemes (left side and center) for the 1957 Bel Air convertible were unique to the model and included this raised dot pattern. Five convertible-top colors (right) were offered.

All closed Bel Air models, including the Nomad, were equipped with these combination fabric and vinyl schemes for 1957. Each series had a fabric design unique to it, though the Bel Air convertible made use of all-vinyl upholstery.

dimmer dubbed Autronic Eye, power front seat and windows (not offered separately, option code 397), two-tone paint, and air-conditioning.

Several two-tone paint schemes were offered for the Bel Air and Two-Ten lines. The body side trim of both series made possible two types of two-toning dubbed "conventional two-tone" and "special two-tone." Conventional resulted in a roof and lower body of contrasting colors while the latter had the roof, deck, and upper quarters one color and the rest another. An extra molding was added between the rear bumper and the tip of the quarter panel molding to complete the break line for the special two-tone scheme. Two-tone paint could also be had on the One-Fifty series with the roof panel one color and the lower body and window frames the other.

Two-tone paint (Navajo Tan and India Ivory) is among the options on this 1955 Two-Ten two-door sedan with 34,000 actual miles. It also has the optional 265 2-barrel coupled to the standard 3-speed manual transmission. With production of nearly a quarter-million units, it was the third most purchased Chevy passenger car for the model year.

Nylon-faced fabric, ripple-weave Gabardine, and leather-grained vinyl upholstery was standard on the Two-Ten sedan models. Note the radio delete plate on this original car.

positional relationship as they would be when installed inside the car's engine compartment. This procedure prevented twisting or stress on the refrigerant hose as the unit was lowered into the car at the assembly plant.

Not surprisingly, the design of the air-conditioning unit took quite some time. A little more surprising is the amount of thought that was needed to determine how to move it from the processing rack to the shipping crate, the design of the crate, and how to install it at the assembly plant. To move it from the processing rack to its specially designed shipping crate, the compressor and evaporator were fastened to the base of the crate and the condenser to the top prior to moving these assemblies from the rack. The base and top were then turned over as the assemblies were removed and then the crate's four sides were nailed in place. During the preparation to install the A/C system, the crate was turned upside down so that both the evaporator and compressor assemblies were suspended from the base of the crate. The base was supported by mechanical handling equipment while the sides of the shipping crate were removed. The condenser was then unbolted from the top of the crate and suspended from the base by a bracket and hooks.

Air-Conditioning/Heater/Defroster System for 1955

A couple of months after the 1955 models went on sale, air-conditioning was released as an extra-cost option. It was a new and innovative option for Chevrolet, though not new in automotive use, having first been introduced by Packard for 1940. This option was quite expensive and only a small percentage of Chevrolets were ordered with air-conditioning.

During the early part of the design phase of the 1955 Chevrolet, the decision was made to include factory-installed air-conditioning in the Bel Air (except the convertible) and Two-Ten series; the purchase of a V-8 was required with either series to get factory air. At the time, no other car air-conditioning system paralleled the system's ease and accuracy in controlling humidity. The entire assembly, designed by the Chevrolet and Frigidaire divisions of General Motors, was installed completely within the engine compartment, which differed from other systems of the day that took up a portion of the trunk space. The air conditioning system was built as a ready-to-drop-in unit at the Frigidaire plant in Dayton, Ohio. There, it was pre-charged and placed on a pallet for shipment to the assembly plant. While on the assembly line, the car was fitted with the air distribution system, controls, and mounting brackets. Once it reached the end of the assembly line, the car was taken to an open area where the air-conditioning system was lowered into the engine compartment and bolted in place. Connecting the wiring harness and heater hoses completed the process.

The air-conditioning system was assembled on a processing rack where the refrigerant hose was connected to the fittings on the compressor, condenser, and evaporator. Then the components were placed on the rack in the same

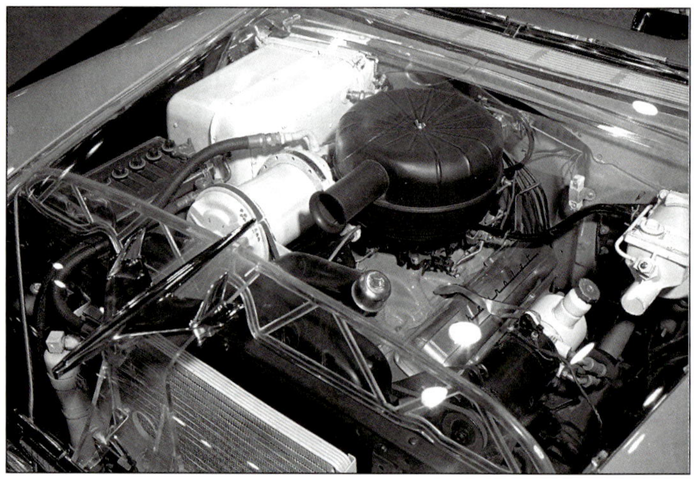

Among the many new features offered for Chevrolet's 1955 models was air-conditioning. While air-conditioning in an automobile was not new, having been introduced by Packard for 1940, offering the option in a low-priced automobile and having it fully contained within the engine compartment was new. This Bel Air was fitted with a transparent hood to show off its V-8 and air-conditioning system. (A V-8 was required to obtain air-conditioning.) The special hood allowed the engine compartment to be shown with the hood down, a novel way to see the show car and its innovative features. (Photo Courtesy GM Media Archive)

When air-conditioning was ordered, the vents were placed at the far ends of the dash of the 1957 Chevrolet passenger cars. The air-conditioning system was redesigned to work in combination with the deluxe heater, and the control panel was also redesigned to simplify operation.

The unit was a package-type combining cooling and heating capabilities, and it was a first of its kind. Early automotive air-conditioning systems consisted of multiple subassemblies installed in or on the car prior to the final assembly operations. Oldsmobile, Buick, and Cadillac were the first GM brands to get factory air as an option (1953). Frigidaire's, which supplied both cooled and heated air for all-year comfort, consisted of just three major components: compressor, evaporator, and condenser-receiver-dehydrator-filter assemblies. The systems for the higher-echelon GM cars consisted of a compressor, condenser, receiver, dehydrator-filter, evaporator and blower assembly, and the refrigerant lines and fittings. These were installed independently of each other in or on the various units of the car, such as the installation of the compressor on the engine, the condenser to the radiator, the evaporator and blower assembly in the trunk, etc. The independent components were connected by approximately 10 sections of copper tubing. Not surprisingly, this type of air-conditioning system was complicated to test because each component had to be leak tested prior to installation, plus it created problems in handling and assembly operations. Frigidaire's air-conditioning was completely fabricated, assembled, evacuated, charged, and leak tested prior to shipment to a Chevrolet assembly plant.

The package-type design was made possible through two critical features in combination with others less challenging to develop: (1) the creation of the flexible hose for use with Freon 12 to replace the copper refrigerant lines used on previous systems, which provided necessary flexibility between the major air-conditioning components, and (2) the development of a thin condenser, which permitted ease of installation between the radiator and the grille. Other contributing factors were the use of cowl intake vents to bring outside air into a front-mounted evaporator, negating the need for expensive ducts, and combining multiple components into one assembly (condenser, receiver, dehydrator, and filter). To combine the cooling and heating capabilities into a single system, a hot-water coil was added to the downstream side of the evaporator.

The system was said to be the equivalent of 24 household refrigerator compressors, could drain $1^1/_2$ gallons of water out of the air in an hour, could drop the temperature in the passenger compartment to 15 degrees below the outside temperature in 5 minutes, and could hold the inside temperature to 20 degrees below the outside temperature for as long as desired.

The small-block was enlarged to 283 ci of displacement for 1957, although a 265 remained available. The base 283 developed 185 hp at 4,600 rpm. A Power-Pack version, like the one shown here, was rated at 220 hp at 4,800 rpm and used an air cleaner with a paper filter element while the lower output small-blocks retained the oil bath air cleaner. This car has factory air-conditioning, though the compressor has been upgraded to a modern unit.

The Components

The air-conditioning system used an axial-type compressor with five cylinders. The axial compressor was chosen over other types because it offered the advantages of a relatively small size and was lightweight. An internal solenoid placed within the seal housing, which was part of the compressor assembly, activated a friction-type electromagnetic clutch. The clutch plates were located inside the pulley. When the solenoid was disengaged, the pulley would rotate freely on its sealed ball bearing mounted on the compressor shaft.

All-steel construction was used for the condenser, composed of 10, 3/8-inch-diameter tubes in parallel, grouped in two winding rows of 5 tubes each. The winding, or serpentine, layout minimized the number of joints needed. Corrugated fins stacked between the rows of tubing were copper brazed as a unit for good thermal contact and rigid construction. This design resulted in a condenser with a large frontal area and minimized thickness, allowing air to freely pass through it to the radiator.

The receiver-dehydrator-filter assembly combined two components that had been separate in the past. Other automotive air-conditioning systems had a receiver that was a straightforward tank that ensured a liquid column at the expansion valve no matter the load on the evaporator. Frigidaire placed the filter screens and drying agent within the receiver shell, which eliminated the dehydrator shell and its associated fittings. A liquid refrigerant line from the condenser to the receiver was part of the brazed assembly. This setup eliminated the connector and flair joint that had been used at the condenser outlet of earlier types. The receiver-dehydrator-filter assembly was easily replaced when necessary since it was fastened by two screw clamps to the condenser mounting bracket.

Only a single blower was needed since the cooling and heating features were together in one system. It was located within the passenger compartment under the dashboard but took nothing away from passenger space. A redesign of the distribution duct eliminated the heater core housing, and a regular heater damper was used to direct heated or cooled air to either the heater discharge or the defroster nozzles while another damper directed cooled or heated air to the two adjustable discharge nozzles in the lower dash or to the second damper (splitter). A Frigidaire core integrated into the packaged air-conditioning unit under the hood eliminated the heater core from inside the passenger compartment.

Cowl ventilation allowed the cooling coil and heater core, which were contained within an insulated housing, to be in front of the firewall. These components were made from individual finned tubing, which, at the time, was the type used by about half of the manufacturers of room air-conditioning units. Rounded or button-type fins were secured to the tubing except where the tubing was to be bent. Both outside and recirculated air was needed to maximize comfort; for this purpose, openings were placed in the ventilation duct and firewall along with air valves to control the flow of air. The desired level of heating was obtained simply by metering the flow of engine coolant through the heater core.

Other than the typical heater and defroster controls, a thermostatic switch was needed to maintain the temperature inside the passenger compartment when cooling. A duct valve control operated the valve inside the air distribution duct to direct air to either the heater air valve or the nozzles in the dash, or to both. The thermostatic switch, which was mounted on the air distribution duct on the passenger side of the firewall with the thermobulb extending inside the duct, was operated at the blower outlet. Occupants could adjust the setting of the two-speed switch to control the inside temperature. The switch cycled the compressor to maintain the selected setting; Chevrolet was one of the first to offer this feature. The switch for the air-conditioning was part of the control assembly used for the heater and defroster. A single lever served as a switch in the first part of its travel and as an adjustment for the thermostatic switch through the rest of its travel.

Leak Test, Evacuation, and Charging

Prior to shipment to the assembly plant, each air-conditioning unit was tested. This process began by evacuating the system then charging it with a mixture of Freon 12 and nitrogen for the leak test. Then the system was evacuated to an absolute pressure within 3 mm of mercury for a minimum of 45 minutes. Afterward, the unit was charged with oil and refrigerant with automatic equipment that was accurate to within plus/minus 1 ounce for the oil and plus/minus 0.03 pound for the Freon 12. The automated system would not charge the air-conditioning system if the initial absolute pressure exceeded 9 mm of mercury. Last, the charged system was tested for function in a humidity- and temperature-controlled environment.

After the air-conditioning unit was installed in a car, it was tested again. The engine was run for several minutes at low idle with the compressor clutch engaged, which established normal distribution of the refrigerant throughout the system. Then the thermostat was set to the coldest setting, the blower set to its maximum speed, and the damper adjusted for maximum recirculation of air. The engine was allowed to run for approximately 5 minutes, by which time the compressor was cut out by the thermostat and the temperatures of discharge air and the recirculated air were checked. Last, the controls were adjusted to the heating cycle and the temperature of the discharge air was checked. If the respective temperatures were within design specifications, the system passed inspection.

Seldom Ordered

Few purchasers of a new Chevrolet ordered air-conditioning; only about 3,500 of the 1.7 million cars built for

1955 were equipped with the option. The reason was simply the price tag of $565. With the base prices for the two most popular models, the Two-Ten four-door sedan with V-8 and the Bel Air four-door sedan with V-8, being $1,918 and $2,031, respectively, one can easily see how tremendously expensive air-conditioning was to the average buyer of a new 1955 Chevrolet. In fact, the $2,596 required to purchase a Bel Air four-door sedan with air-conditioning was enough to purchase a new Oldsmobile 88 Holiday four-door hardtop minus air-conditioning, of course. Chevrolet executives expected that only a small percentage of buyers would opt for the air-conditioning option at first. They also expected the price for the option to drop over time as more and more people bought it, which was exactly what happened.

The Bel Air Sport Coupe of 1956 accounted for 128,382 of the 1,574,740 Chevrolet passenger cars sold that model year, which began in November 1955. This example is painted Sierra Gold and Adobe Beige, one of 14 two-tone paint schemes offered. (Photo Courtesy Phil Aubrey)

The recirculating-type heater, one of two heaters offered, now incorporated a limited amount of outside air into the car's interior through the heater, giving it the ability to operate as an outside air heater or as a recirculating air heater.

1956: Hotter Than Before

Writing the introduction for the *1956 Chevrolet Engineering Features* manual, Ed Cole (by then Chevrolet's general manager) wrote, "We are pleased to present the outstanding new features of the passenger car, which will make this model year one of achievement and distinction. Extensively restyled, and with a number of engineering improvements, the new car carries the previous year's complete design change to a still higher point of beauty and mechanical excellence."

The 1956 twin-carb setup could be ordered through the Chevrolet parts department and installed by the dealer or acquired with the purchase of the optional 225-hp Corvette engine.

Chevrolet's advertising presented a theme similar to Cole's foreword, though at times with more dramatic language, such as, "The Hot One Is Even Hotter!" Its boastfulness was based upon the availability of a more powerful 265 V-8 producing a peak output of 205 hp at 4,600 rpm; torque maxed out at 368 ft-lbs at 3,000 rpm. All three transmissions offered (3-speed manual, 3-speed with overdrive, and Powerglide) could be had with the 205 hp engine. Labeled "Super Turbo Fire," the 205-hp engine featured a 4-barrel carburetor, high-lift camshaft, and 9.25:1 compression ratio. The 265 2-barrel remained listed at 162 hp at 4,400 rpm and 257 ft-lbs at 2,200 rpm with the manual transmission, but when coupled to the Powerglide it received a higher-lift camshaft boosting output slightly to 170 hp at 4,400 rpm and 257 ft-lbs at 2,400 rpm. Additional improvements to the 265 included replacing the bypass oil filter with a full-flow oil filter and increased protection against carburetor icing via a modified exhaust manifold heat riser. The 4-barrel carburetor also had a deeper heat grooving in the throttle-body similar to the 2-barrel's for improved warm-up characteristics. Station wagon models could now have the full benefit of the Power-Pack engine thanks to a reshaped fuel tank that accommodated twin exhausts.

Furthermore, the base 6-cylinder Blue Flame received revisions; the 123- and 136-hp engines were no longer available and in their place was a more powerful Blue Flame with hydraulic lifters and extra-alloy aldipped (special aluminum treatment) exhaust valves. The latter had an advantage in resisting combustion deposit accumulation and was a feature transferred to the inline-6 from the 1955 small-block. This version of the Blue Flame had a greater compression of 8.0:1 and a high-lift camshaft, naturally resulting in higher performance. Output ratings were advertised as 140 hp at 4,200 rpm and 210 ft-lbs at 2,400 rpm.

Not surprisingly, performance with the 205-hp V-8 was significantly improved over the 180-hp version. While a 1955 Chevrolet with the Power-Pack engine could run 0–60 mph in 9.7 seconds, the hotter 1956 version needed only 8.9 seconds for the task. The standing quarter-mile time also improved to 16.6 seconds, which was also 0.8 seconds better than the 1955 Chevrolet. The comparison is somewhat inadequate in making the point, though, without noting that the axle ratios varied between the cars tested. The 1955 model was equipped with a 4.11:1 axle ratio while the 1956 had the 3.70:1 ratio. If the same axle ratio had been used for both cars, the results for the 1956 Chevrolet would have been a bit more impressive. As it was, the 14 percent increase in horsepower more than offset the 10 percent reduction in axle ratio.

Even more remarkable was the release for all models of the 225-hp Corvette engine in time to qualify for that year's annual Daytona Speed Weeks competition held at Dayton Beach. The Corvette engine featured twin 4-barrel carburetors and the high-lift "Duntov" cam. It reached its maximum horsepower at 5,200 rpm while peak torque was rated at 270 ft-lbs at 3,600 rpm. It could be had with any of the three transmissions offered.

Tom McCahill, writing for *Mechanix Illustrated*, evaluated a new Chevrolet One-Fifty two-door sedan with the 225-hp engine and reported, "Chevrolet has come up with a poor man's answer to the hot Ferrari . . . You blast up the road as if you had a barrel of nitro in the tail. Zero to 30 mph averages 3.2 seconds; zero to 60 mph 8.9, and in 12 seconds you're doing 70 mph . . . Absolutely perfect camshaft and a light valvetrain make this mill the greatest."

A Better Chassis

The 1956 passenger car chassis was revised to improve handling characteristics, directional stability, and durability, and provide a softer ride.

A 1-degree change in the caster angle provided improved handling and directional stability; however, this simple modification required a few adjustments to offset the change in the front suspension alignment it caused. The steering arm ends were raised slightly to maintain the correct steering geometry, and shims were added at the steering knuckle stops to prevent the possibility of the front wheels striking the frame in the event of especially hard turns. These changes caused a slight increase in the turning diameter of the 1956 Chevrolets.

Front wheel-bearing durability was improved with higher-capacity outer bearings in the front hubs. Widening the rear hanger of the rear spring from 2 to 3 inches increased durability of the rear suspension. This allowed for the use of additional rubber in the bushing to reduce the effects of compression forces produced by axle side thrusts. Wheel bearings in the rear axle were lubricated for the life of the unit at the factory, and then they were completely sealed. Furthermore, a sixth leaf was added to the new nine-passenger wagon.

This photo of a 1956 Bel Air convertible chassis offers a look at the X-frame member used for this body style, the Hotchkiss drive, Powerglide, and the V-8 engine. Hotchkiss drive replaced the heavier torque-tube drive starting with the 1955s. Both the convertible and hardtop models had more body mounts than others in the Chevrolet passenger car lineup.

Standard tires for 1956, except on the nine-passenger wagon, were 6.70x15-4–ply; the nine-passenger wagon received 6-ply tires. The latter were optional for other models.

Other Improvements

Additional changes introduced for the 1956 Chevrolet line included upgrades to the headlights, battery, voltage regulator, and temperature gauge; a new woven asbestos-faced clutch and pressure plate for use with the V-8; and self-canceling directional signals as standard equipment.

Guide T-3 sealed beam headlamps with 3-point quick adjustment aiming were new for 1956. (Guide Lamp Corporation was owned by General Motors. It was purchased in 1928 when the company was known as the Guide Motor Lamp Corp.) The headlights had three tangs, or gauge points, against which headlight aiming equipment could be positioned to provide precise alignment. The revisions to the optics of the headlight lens for farther low-beam visibility performed in the middle of the prior model year were, of course, carried forward.

A more durable 12-volt battery, waterproof voltage regulator, and an electric temperature gauge were issued for 1956 by GM's Delco-Remy Division. The temperature gauge, with a sending unit relocated to the water manifold section of the intake manifold, provided a more accurate reading.

The new clutch used with the V-8 and manual transmission powertrain provided greater torque capacity and better recovery from fade, and the revised pressure plate used nine heat-treated coil springs that replaced the diaphragm spring. This setup was more adaptable to the higher torque of the optional high-performance V-8s.

New Safety Features

Archrival Ford introduced its "Lifeguard Design," an

optional safety package for the 1956 model year. It consisted of padded dash, sun visors, and seat belts. They promoted it heavily, but few buyers were interested. Chevrolet offered a padded dash, seat belts, and even shoulder harnesses. Few buyers took notice of Chevrolet's safety equipment either. Still, the automakers were at least offering safety features and Chevrolet was quite innovative in taking the extra step of making shoulder harnesses available. The shoulder harnesses, by the way, could be had for both front- and rear-seat passengers.

Each of the belt links was looped through a steel bracket bolted to the floor. The underbody was reinforced at this point from underneath with a large steel washer. As for the shoulder harnesses, one end of each of the two harness straps attached to the seat belt; the opposite ends were then joined to a single strap attached to the car body. The anchoring point for the front-seat harness was the floor, while the package shelf of sedans and coupes was the anchoring point for the rear. More details regarding the seat belts are presented in the final chapter of this book.

The padded dash, released as a regular production option not long after the new model introduction, was constructed of fiberglass and covered with leather grain Elascofab (a leather-like vinyl material). It was offered in red, copper, black, green, and turquoise.

Styling Updates and Body Style Additions

A wide lattice-pattern grille replaced the Ferrari-inspired grille for 1956. Also different were restyled headlight hoods, rectangular parking lamps, new bumpers and bumper guards, hood and trunk ornamentation, flared and elongated wheel openings, side trim, wheel covers, taillamps, and a longer (by 4 inches) flatter hood with a greater downward slope. Overall length for coupes and sedans, however, increased only 1.9 inches because of changes in the bumper guards. Station wagon models were 3.7 inches longer.

Two-tone paint schemes were now available on all series; a change to the side trim on the One-Fifty series cars allowed for the extra-cost option. A lot of consideration went into the arrangement of the side trim for all models, with the overall goal of creating a lower, longer, wider look for each series. Particularly novel, though, was the hidden fuel filler inside the driver's side taillamp. By twisting a small latch above the lens, the entire assembly could be pivoted downward to access the filler cap. The hidden fuel filler eliminated the filler door cut lines, providing a cleaner look.

Interior appearance for the Bel Air series (except the convertible) was enhanced with new jacquard-weave nylon-faced fabric and leather grain vinyl. A new flexible plastic material with the appearance of bright metal was introduced. Extruded welts of the material were used to outline backrest bolsters and cover the small buttons applied at the points of the backrest panels. The Bel Air convertible was equipped with full leather-grain vinyl upholstery, also with the bright welt outlining the backrest bolsters.

Other important changes for 1956 included the addition of two body styles to both the Bel Air and Two-Ten lines: the four-door hardtop Sport Sedan and the nine-passenger four-door sedan Beauville station wagon that replaced the

Racing Raises Chevrolet's Image

In his book *Chevrolet 1955: Creating the Original*, Michael Lamm included portions of his interview with Walter R. Mackenzie, an engineer working at the GM Proving Grounds in Milford, Michigan, and the performance liaison for Chevrolet. The 265 V-8, Mackenzie said, "was certainly conceived as competition to Ford's flathead V-8, because Cole had always been interested in racing. I can't say he had definite plans for Chevy to get into stock car competition with that engine, but I can say he intended this new and very sophisticated engine to be something that was easy for the competition people to modify, something they'd really fall in love with. It was a lightweight, high-heat-rejection engine, quite simple, and as such it proved a tremendous success. But no, I wouldn't say he was planning to get into stock car racing when he did that engine. First and foremost he wanted to revitalize the Chevrolet product. . . ."

While Cole may not have had any intention for Chevrolet to become involved in professional racing while the small-block was in development, he definitely took an interest in the prospect not far into the model year. He was not the only one. Some within the organization were pushing for more attention to performance to improve Chevrolet's image and help increase sales. They could see that professional stock car racing was gaining in popularity in the 1950s; factory participation in NASCAR was an important sales tool. "Win on Sunday, sell on Monday" became the mantra once the often-quoted phrase was coined in the 1960s.

On the flip side, though, another truth was becoming clear. Performance attention was starting to lead to some negative publicity as the 1950s progressed. The horrific crash during the 1955 Le Mans competition in which more than 80 spectators were killed when a Mercedes swept through the crowd after a collision brought an intense spotlight on the sport of automobile racing.

A 1955 Bel Air convertible painted Gypsy Red and Ivory White driven by Chevrolet Division chief Thomas Keating was the official pace car at that year's Indianapolis 500. An unverified claim was that the official pace car was equipped with two 4-barrel carburetors, a setup similar to that released for the following model year. (Photo Courtesy GM Media Archive)

Herb Thomas, who drove a Chevrolet-sponsored, Smokey Yunick–prepared car, finished first in NASCAR's Southern 500 race held at Darlington, South Carolina. Chevrolets also took positions 2, 4, 7, 8, 9, and 10. Though Chevrolet did not win many NASCAR events in 1955, its wins favorably impacted the public's perception of the division.

This was the same year in which Chevrolet took its new V-8 cars to the racetrack and won five major NASCAR races.

Legendary race-car builder Smokey Yunick reportedly claimed that NASCAR founder Bill France planned to "hook Ed Cole" on the idea of factory sponsorship of Chevrolet race teams. The story is that Cole met with France in North Wilkesboro, North Carolina, early in 1955, and agreed to pursue the proposal. Ed Cole is said to have told Yunick, "We have an old man's car, and we don't have 20 years for the kids to catch on. I want to get to young people now, and I think I can do it through racing." According to Zora Arkus-Duntov, however, a more significant turning point took place the following year when Chevrolet hired 1956 Grand National champion Buck Baker away from Chrysler. Baker went on to win the 1957 Grand National championship driving a Chevrolet, a first for this division of General Motors. The "old man's car" image was a thing of the past.

In June 1955, the Super Turbo-Fire V-8 became an option. It produced 195 hp at 5,000 rpm with the hotter camshaft and valve springs that were installed in the Corvette engine. Also adding to the performance image were wins by Chevrolet drivers in the increasingly popular sport of automobile racing, particularly the stock car variety offered by the National Association of Automobile Stock Car Racing, or NASCAR. Chevrolet's first win of the race season came in a short track event (200-lap, half-mile oval) at Columbia, South Carolina, and later came a big win at Darlington, South Carolina. The latter race, the Southern 500, produced not only a first-place finish, but had Chevrolets finishing in positions 2, 4, 7, 8, 9, and 10. The winning driver was Herb Thomas in a Chevrolet-sponsored, Smokey Yunick–prepared car. Of the 69 stock cars entered in that race, 23 were Chevrolets. Though Chrysler ruled the winner's circle that year, these wins were a nice start for Chevrolet.

At first Chevrolet was not sponsoring professional race car drivers; instead, various drivers were simply buying the cars and engines then discovering just how well the cars ran on the tracks. Race-car builder and crew chief Smokey Yunick called Ed Cole to tell him how well the 1955 Chevys were performing on the racetrack. That started some unofficial assistance from Chevrolet to race teams by the middle of 1955. Heavy-duty suspension components, for example, such as springs, wheels, and hubs, were provided because of the tremendous forces applied to the chassis during racing; stock parts were sometimes breaking under the stressful loads. Ed Cole

This 1956 Chevrolet Two-Ten was driven at the speedway at Darlington, South Carolina, in a record-breaking 24-hour closed-course endurance test in late April. (Photo Courtesy GM Media Archive)

Buck Baker is shown speeding around one of the turns at Daytona followed by another driver. Both 1957 Chevrolet One-Fifty race cars were powered by the 283-hp fuel-injected engine. Partway through the race season the ban on performance promotion agreed to by the auto manufacturers went into effect with the aim of ending factory-sponsored racing activities. (Photo Courtesy GM Media Archive)

assigned Mauri Rose, a three-time Indianapolis 500 winner (1941, 1947, and 1948) hired by Chevrolet as its special engineer and vehicle development engineer, to speak with drivers, such as Herb Thomas and Jim Reed, to learn what they needed from Chevrolet to help them in their racing efforts. (Competitor Ford Motor Company made a similar move by hiring the 1925 Indy 500 winner, Pete DePaolo, as its consultant.) For some, just owning a car resembling the one that won the big race was desirable, even when it did not have the most powerful engine offered by the manufacturer.

For the 1956 race season, Chevrolet spent millions of dollars to improve its chances on the racetracks. Even so, Chryslers, Dodges, and Fords crossed the finish line first with great regularity. Herb Thomas got Chevrolet's first win of the season in December in a 100-mile race at Palm Beach Speedway followed by another win in March. Chevrolet's third and final Grand National win that year came at a 300-mile race at Langhorne Speedway in a car driven by Paul Goldsmith. At that year's Daytona Speed Weeks, Chevrolet overtook Ford by averaging 121.335 mph versus Ford's time of 118.13 mph in the flying mile two-way average competition (259–305-ci class). However, Ford edged out Chevrolet to win the Pure Oil Manufacturer's trophy by scoring 584 points to 566 for Chevrolet. Both Chevrolet and Ford offered a 225-hp engine that year, but then Ford upped the ante by releasing a 260-hp version of its Y-block V-8 later in the model year.

For 1957, Chevrolet drivers had the so-called "Black Widow," a One-Fifty utility sedan painted black and white and equipped with the 283-hp fuel-injected engine upgraded for racing. The One-Fifty sedans were beefed up underneath using stronger truck springs, rear axle, spindles, and brakes. Wheels were six-lug 15 x 6 units (listed in Chevrolet's parts catalog at $19.50 each). A larger radiator from a Buick or Cadillac, a 20-gallon Chevrolet taxi fuel tank, four additional shock absorbers, and Fenton cast-iron exhaust manifolds with exhausts through the frame rails were also employed. Chevrolet, though, did not build these cars. After the terrible accident at Le Mans in 1955, politicians in Washington, DC, focused on the dangers of racing and considered banning it. There was also talk that General Motors should be broken up on antitrust grounds. Ed Cole decided to farm-out the racing program to Vince Piggins, formerly Hudson's chief engineer, who had been very successful in putting Hudson across the finish line first. Piggins set up a company, Southern Engineering and Development Company (SEDCO), to build the cars for Chevrolet. The company reportedly built six Black Widows, a nickname for the mostly black cars, which apparently originated at SEDCO. Another identical car was built elsewhere for Johnny Beauchamp.

In late February, NASCAR officials made a rule change specifying that only a single 4-barrel carburetor could be used; therefore, the Black Widow race cars' fuel-injection systems had to be replaced or they could not be raced on NASCAR tracks. In the end, Chevrolets took the checkered flag in 21 Grand National races for 1957. Despite the vast improvement, it fell short of Ford's 26 wins, but Chevrolet's image with the public had greatly improved. With Chrysler having dropped out, the races were largely between Ford and Chevrolet, though a smattering of Pontiacs and Oldsmobiles also competed.

Chevrolet's support for race teams continued until the ban on performance promotion agreed to by members of the Automobile Manufacturers Association (AMA), a trade group formed in 1911 operating under variations of their name. The September 1956 meeting of the AMA resulted in a verbal understanding that performance promotion would cease. Even so, Chevrolet's racing activities continued, though its involvement was hidden as much as possible. Harlow Curtice, president of General Motors at the time, and representatives of the other auto manufacturers signed the agreement the following February and it took effect on June 1, 1957.

Concurrently, members of congress were also voicing their opinion that General Motors should be broken up under antitrust laws because of its sizable market share, which was more than 50 percent. That was likely another motivator for Curtice to sign the AMA agreement; the company was getting too much negative attention from the feds already. Curtice was concerned that Congress would get involved in the matter of performance promotion. Congress was beginning to openly discuss the rising highway death toll and partially blaming the way cars were promoted. Curtice explained his decision publicly: "The factory speed wars would escalate costs of doing business dramatically, would enrage the government and perhaps even the public over safety issues, and competing against your customers would in effect discourage sales."

Another motivator for Curtice, according to former GM designer Pete Brock, was not so widely known at the time. According to Brock's book *Corvette Sting Ray: Genesis of an American Icon*, ". . . reports of unsanctioned night drag racing by midlevel factory execs and engineers on Woodward Ave in Detroit" potentially could result in some major embarrassment for General Motors in the event of an accident. The factory hot rods offered too much temptation for "corporate egos."

Conversely, a road test report on the 1957 Chevrolet published in the March 1957 issue of *Speed Age*, asserts a strong link between manufacturers' support of racing and better cars: "Chevrolet and many other futuristic-minded manufacturers have learned a great deal from stock car racing throughout the country, and have put their knowledge to good use. The sport has proved many ideas and disproved many others, while the automobile world has benefited." The competition to win did help to some degree in the development of better automobiles for the public, but its primary purpose was simply to help sell cars.

Harlow Curtice favored performance promotion in the beginning, but he came to a new realization. Pete Brock noted in his book, "This reversal of corporate policy was surprising as Curtice had been an early advocate of performance-oriented programs; their proven, positive influence on sales had made him a believer. Ultimately, though, Curtice was a bottom-line guy. Ever escalating costs related to performance and racing were now threatening to cancel profits. As a high-ranking member of the AMA, Curtice wielded considerable power and influence within the industry. Despite the fact that his well-intended decision to assist in creating the AMA's racing/performance ban was counter to the ever increasing influence of racing on sales and the popularity of performance-related activities with the general public, Curtice forged ahead, concerned only about short-term corporate profits."

The May 1957 AMA's no-racing edict did little to stop most manufacturers, including Chevrolet, from racing. Chevrolet dealers remained a source for speed parts and Vince Piggins continued providing engineering assistance to independent teams for years to come while hardcore racing enthusiasts such as Bill Mitchell, who became VP of GM Design in late 1958, largely ignored the ban. Chevrolet and Pontiac continued to offer high-performance equipment to racers, though ostensibly such equipment was for police use only. Factory support from Chevrolet as well as Pontiac finally came to an end in 1963, when top management demanded such activities cease partly because it was costly, but mainly because the federal government could construe such activities as having a direct relationship with traffic fatalities caused by high speed. In the end, Chevrolet and Pontiac sales during the 1960s do not appear to have been hurt by the decision to drop factory support for race teams.

six-passenger version from 1955. The six-passenger, four-door sedan wagon in the Two-Ten lineup became the Townsman.

Body structure details of the Sport Sedan and the nine-passenger station wagon differed significantly from other Chevrolets. The stub center pillar of the Sport Sedan was flared widely at its base to ensure its rigidity to function as both the rear door hinge pillar and the front door lock pillar. Two body mounts were repositioned directly under this pillar for extra support. The full-width U-channel brace welded to the underbody was reshaped to conform to the wide-based center pillar. It was attached with four body bolts to reinforce outrigger frame brackets. As for the wagon, a depression in the floor extending rearward between the frame side members to the kick-up provided additional leg and foot room for backseat passengers. This change forced relocation of two body mounts and the fuel tank to behind the spare tire well. The intermediate seat of the nine-passenger wagon was positioned slightly closer to the front seat and the back seat was removable to provide increased cargo capacity when needed. Furthermore, the intermediate seat was divided into two individual units in a one-third/two-thirds arrangement. The one-third right-hand portion could be folded vertically to serve as a jump seat, folded forward to facilitate entry and exit for backseat passengers, or be folded downward to form part of the load platform; the left-hand two-thirds section could be folded down to complete the cargo space. With the back seat removed and the intermediate seat completely folded, 87 cubic feet of cargo space was available.

This 1956 Bel Air Sport Sedan painted Dawn Gray (a metallic color) and India Ivory is one of 103,602 built for this model year. The four-door hardtop was a new addition to the Chevrolet line of passenger cars. Oldsmobile and Buick introduced it the previous model year, and for 1956 all GM passenger car divisions offered a four-door hardtop. The introduction of the four-door hardtop forced Ford to respond with one, too, which was dubbed Town Victoria. Chevrolet's sport sedan easily outsold Ford's Town Victoria.

The V themed instrument panel from 1955 continued to be used for 1956. Bi-level instrumentation was grouped with the speedometer, coolant temperature, and gasoline level instruments at top and the generator warning, odometer, and low oil pressure warning below. The bright molding spanning the dash had the bowtie cutouts of 1955 replaced with thin, rectangular slots for 1956.

The Beauville station wagon became a nine-passenger model offered in both the Two-Ten and Bel Air series for 1956. Shown here is the Two-Ten Beauville in Pinecrest Green and India Ivory. It is one of only 17,988 built and is equipped with the 205-hp 265, Powerglide, and air-conditioning. The following model year, the name "Townsman" was used to identify the Bel Air four-door wagon and "Beauville" the Two-Ten version.

DUNTOV'S RUN UP PIKE'S PEAK

Zora Arkus-Duntov drove this well-disguised 1956 Chevrolet Sport Sedan up Pike's Peak to establish a new, though unofficial, record on September 9, 1955. The purpose of the disguise was to conceal the look of the as-yet-unreleased 1956 models. Chevrolets later finished 1st, 2nd, 5th, 6th, and 10th at that year's annual Pike's Peak Hill Climb. (Photo Courtesy GM Media Archive)

After several weeks of practice, on September 9, 1955, Zora Arkus-Duntov raced a strangely striped 1956 Chevrolet Sport Sedan through 170 turns to the 9,400-foot summit of Colorado's Pike's Peak. He accomplished it in only 17 minutes, 24.05 seconds. This was more than 2 minutes faster than the official record held by an American stock car sedan. NASCAR officials timed the event, but NASCAR was not an official sanctioning body for the Pike's Peak hill climbs. Therefore, Duntov's time did not establish an official new record. He repeated the drive in a 1956 Chevrolet four-door sedan, though not quite as fast at 17 minutes, 41.91 seconds.

The cars, incidentally, were disguised because Chevrolet's 1956 model year had not yet started. Back then, the official release date was a significant day for new car browsers. Dealers papered their showroom windows to keep the new cars from view until the official start of the new model year. Fiberglass fender skirts and quarter panel extensions were used along with wide horizontal paint stripes along the body sides. The Pike's Peak cars almost looked like Packards!

Chevrolet advertising promoted the achievement but did not mention its record was not an official one. Regardless, few Chevrolet owners (if any) would have cared whether it was official or not!

In July 1956, at the Pike's Peak Hill Climb, Chevrolets took first, second, fifth, sixth, and tenth place with the lead driver, Jerry Unser, conquering the mountain in 16.08 minutes. That was 1 minute and 16 seconds better than Duntov's run!

Chevrolet's 1956 model year announcement ad promoted the record run up Pike's Peak, but did not mention it was not an official one, though that fact probably would not have mattered to the public. Chevrolet's emphasis on high performance was greatly improving the image of the division and increasing sales.

Upholstery for this 1956 Two-Ten Beauville is Starfrost vinyl and Dark Green pattern vinyl, one of the two "Custom-Colored" interiors offered. Starfrost vinyl and Charcoal Gray pattern vinyl was standard. More sophisticated fabrics and vinyls became available during this decade.

Hiding the fuel filler was a styling innovation of the era. It allowed for a cleaner look since it eliminated the fuel filler door in the quarter panel. The filler was hidden behind the driver-side taillight on 1956 Chevrolet passenger cars.

1957: More Advancement

Chevrolet Chief Engineer Harry Barr wrote the foreword to the *1957 Chevrolet Engineering Features* manual, stating, "Styling changes bring new and advanced lines to the current models. New 283 cubic inch displacement V-8 engines, the Turboglide 'luxury' automatic transmission, a fuel-injection system of revolutionary design, and numerous chassis improvements are illustrative of the mechanical advances available to the customer in 1957."

The 1957 model year ushered in the fuel-injected small-block, which spiced-up the image of Chevrolet all the more. A bore increase of 0.125 inch to $3\frac{7}{8}$ inches pushed the displacement of the small-block to 283 ci, which was offered in five states of tune. Transmission choices increased by one with the addition of another automatic transmission.

The base 265 Turbo-Fire V-8 with 2-barrel and 8.0:1 compression was essentially the same as the new and improved 283, but with a smaller bore. It was the only 265 offered for 1957

A trolley system brought freshly assembled bodies along the assembly line. Note that the trolley and body were attached to the body-mounting locations. The assembly line process required as much innovation as the car design itself. Shown here is a 1956 two-door sedan. Holes drilled into the quarter panel indicate it was destined to become a Bel Air or a Two-Ten rather than a One-Fifty, which lacked body side trim. A four-door sedan followed it. (Photo Courtesy GM Media Archive)

The 1957 Chevrolets reached iconic status many years ago. They are among the most recognized cars of the 1950s, even by non-enthusiasts. Shown here are two of the most popular models, a Matador Red Bel Air convertible and a Larkspur Blue and India Ivory Nomad. Both are part of the collection at the GM Heritage Center.

A black mesh screen incorporated into the headlight bezel allowed outside air to flow into the interior. This means of passenger car compartment ventilation was said to provide 20 percent more outside airflow than the previous plenum chamber system. Also of note is the Guide T-3 sealed-beam headlamp with three-point quick adjustment aiming seen in this photo. This marked the second year of its use.

in the passenger car line. (Interestingly, it was painted chartreuse for passenger cars and gray for pickups.) For higher performance, a variety of 283s was offered. The Turbo-Fire 283 with compression ratio of 8.5:1 gave 185 hp at 4,600 rpm, 5 more than the Power-Pack 4-barrel version of 1955, and 275 ft-lbs at 2,400 rpm. Next up the performance ladder was the Power-Pack Super Turbo-Fire, again with a 4-barrel and a dual exhaust system, rated at 220 hp at 4,800 rpm and 300 ft-lbs at 3,000 rpm; its 9.5:1 compression ratio required premium fuel. While those engines would have given most buyers complete satisfaction in terms of improved performance, even greater power was offered via the hotter camshaft used in the 245-hp Corvette engine. With it, a 283 with twin 4-barrel carburetors delivered 245 hp at 5,000 rpm and 300 ft-lbs of torque at 3,000 rpm. (As best as can be determined, no 1957 Chevrolet passenger car left the assembly line with this camshaft; it was either dealer-installed or owner-installed.) Yet another twin-four type, a competition V-8 with solid lifters, pumped out 270 hp at 6,000 rpm, also with 300 ft-lbs of torque but at a higher winding 3,800 rpm.

Then there was the 283 with Rochester fuel injection developing 283 hp at 6,200 rpm, or, as Chevrolet advertising liked to point out, 1 horsepower per cubic inch. The price for this optional engine was an expensive $484.20. This high cost kept orders for the fuel-injected engine low; total production of 1957 Chevrolet passenger cars equipped with either of the fuel-injected engines is reported to have been only 1,530 units.

A Better Small-Block

The *1957 Chevrolet Engineering Features* manual stated, "The new 283 cubic inch displacement V-8 has many advanced features designed to bring improvements over previous V-8 engines in virtually every characteristic. These range from freer breathing, more accurately timed and more uniform mixture burning, to improved lubrication and greater overall durability." The new engine also featured improvements to the oiling system, a revised camshaft, a new distributor, increased hot air supply to the automatic choke, a new clutch, and more.

Freer breathing was the result of enlarging the cylinder head inlet ports and the exhaust ports in combination with ram's-horn-type exhaust manifolds. Engines with a dual exhaust setup also had a balance tube added to equalize exhaust flow through both mufflers. Spark plug electrodes protruded farther into the combustion chamber, resulting in shorter flame travel and more uniform combustion of the fuel-air mixture. The contour of the combustion chamber at the location of the spark plug had a small boss to keep the spark plug flush with the combustion chamber wall and inhibit buildup of deposits on the spark plug threads.

Another improvement to the ignition system was a metal heat shield installed between the exhaust manifolds and the spark plug wires, which of course protected the spark plug wires and boots. The cylinder block top deck was made more uniform in thickness to reduce localized stresses. This also resulted in more secure head bolts and minimized distortion of the cylinder bore. Wider (by 0.0625 inch) main bearings reduced loading and increased the life of these bearings. Compression and oil control were better maintained by changing the location of the inside bevel of the second compression ring from the top to the lower portion. Furthermore, the combination expander and spacer for the oil control ring was changed to stainless steel, replacing the heat-treat hardened, drawn steel component. Stainless steel offered superior manufacturing tolerances.

Oil was now supplied to the valve lifter galleries under full pressure rather than the previous metered-pressure oil system. This setup provided better filling of the hydraulic valve lifters, reducing the chance of oil aeration at high speed. The hydraulic and solid lifters used exclusively on the high-output 283s were designed to meter the oil supply to the upper valvetrain. However, a full-flow oil filter remained as an option.

A new camshaft with a higher lift for both the intake and exhaust valves was installed on all 283 engines except the competition Corvette engine. Valve overlap was reduced to improve idle stability. Spring dampers helped to quiet valve noise and improve the performance of the valve-opening mechanism.

Except for the Corvette engines, a new distributor was installed on all 283s, which allowed for the accurate setting of the point gap with the engine running.

A new semi-centrifugal clutch was included on cars powered by a 283 and synchromesh transmission. It offered a reduction in clutch slippage at higher engine speeds. Six-cylinder and 265-powered cars with manual transmission also received an improved, higher-capacity clutch.

This fully documented, low-mileage, Canyon Coral and India Ivory 1957 Bel Air two-door sedan is equipped with the 283-hp fuel-injected small-block and 3-speed synchromesh transmission. At the time these photos were taken, it was in the collection of only its fourth owner. Prior to that it was part of the Milt Robson collection for many years. It sold for $121,000 in 2015 at the RM Auction sale held at Amelia Island, Florida.

Fuel Injection: A Step into the Future

In a sense, the release of fuel injection was perfectly timed. During 1957, an F-101 Voodoo was flown to about twice the speed of sound at more than 1,200 mph, an impressive achievement at the time; later that year, the Soviet Union ushered in the start of the "space race" by launching the first artificial satellite into orbit around Earth. Something as exotic sounding as "fuel injection" certainly fit the fast-paced times.

Like those scientific achievements, Chevrolet's release of fuel injection received its share of press attention. The January 1957 issue of *Speed Age* featured an article titled "GM gets the Needle," in which the benefits of Chevrolet's fuel-injection system versus carburetion were detailed. The story began, "Carburetors were never worth the gasoline it takes to blow them to heaven. When you consider all their shortcomings when compared to an ideal fuel system, it isn't surprising that General Motors has chosen to offer a fuel-injection system as an optional replacement for their present carbs. . . . In order to get good performance, each cylinder must receive exactly the same amount of air-fuel mixture at all speed ranges. This never happens."

The reason for this imperfect situation is simple: There is no way to place a carburetor, or even multiple carburetors, on an intake manifold such that the paths of fuel delivery to each cylinder are equidistant. The result is that an engine using carburetion to meter fuel to the combustion chambers has virtually ideal flow to some cylinders while others are somewhat starved of fuel. Another problem encountered with carburetion is full flow at higher revolutions per minute. If fuel flow is represented by "X" at, for example 2,500 rpm, then fuel flow at 5,000 rpm will be 1/2 X at this point simply because there is less time for the combustion chambers to receive fuel unless the carburetor can adjust to the higher revs; indeed they do, but not perfectly. Fuel injection solves these problems and is commonplace today. It also offers better accelerator response and smoothness of operation in both cold and hot operating conditions. It does not need the warm-up period that carburetion requires since the fuel is supplied to the cylinder head intake ports under pressure through individual fuel lines, so cold starting is easier.

The crossed flags emblem and fuel injection script were mounted on the front fenders of 1957 Bel Airs and Two-Tens. Both the emblem and script were also used for the 1957 Corvette. Three different scripts were used from 1957 through 1959.

This "fuelie" is the 283-hp version. Though officially rated at 283 hp at 6,200 rpm, it actually produced 290 hp. The official rating was simply a marketing ploy to emphasize 1 horsepower per cubic inch.

In 1957, fuel injection was exotic. Unfortunately, it needed more development time before release and was very expensive. It was definitely not for the average driver of the day.

Chevrolet claimed they were the first to offer 1 horsepower per cubic inch for an American production car. However, they must have overlooked the previous year's Chrysler 300B, which could be had late in the model year with an optional 355-hp 354 Hemi. However, it was intended for competition purposes and no 1956 300B built for routine street use is known to have been equipped with this engine. The claim, while inaccurate, was not entirely false. Inserting the phrase "in the low-priced field" would have made Chevrolet's advertisement completely true.

The use of fuel injection started getting traction when Mercedes included it on its 1955 300SL Gull Wing sports car, though metering fuel to an engine's combustion chambers in this way was not a new idea. A rudimentary fuel-injection system for an internal combustion engine for marine use was patented in 1817. Rudolf Diesel developed fuel injection for the engine that bears his name. Many aircraft in World War II also made use of fuel injection. Racer Stuart Hilborn designed and built the first constant flow mechanical fuel injector and used it in 1948 on the dry lake bed at El Mirage, California, to propel his car to 150 mph, the first car to reach that speed. His Hilborn fuel-injection system went on to dominate Indianapolis 500 races throughout the 1950s.

GM's Rochester Products Division manufactured the "Ram Jet" system for Chevrolet, though GM's Engineering staff actually performed the R&D work to develop it. Among the staff there was Harry Barr, John Dolza, and Zora Arkus-Duntov. Incidentally, John Dolza's theoretical work in the areas of mass airflow, fuel flow, equations, and more is in use on fuel-injection systems still today.

The Ram Jet system, though complex, generally worked well once some of its early problems were remedied. Its biggest drawback, other than its cost, was the lack of trained technicians to work on the units when repairs were needed. Few people ordered Ram Jet, and staffing technicians who were fully trained to work on the fuel-injected engine at dealerships all over the country was impractical considering the low production rate of the engine. It needed more periodic maintenance than a carburetor, too. Only a little more than 1,500 of the 1957 Chevrolet passenger cars were ordered with the optional fuel-injected engine (option code RPO-578).

After the 1959 model year, Chevrolet dropped the option from its big car line but continued offering it on the Corvette through 1965. By then it had been refined and was feeding fuel to a 327-ci version of the small-block producing 375 hp, well past the 1 horsepower per cubic inch barrier that was so magical less than a decade earlier.

Transmissions

Transmission choices remained nearly the same as they had been in 1956. Several changes to the Powerglide increased its durability in mid-1956, and these were carried forward to the 1957 model year. Three of the changes resulted in better flow of cooling oil over the clutch plates. Also, the 3-speed and overdrive received a new cam and roller detent cover assembly to improve shift feel and operational dependability. This change reduced dependence on the driver's precision of shifting motion. Completely new for 1957 was the Turboglide automatic transmission.

These transmissions were the only ones officially available and advertised. However, claims persist of 1957 Chevrolet passenger cars being factory-equipped with a 4-speed. I have personally spoken to the son of a man who had a good "war buddy" who ordered a new 1957 Sport Coupe with the 270-hp 2x4–barrel Corvette engine, 4-speed transmission, and 4.11:1 gears. The son, D. J. Moore, remembers the car well from his early childhood. His father owned a Dodge with the police engine and raced against his friend in the 4-speed Bel Air. Moore said his father's Dodge was outraced by the Bel Air in the quarter-mile, but the Dodge easily outraced the Chevrolet in the half-mile. Moore later "tracked it down" and bought it. He added the usual speed equipment, such as Headman headers and Hurst shifter, and noted the cutout for the shifter was smooth as though it was a factory cut. It was not the butchered kind of cutout that many people performed when swapping the Powerglide or 3-speed for a 4-speed back in the day.

While I always believed such cars had the transmission either dealer- or owner-installed, I now suspect that someone could get a dealer to order a 1957 Chevrolet with a 4-speed transmission. Still, I expect this seldom happened. Furthermore, I doubt the transmission would have been installed on the assembly line, but rather at another facility much like the situation with the few 1958 Chevrolet passenger cars equipped with a 4-speed. That topic is detailed in chapter 6. By the way, that 4-speed Bel Air did not have a good ending. Moore eventually sold the car and it was totaled within 48 hours.

Turboglide

A new automatic transmission called Turboglide made its debut for 1957. This 2-speed transmission had a torque converter designed with three separate turbines, one for each of the transmission's speeds; multiple disc clutches; and an accelerator-controlled dual-pitch stator. It was intended as an improvement over the Powerglide's somewhat lackluster performance. According to the *1957 Chevrolet Engineering Features* manual, the Turboglide "features low weight and inherently trouble free design. Turboglide, which features excellent torque multiplication that extends to higher vehicle speeds far surpasses the previous non-shifting automatic transmissions . . . A perfectly smooth torque multiplication transition from standstill to highway cruising speed is the unmistakable identification of Turboglide." With the stator at its high, or performance, position the maximum torque multiplication ratio was 4.3:1; in the low position it was 3.8:1. Its aluminum case housing, weighing slightly more than 15 pounds, at the time was the largest single die-cast unit in the world.

Though it was acknowledged for its smoothness, unfortunately it was not "trouble free." Its cast-aluminum case, a key aspect of its lightweight advantage, did not have a tolerance for high torque loads, making it prone to cracking. It soon received a reputation for being unreliable. It could also crack when overheated. Casting large pieces of aluminum was still on the ragged edge of engineering capabilities in 1957. All the bugs in the design were not fully resolved until the 1961 model year. The Turbo Hydra-Matic ultimately replaced it the following model year.

The Turboglide was an entirely new automatic transmission with a design that eliminated the necessity for a low range; it was inherently speed and load sensitive and capable of unusually broad ratio coverage. Downhill braking, typically achieved using low range, was accomplished by the Turboglide utilizing its converter as an energy-dissipating device. As explained in the *1957 Engineering Features* manual, "Kinetic energy transferred to the converter oil supplements engine braking to provide up to 15 percent greater braking effort, while engine speed is increased less than with Powerglide." This feature was known as "Hill Retarder."

Though the aluminum case was a significant weight saver, fewer internal components also contributed to the transmission's light weight as well as resulting in reduced maintenance. Its hydraulically applied clutches did not require periodic adjustment to compensate for wear. The typical intricate shift timing mechanisms were eliminated with this design. Turboglide's hydraulic control system was simplistic. It utilized a small cast-iron valve body with a heat expansion rate nearly the same as that of the steel valve spools. The material used made

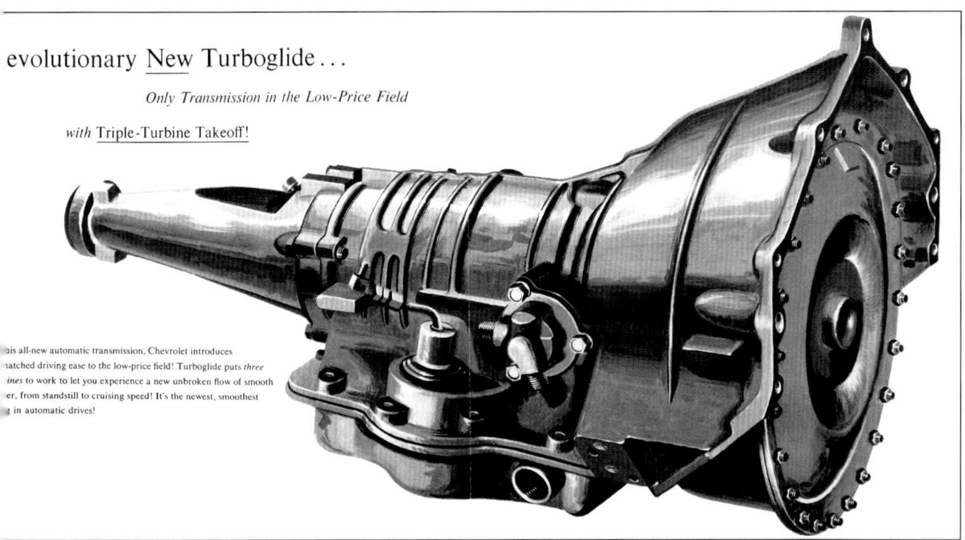

The Turboglide automatic transmission was introduced for 1957. It was the only triple-turbine type offered in the low-priced field. This transmission was designed to be of relatively light weight through the extensive use of aluminum. Its design concepts were good. However, the science of casting aluminum components was not fully understood and, as a result, the Turboglide often experienced early failures. The problems were eventually remedied, but by then another new transmission was ready to be released.

A tremendous amount of instrumentation was required to monitor the performance characteristics of this 283 V-8 in the engine dynamometer room of the Chevrolet Engineering Center. The large round gauge at center registered the torque output up to 500 ft-lb. Constant testing helped to refine the division's cars and trucks. The 638,000-square-foot facility was completed in 1955 for research and testing of Chevrolet's vehicles. (Photo Courtesy GM Media Archive)

This photograph was likely taken inside the Chevrolet Engineering Center and shows a 1957 Bel Air Sport Coupe undergoing what appears to be a variety of tests. Plenty of cables and sensors are around the front wheel and heat lamps appear to be above the car. Ahead of it is what seems to be a large vent. Perhaps some tests were of the effectiveness of the air-conditioning system under extreme conditions as well as the car's cooling system. (Photo Courtesy GM Media Archive)

it less sensitive to dirt contamination, as was the case with a cast-aluminum valve body. It also eliminated the compromises in tolerances required with the use of a die-cast aluminum valve body in conjunction with steel valve spools under widely varying temperatures. With other transmissions the use of dissimilar metals required the use of large clearances when hot to provide the proper clearances under cold operation. This situation could cause foreign matter to hinder proper valve function.

Chevrolets equipped with the optional Turboglide could be identified by the shift quadrant labeled "P-R-N-D-HR." The sequence provided greater ease in rocking the vehicle back and forth in mud or snow. This selector sequence required the driver to lift the lever only when engaging park or Hill Retarder; otherwise the driver only needed to push the lever back and forth between the gating limits to engage reverse and drive alternately. A safety switch prevented the vehicle from being started in anything other than neutral or park.

The Turboglide had a lot going for it; too bad for Chevrolet that it was not perfected much sooner.

Chassis Upgrades

Once again, the basic 1955 chassis received more improvements for the 1957 model year. These resulted in a softer ride, improved handling and braking, and increased structural rigidity and durability.

Various changes pushed the weight of the 1957 Chevrolets upward by approximately 100 pounds. To compensate for the increased sprung weight, the front suspension deflection rate was increased from 100 to 109 pounds per inch. New tires (7.50x14-4 ply) requiring 22 psi of pressure (compared to 24 for the 6.70x15-4 ply previously used) that were 0.8 inch wider in section also softened the ride. The greater section width permitted lower pressure without compromising stability or load-carrying capability. Station wagon models received a 6-ply version of the tire to accommodate their additional weight. A change to the shock absorber valving also contributed to the softer ride.

The upgraded rear suspension was less likely to bottom out against the chassis frame on rough surfaces. An increase in the rear axle clearance was accomplished by raising the rear spring front mounting and changing to a positive spring camber. Nearly horizontally mounted rear springs contributed to neutralizing any understeer and oversteer tendencies.

The redesigned front crossmember-to-side-member braces welded to the frame side members formed a rigid box structure that served to increase the strength of the entire front of the frame and strengthen the front bumper mountings.

Adoption of higher-capacity ball bearings, improved lubrication, phosphate treatment of the gears, and a stronger differential carrier and case via increased thickness and reinforcing ribs, led to a quieter and more durable rear axle. Tapered roller bearings replaced the barrel roller type formerly used at the sides of the differential.

A new drain plug in the bottom of the axle housing made it easier to periodically change the lubricant and eliminate contaminants.

Road Testing

The March 1957 issue of *Speed Age* provided readers with a drive report on the new 1957 Chevrolet. Its Bel Air test car, which was equipped with the Super Turbo-Fire 283, Powerglide, power steering, and power brakes rode, handled, and performed well in the opinion of the test driver. He stated, "Driving the new Chevy was pretty pleasant duty." The power-assisted options were evaluated under sudden loss of power; the driver noted that shutting off the power while driving had no adverse effect on steering or braking effectiveness. He added that "the engineers did a bang up job on the design of the power brake reserve tank . . . It is made of metal, pressed together in two parts, and then welded like a gas tank." However, brake fade was rated as "considerable" in heavy stop-and-go traffic, though once the brakes cooled the stops were straight without pulling to one side.

Other observations included: "Steering was not oversensitive . . . Cornering, I could feel a slight road pull which I think is best anyway, and yet the power made it easy. I got into one turn a little too hot and had to correct in a hurry but when I did, the car recovered quickly and I never lost the feel of the front end at all . . . The suspension was firm, handling the bumps and dips nicely, and still it was comfortable . . . As for acceleration, the engine packed plenty of punch." The Powerglide was judged as having "more direct drive with less slippage" compared to earlier versions of the transmission.

Styling Changes

Major sheet metal alterations made the 1957 Chevrolet passenger cars distinctly different from the preceding model years. With a commitment to a three-year body styling cycle, the 1957s maintained the basic shell (the roof, doors, and deck) while the rest was changed. In Pat Chappell's book *The Hot One: Chevrolet 1955–1957*, designer Clare "Mac" MacKichan was quoted as saying in regard to the styling, "As I recall, there was a great deal of pressure on us in the Chevrolet Studio [to add distinction to] the 1957 car . . . So what we were supposed to do [on the 1957 Chevy] was . . . beat Chrysler and Ford but not change the basic shape of the thing. We did manage to get entirely new graphics in the front, and the back was pretty different looking, too. We did such obvious things as moving the taillights to a new location, changing that whole corner. From the side we did a similar thing with the aluminum panel and trim molding. We did everything we could to change those cars, within the ground rules that we were stuck with."

The change in "graphics" in front included a new bumper-grille combination, new headlight bezels with an air

The Sport Sedan model continued to be offered for the 1957 model year. This Larkspur Blue and India Ivory Bel Air Sport Sedan is one of 137,672 built. Though Ford beat Chevrolet in the sales race this model year, Chevrolet's Bel Air Sport Sedan again easily outsold Ford's Town Victoria by roughly a two-to-one margin.

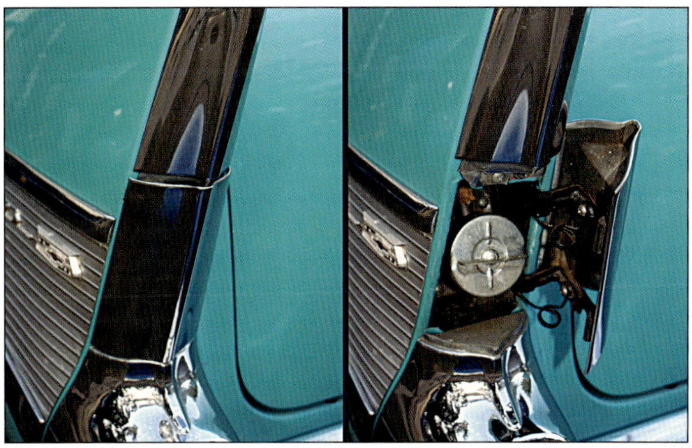

The fuel filler was again hidden for 1957. This time it was placed behind the stainless-steel molding wrapping around the edge of the quarter panel and just above the taillight on the driver's side. A redesigned filler pipe allowed for faster filling of the tank. In the previous design, air was forced out as fuel flowed into the tank, slowing the process. A new fuel cap prevented loss of fuel when cornering or parking on grades. New air passages in the gasket and cap allowed the fuel tank to vent.

Like other Bel Air models, the Sport Sedan featured a "Color-Fashioned" interior composed of nylon-faced woven fabrics with grain and patent leather vinyls. Foam-rubber seat cushions and deep-pile carpeting were standard. Note the dash-mounted rearview mirror, a seldom-ordered option. Another uncommon option on this car is air-conditioning.

inlet to duct air into the passenger compartment, and twin hood "bullets." The hidden fuel filler was again included for 1957. This time it was placed behind a pivoting door integrated with the stainless-steel molding wrapping around the edge of the quarter panel just above the driver's side taillamp.

Sales Not As Predicted

At the auto show dubbed "America on the Move" held at the Waldorf-Astoria Hotel in New York City in November 1956, GM president Harlow Curtice predicted, "The industry in 1957 should produce, and the domestic market absorb, approximately 6.5 million cars and 900,000 trucks. Including export, production should approximate 8.3 million cars and trucks." Unfortunately, the usually accurate Curtice was off considerably in his estimates. While production was, indeed, up from 1956, it fell far short with the actual total being about 7.2 million cars and trucks. As for General Motors, its market share fell from 52.8 to 46.1 percent with Ford Motor Company and Chrysler Corporation getting the benefit of

A new instrument panel was created for the 1957 Chevrolet passenger cars. Flanking the round speedometer, which registered to 120 mph, were round housings containing the coolant temperature gauge and the gasoline level gauge. The odometer was placed within the speedometer housing at center with a chromed surround. A full-width textured panel decorated the dash and replaced the slotted design of the previous model year. This car, a Bel Air two-door sedan powered by the 283-hp fuel-injected engine, also has the optional padded dash. Mileage shown on the odometer, less than 41,000 miles, is believed to be actual.

A freshly built 1957 Chevrolet One-Fifty two-door sedan with a 6-cylinder followed by a One-Fifty Handyman two-door station wagon near the end of one of Chevrolet's 11 assembly lines located across the United States. Even though the One-Fifty line was the lowest priced of the three offered, it sold in relatively few numbers compared to the Two-Ten and Bel Air series of cars. A total of 70,774 of the six-passenger two-door sedans were built and only 8,300 of the three-passenger two-door utility sedans were built. In the background appears the truck assembly line. (Photo Courtesy GM Media Archive)

This photograph was taken inside Chevrolet's Van Nuys, California, assembly plant, which began operations in 1947. It shows a One-Fifty Handyman station wagon body passing an inspector. A total of 14,740 of this two-door station wagon were built for 1957 at a base price of $2,307 with the 6-cylinder and $2,407 with a base V-8. (Photo Courtesy GM Media Archive)

During the last few years of Harley Earl's command of GM Design, he hired a team of female designers to add a woman's point of view to styling automobiles. They became collectively known as the "Damsels of Design." The woman's viewpoint had become especially significant because by 1955 women much more often than not were given the final say on what car the family purchased. In 1957 and again in 1958, the "Damsels" were assigned to makeover cars from each of the five divisions of GM. This 1957 Bel Air convertible, renamed "Mademoiselle," had its interior altered with multicolored fabric inserts and pleated vinyl upholstery. Note that the side panels match the woven fabric. (Photo Courtesy GM Media Archive)

The bumper and grille combination was just about finalized when this photograph was taken of a full-size clay mockup of the 1957 Chevrolet in September 1955. Bumper guard shape, however, was still a matter to be resolved. (Photo Courtesy GM Media Archive)

GM's losses. Chevrolet fell from 27.9 percent of the market to 24.9 percent. Ford and Plymouth both experienced increases in their respective market share. When asked who was at fault for the faltering sales and the "static styling" in June 1957, Curtice responded frankly, "Management."

Of the five passenger car divisions, only Chevrolet and Pontiac were not totally redesigned. Chevrolet's competition had new cars with which to compete. Furthermore, price increases for Chevrolet cars did not help the situation. *Motor Trend* had predicted Chevrolet would come out ahead for 1957, while *Motor Life* said of Chevrolet, "Never before has it had so much to offer. And—as a matter of fact—never has it needed it more." With the trend having been on the side of Chevrolet and all the new features, those responsible for the design of the car must have been quite disappointed. By about 1960, though, the 1957 Chevrolets were hot sellers on used car lots and have since become an icon among vintage car enthusiasts.

Power windows and power adjustable seat, a combined option first offered by Chevrolet for 1954, continued to be available for 1957. Since 1954, the power seat adjustment went from two-way to four-way.

CHAPTER 4

THE CHALLENGING CORVETTE

1953–1959

The Chevrolet Corvette is an automotive icon with origins dating back to the fall of 1951. When GM Styling Chief Harley Earl attended a sports car race at Watkins Glen in mid-September of that year, he conceived the idea of an American sports car. Designing it began in secret. In fact, Earl had the first plaster model built before informing the head of Chevrolet Engineering, Ed Cole, about the project. As the story goes, when Cole saw the model on June 2, 1952, along with the other engineers, he demanded of his staff that he never be surprised like that again, though upon seeing the model, he reportedly literally "jumped up and down."

The small assembly line at Flint helped refine procedures for assembling the Corvette. Lessons learned were applied to the St. Louis plant, where full-scale production was performed. Shown here are three 1953 Corvettes at the trim line where windshield assembly, bumpers, grille, and other trim pieces were installed. (Photo Courtesy GM Media Archive)

This 1957 Corvette is one of just 1,040 built with the optional fuel-injected 283. Its 4-speed transmission was a new and welcomed option for the model year. Fuel injection and the 4-speed offered the kind of performance that made the Corvette finally respectable in the eyes of sports car enthusiasts. The car was posed in front of the former General Motors building in Detroit.

Sportsman Red was the sole color choice for the 1953 Corvette. Stitching was in white. Shown here is the interior of the first prototype show car displayed at that year's GM Motorama. Note it had a red knob for both the choke control and the gear shift lever while production cars had white knobs. (Photo Courtesy GM Media Archive)

Visually, the 1953 Corvette prototype was little different from the production version. However, it was about 100 pounds heavier and its fiberglass panels were made using a resin mixture somewhat different from that for production. This photograph shows the original prototype in Dallas, Texas, the next-to-last venue of the 1953 GM Motorama. (Photo Courtesy GM Media Archive)

According to Clare MacKichan, who headed the Chevrolet Studio at GM Styling at the time, "Cole could see the enormous benefits to Chevy's image, which at that time was really deteriorating." The division "was bringing out a radical new V-8 for 1955, but we were still in 1952. Cole then brought Tom Keating, Chevy's general manager, over and got his approval to proceed." Harlow Curtice, executive vice president of General Motors at the time, gave his approval for the sports car, too.

Again according to MacKichan, "Cole insisted on seeing this car on the road and in the showrooms and newspapers as soon as possible . . . Cole personally was at the center of action. He came to styling almost daily. As the design progressed, he often brought manufacturing, engineering, and financial people to show them what could be done and to inspire them to try harder to build difficult parts or to show them the necessity for higher expenditures." Without the support of Earl, Cole, and, later, engineer Zora Arkus-Duntov, the Corvette would not have survived beyond 1954 to become an automotive icon. Producing the body of the fiberglass car involved a learning curve. Saving the sports car from cancellation, though, presented some tremendous challenges.

It was not the first American-built sports car, but rather among the first to be built since long before World War II. In the teens and 1920s, sporting-type cars, such as the Stutz Bearcat and the Jordan Playboy, were sold. Even earlier were the Kissel Kar Model 4-40 and the Mercer 35R Raceabout. Others tried to develop a sports car at about the same time as Chevrolet, but only the Corvette became highly successful, eventually.

The Beginning

As Harley Earl watched the little Allard J2s, Ferrari 166s, Cunningham C2-Rs, Jaguar XK120s, MG TCs, and other sports cars speed around the track at Watkins Glen on a comfortable, sunny September day in 1951, an idea began to gel in his mind: Chevrolet should build an American version of the European sports car. This was a revolutionary concept because no division at General Motors built sports cars simply because the market for them was perceived as almost nonexistent. However, the sports car was increasing in popularity in postwar America. Despite the increase, the number of people who owned, or at least seriously wanted to own a sports car, represented a small segment of the motoring public. Almost all the sports cars offered were European models such as the MG TD and the Jaguar XK120, far and away the most popular ones in the United States.

As of 1952, the sports car accounted for only 11,199 registrations in the United States, a mere 0.27 percent of total registrations. Such a narrow market segment did not appear to offer an opportunity for any major automobile manufacturer; the cost of designing and producing a sports car to compete with the European models did not seem to be a profitable venture. Nash had tried its luck in the sports car market in 1951 with its Healy, hoping to sell just 500 per year. When the car was terminated at the end of the 1954 model year, only 506 had been sold in all. Then there were the failed attempts by private parties, such as Earl "Mad Man" Muntz with his Muntz Jet and the Edwards from Sterling Edwards, of which only six were built over a six-year period. Considering such facts, getting Harlow Curtice to approve "Project Opel," the code name for what became the Corvette, may have required especially persuasive talk from Harley Earl, but regardless of how lengthy the discussion was, the plan to produce a sporty two-seater was strongly supported by Curtice.

Chrysler Corporation and Ford Motor Company also investigated the sports car market. Dodge built a prototype, the 1953 Storm Z-250, but found the costs of production too high to make it worth the effort. The same fate befell Chrysler Corporation's 1954 Firearrow and 1955 Falcon. Ford chose to design its 1955 Thunderbird as a sporty boulevard cruiser rather than a true sports car, believing the market for a true sports car was too limited. (Incidentally, according to the book *The Man Who Saved the V-8* by Chase Morsey, while the Corvette design began in total secrecy, Ford soon learned of the car's development from someone who left General Motors to join Ford. He even brought sketches! This windfall of information led to the Thunderbird.) Even with sales exceeding 15,000 units, Ford Motor Company executives agreed that sales were too low to justify continued production of the Thunderbird with a single bench seat and opted to add a back seat. Doing so increased sales of the Thunderbird many times over.

Owners of sports cars had to be very serious enthusiasts to appreciate driving them. To most Americans, these cars had enough eye appeal, but they were not particularly comfortable and were more expensive than other more practical alternatives for transportation. No doubt many young men fantasized about owning an XK120, a Ferrari, or any one of the other sports car offerings but simply could not afford the cost or talk the wife into going along with the purchase of one of them. For the price of, for instance, a 1950 Jaguar XK120, one could have bought a 1950 Cadillac Club Coupe or they could buy both a Chevrolet Bel Air and a Deluxe convertible with money left over. Even so, Zora Arkus-Duntov told a group at a Society of Automotive Engineers meeting in 1953 that while statistics showed most Americans did not want a sports car, he questioned if the statistics gave a true picture. He told the group, "As far as the American market is concerned, it is still an unknown quantity since an American sports car catering to American tastes, roads, way of living, and national character has not yet been on the market." He suspected a sports car designed to correspond to the wants of the *American* driver might have a significant following. His hunch, of course, later proved to be on the mark.

Perhaps Harley Earl had had the same impression as Duntov. According to Earl, he conceived the idea of the Corvette while driving his experimental 1951 GM LeSabre on the racecourse at Watkins Glen. Briggs Cunningham, who brought C4Rs to the Grand Prix, reportedly suggested to Earl he should have brought a car he could have raced. Maybe Cunningham's alleged ribbing of Earl gave even greater motivation to move forward with his idea.

The Opel Passenger Car Development Project, as it was officially known, began very quickly. Opel, incidentally, was a name borrowed from GM's German division, so it served to conceal the true nature of the project. At the time, there were no plans to produce the Corvette with a fiberglass body; only prototypes were intended to be built with the relatively new material simply as a matter of expediency. However, fiberglass (or Fiberglas, the trademarked name) was eventually found to be quite suitable for the expected level of production. Time was required to learn how to build the Corvette's fiberglass body to the same fit and finish standards as steel-bodied cars. In the end, the molds used in shaping the fiberglass components were able to endure a production run of 10,000 units per year.

During the fall of 1952 and through the first couple of months of 1953, three prototypes were completed, two for auto shows and one for testing. The first of the two show cars debuted at the Waldorf-Astoria Hotel in New York City, the starting point of the 1953 GM Motorama multicity tour. Many of those who waited in line to see the Corvette and the other show and production cars on display there indicated a serious interest in buying Chevrolet's sports car.

According to an internal GM document, "Reactions to the Show Car—The Corvette," some people said they would cancel their order for an Eldorado to buy a Corvette. Others were inquiring as to when it would be produced and what its price would be. Some sports car owners said the Corvette had the Jaguar XK120 and the MG beat for styling. At least as many women as men showed great interest in the Corvette.

Chevrolet engineer Zora Arkus-Duntov performed much of the test driving done with the 1953 Corvette at the GM Proving Grounds in Milford, Michigan. Duntov was one of the key figures in developing the Corvette into a true sports car. (Photo Courtesy GM Media Archive)

Only 300 Corvettes were built for the 1953 model year with production ending on December 24. This is the last of them, serial number E53F001300. This fully restored car has been displayed at Pebble Beach and won numerous awards and honors, including a two-time selection to the Bloomington Gold Special Collection and a Bloomington Gold Hall of Fame induction.

Allegedly, because of this enthusiasm, production of the car was advanced and set for the middle part of the 1953 model year. In fact, the Corvette was authorized for production from the beginning and scheduled for release sometime during the latter half of the 1953 model year. Indeed, according to an internal GM memo dated November 28, 1952, a total of 100 Corvettes were to be built in the month of June alone with production of 300 per month thereafter until the start of the 1954 model year, when 10,000 were expected to be built. Production beyond that would "depend upon circumstances." However, Thomas Keating announced on March 16, 1953, at a press reception held at the Chicago Auto Show that 300 were to be built starting in June. The press saw the first two cars ceremoniously leaving the assembly line on June 30; they had actually been carefully hand-built some weeks prior to the photo op and, in reality, were prototypes with production car serial numbers. The final car of the 300 assembled left Chevrolet's Van Slyke Road plant on December 24, 1953.

This Corvette prototype was not finished to show-quality standards. This photograph was taken at the "Press Party" held in September 1953 at GM's Proving Grounds and shows a demonstration of the toughness of the fiberglass body. Note the holes for engine heat ventilation in the front fender behind the wheel opening, a unique feature added some time after the car was built. (Photo Courtesy GM Media Archive)

In a sense, the 1953 Corvettes were pilot line cars with various improvements made throughout the run. Even the way the fiberglass body parts were made changed a couple of times. As an example, the earliest production cars had a one-piece floorpan with subsequent ones getting a two-piece affair for more exacting dimensional control. Cars number 1 and number 2 were hand-built cars given extreme attention to fit and finish, economically impossible to perform for the entire production line. The frames for both cars were determined to be too weak for retail sale and were retained by General Motors for test purposes. Poor panel fit was a major and justified complaint concerning the cars. Of much less consequence, the earliest cars, roughly the first couple dozen or so, did not receive the intended wheel covers because the tooling was not quite ready; therefore, the Bel Air type was substituted. Because of all the improvements made during 1953, Corvette number 1 and Corvette number 300 were considerably different from each other. As time went by, forming and assembly techniques improved, so the last of the 300 1953s were better than the first ones.

Fiberglass: An Unexpected Innovation for the Corvette

Coinciding with the decision to build the Corvette was the increasing use of glass-reinforced plastic (GRP), or simply fiberglass, as it's widely known today. During World War II, GRP was used to form radomes for aircraft. After the war, aircraft were built with an increasingly greater number of fiberglass components. Fiberglass was soon used to build storage tanks, pipes, laminates, sports gear, boats, and more.

The material was even considered for use in constructing automotive bodies as early as 1944 when Owens Corning began working with Henry Kaiser and aviation pioneer William Stout. Soon a prototype designed and built by Howard "Dutch" Darrin debuted in 1946, as did the "Project Y" car for Stout. Another prototype by Dutch Darrin, a Kaiser sports car named for its designer, was revealed to the public in 1952 and put into production for 1954; only 435 Kaiser Darrins were built and production of it was terminated when Henry Kaiser moved his automobile business to Argentina. Then there was the fiberglass-bodied Kurtis Sports Car in 1949 and 1950, of which only 16 were built before Frank Kurtis's company was purchased by Earl "Madman" Muntz, who chose to use steel for body construction. Other private ventures produced fiberglass sports cars in the early 1950s as well, but at best, production numbers were low.

A larger link in the chain of events leading to the fiberglass Corvette was the construction of fiberglass prototype cars by the Glasspar Corporation, a manufacturer of fiberglass boats, which eventually produced roughly 100 of its fiberglass G2 sports cars as well as bodies for the Woodill Wildfire. One of the two nearly identical prototypes was named "Alembic I." (Glasspar was a customer of Naugatuck Chemical, a division of U.S. Rubber, and the division's logo was the alembic, the hexagonal-shaped benzene ring.) The *Alembic I* was illustrated in an article arranged by U.S. Rubber for the February 25, 1952, issue of *Life* magazine about the increasing use of fiberglass. The article mentioned it was to appear at the National Plastics Exposition at Philadelphia's Convention Hall, which opened on March 11. The story got the attention of several GM engineers who went to view the car. Harley Earl also viewed the *Alembic I* when it was driven to Detroit after the event and placed inside GM Styling's 11th-floor auditorium. He was very impressed with the smooth finish and resistance to denting offered by fiberglass. As a result, technicians from Naugatuck Chemical's Mishawaka, Indiana, plant went to Detroit to show how a mold could be made from a fender to make an identical part from fiberglass. GM Styling and Chevrolet Engineering immediately began experimenting with fiberglass. Chevrolet engineers quickly realized that fiberglass was far easier to use for building experimental bodies than traditional materials, such as hand-hammered steel.

Chevrolet engineer Maurice Olley noted how the properties varied with "the percentage of glass in the mixture, the texture of the glass, and the hardness of the resin." Too high a glass content tended to result in flex-cracking or stone bruises in the body panels. With the proper mixture, the properties of fiberglass were much like those of the wood used in early body construction. Olley stated, "What we get . . . is a very usable body, somewhat expensive, costing a little more than a dollar a pound, but of light weight, able to stand up to abuse, which will not rust, will not crumple in collision, will take a paint finish, and is relatively free from drumming noise. [Steel bodies need sound dampening to deaden the drumming sound produced by vibration.] A fiberglass panel of body quality three times as thick as steel will weigh half as much and will have approximately equal stiffness." In addition to the advantages cited by Olley, fiberglass is easier to repair than panels formed of steel. Paint adhesion to fiberglass in various climates was a concern at first, but ultimately did not present significant difficulties.

When the Corvette was approved, fiberglass was viewed as nothing more than a convenient method for building one or a few concept cars. This was significant because with the decision to add the Corvette to the Chevrolet roster was the simultaneous decision to proceed with the GM Motorama. The GM Motorama was a traveling exhibition featuring all the products produced by the company along with an array of concept cars loaded with ideas for future automobiles. In a paper submitted to the Society of Automotive Engineers in 1954, Zora Arkus-Duntov said:

> The body on the show model was made of reinforced plastic purely as an expedient to get the job done quickly.
>
> Although we were going ahead with the building of an experimental plastic body in order to get a car rolling for chassis development work, at the time of the Waldorf Show we were actually concentrating body-design-wise on a steel body utilizing tooling for the projected production of 10,000 units during the 1954 model year. It was some time later that we decided to produce this quantity in reinforced plastic.
>
> About this time, some doubt was expressed that we should build the 1954 model of steel. People seemed to be captivated by the idea of the fiberglass plastic body. Furthermore, information being given to us by the reinforced plastic industry seemed to indicate the practicality of fabricating plastic body parts for automobiles on a large scale.

However, the decision wavered back and forth on whether to use fiberglass or steel. According to Michael Lamm, author of *Corvette: An American Classic*, the founder of the Molded Fiberglass Company (MFG) in Ashtabula, Ohio, Robert Morrison, met with Chevrolet officials shortly after the Corvette prototype's debut at the Waldorf-Astoria. The company eventually contracted with General Motors to mold the body panels for the Corvette.

Morrison told Lamm:

> For the next several weeks, Chevrolet people and I met frequently discussing parts design and problems. I thought I was making progress. One day I went to Detroit to see the Chevrolet purchasing agent and the project buyer. When I got there, I was told they were both gone for the day, which surprised me because I had told them I was coming. Chevrolet purchasing offices were on the second floor of the GM Building. I went to the elevators and pushed the down button. I was standing in front of one elevator which was going up. The door opened and Elmer Gormeson, the Chevrolet director of purchases, stepped out. He said, 'Bob, have you got a minute?' I sure had because I had planned to spend the next morning with the Corvette buyer and Chevrolet purchasing agent. So we went into Gormeson's office. He apologized for the buyer and purchasing agent not being there. He then told me the top management of both Chevrolet and GM had had a meeting on the 14th floor, the sanctum sanctorum of the top GM officials. This meeting had taken place the day before, and GM had decided to go ahead with a steel Corvette body. So the buyer and purchasing agent had been sent out posthaste to investigate sources for steel parts. I asked Gormeson why the decision was made. He said, first because no one, not even MFG, had large enough equipment to mold the Corvette parts. Second, MFG didn't have the money nor credit to finance such a plant. Third, parts this big had never been produced before by the preform-matched-die molding process. Also, the supply of people with technical know-how was too small to solve

The GM Motorama and Its Chevrolets

The contrast between the 1953 Corvette prototype and the Bel Air four-door sedan is striking. Of course, that was the intent of this publicity photo taken outside the Key Biscayne Hotel shortly before the opening of the GM Motorama in Miami. The Corvette's sporty style was something heretofore unseen on any American-built car. It had the looks to get people's attention, but a few years would pass before the car's performance measured up to its styling. (Photo Courtesy GM Media Archive)

From 1949 to 1961, General Motors staged a series of shows (eight in total) that showcased the products of its divisions. Those held in consecutive years from 1953 to 1956 are best remembered since those had a variety of what were then known as "dream cars," which today we refer to as concept cars. The dream cars were the big attraction for the millions of people who ventured to the GM Motorama, an admission-free, extravagant auto show held in major cities across the United States. General Motors of Canada sponsored a nearly identical version in major cities in Canada. Most of the dream car bodies were built of fiberglass.

Of course, the 1953 GM Motorama featured the prototype Corvette, which generated much excitement among the crowds and provided an accurate preview of the production version.

For the 1954 GM Motorama, two Corvette-based concepts along with a modified Corvette were among the Chevrolets on display. The latter had a prototype of

A 1954 Corvette and the Corvette-based show cars were posed together for this publicity photo taken in Miami. The Corvette with the prototype detachable hardtop and roll-up windows forecasted features that would be included on the 1956-and-later Corvettes while the Nomad provided the roof design for a Bel Air version of the station wagon. Low sales of the Corvette kept the fastback body style out of production. (Photo Courtesy GM Media Archive)

The addition of the prototype hardtop to this modified 1953 Corvette required a new windshield frame and windshield assembly. This arrangement was very similar to that of the production pieces used for 1956. In addition to the hardtop were roll-up windows, another feature added beginning with the 1956 Corvette. (Photo Courtesy GM Media Archive)

The Corvette with the prototype hardtop shown during the 1954 GM Motorama show circuit and other venues included waffle-pattern upholstery forecasting 1956 and 1957 Corvette upholstery design. (Photo Courtesy GM Media Archive)

the detachable hardtop that would become available as an option for 1956 as well as for the remainder of production of the first-generation Corvette, along with roll-up windows and waffle-pattern upholstery, which became standard features for 1956 and 1957. The other two show pieces were a fastback Corvair and the Nomad two-door station wagon.

The 1955 GM Motorama featured the Chevrolet Biscayne, a four-door pillarless hardtop. It was more compact than any car offered by Chevrolet, except the Corvette, yet was billed as an "exploration in elegance." An elegant car of the era always meant "big car," so the Biscayne proved luxury could be had in a smaller car.

Then the following year, a five-passenger car combining sportiness with luxury was exhibited, the Corvette Impala.

The Corvair

The 1954 Chevrolet Corvair (a name that seemed to be a combination of "Corvette" and "Bel Air") was essentially a modified Corvette with a fastback roof sweeping back into a jet exhaust–type opening. Other details of the Corvair included a ventilation system comprising a set of three small rectangular intake vents mounted one over the other on the front fenders with exhaust vents located on the C-pillars that could be opened and closed with a manual control. Engine compartment heat was vented through chromed, slotted vents integrated into twin bulges on the hood. The so-called jet exhaust opening was fitted with the license plate mounting, a license plate lamp, and a pair of backup lights, and was filled with a bright metal plate with hundreds of Chevrolet bowtie emblems cut into it. Incidentally, the Corvair's rear styling was considered a styling update for the 1955 Corvette, but no money was released to fund the necessary tooling changes because of poor sales of the sports car. Therefore, the Corvair was evidently intended to forecast styling of the 1955 Corvettes, but in the end it did not.

The interior of all versions of the Corvair was largely upholstered in light beige leather, but the pattern on the seats and door panels differed completely from that of the production Corvette. A bulkhead as on the Corvette sat directly behind the bucket seats while a filler panel covered the section from the bulkhead all the way back to the bottom of the backlight. A convenient storage compartment and an armrest were built into the door panels.

The 1954 Corvair signaled some of the styling changes to be seen on the 1955 Corvette. These changes included the so-called jet exhaust opening filled with a bright metal plate into which a myriad of Chevrolet bowtie emblems was cut. It seems the Corvair was seriously considered for production, but those thoughts dissipated with lower than expected sales of the Corvette roadster. (Photo Courtesy GM Media Archive)

The Nomad

Carl Renner of the Chevrolet Studio of GM Styling was placed in charge of designing what may be the most famous concept car of the 1950s, the Corvette-based Nomad.

The Nomad was 8 inches longer than the Corvette from the firewall to the centerline of the front wheels and 1 inch shorter from the centerline of the wheels to the front-most part of the car. So, while the show car resembled a modified Corvette it was so different that it had to be fabricated from new molds. Other than some mechanical items, only the grille, bumperettes, headlight assemblies, wheel covers, taillight assemblies, and dashboard components were acquired from the Corvette parts bin.

Though the Nomad appears to have much in common with the Corvette, it had to be fabricated from scratch. Only a few of the Corvette's trim pieces could be used, and one of these was its grille. Some designers reportedly favored producing the Corvette-based Nomad, but it was not to be. Its roof design, including the forward-leaning B-pillar shape, was adapted to the larger Bel Air body. (Photo Courtesy GM Media Archive)

Due to the low overall height of the Nomad (just 54 inches) the surface of its roof panel was much more prominent than typical station wagons of the day. Because of this, Harley Earl ordered the roof panel be given a special feature or features to make it more visually appealing. One option strongly favored by Earl was retracting stainless steel panels over the rear half, but the concept proved to be impractical. A compromise (credited to Renner) emerged from the idea. This compromise consisted of a series of grooves running side-to-side aft of the B-pillars.

Styling of the concept car's interior was no less stunning than its exterior. Except for the dashboard and steering wheel, the Nomad's interior shared nothing with the Corvette. Upholstery was composed of white leather with silver-blue fabric inserts. The front bench seat's backrest was split into a one-third (driver's side)/two-thirds arrangement and the rear seat could be folded forward to lay flush with the cargo floor, which when down provided a 75-inch-deep cargo compartment. Chrome-plated bows added some decoration to the car's white headliner, a

The 1954 Nomad's tailgate and lift-gate design was another feature adapted to the Bel Air–based Nomad. Those exhaust ports later inspired nonfunctional versions as an accessory for 1958 and 1959 Chevrolet passenger cars. (Photo Courtesy GM Media Archive)

Styling of the 1954 Nomad's interior was no less stunning than its exterior. Except for the dashboard and steering wheel, the Nomad's interior shared nothing with the Corvette. Upholstery was luxurious white leather with silver-blue fabric inserts. (Photo Courtesy GM Media Archive)

The 1954 Nomad's electrically operated tailgate window was not adopted until the 1959 models were designed. One year earlier the Nomad name was being used for a four-door wagon. (Photo Courtesy GM Media Archive)

feature carried over to the production Bel Air–based Nomad.

When the public got its first look at the 1954 Nomad at the Waldorf-Astoria, it was clearly impressed, so much so that Harley Earl is reported to have made a phone call from the hotel instructing Carl Renner to proceed with adapting the dream car's roof to the Bel Air body. (Not long afterward, Pontiac was also authorized to build its own version, dubbed the Safari.) The production version kept the forward-sweeping B-pillars, sliding side glass, grooved roof panel, tailgate trim, and open rear wheel housings of the show car. Later, the functional exhaust port surrounds on the lower quarter panels of the 1954 Nomad were adopted as a nonfunctional accessory first offered for the 1958 model year. The Corvette Nomad's electrically operated tailgate window would not be adopted until the 1959 models were designed.

As for the production version, it brought relatively low sales but generated a lot of publicity for Chevrolet. However, the concept was dropped with the end of the 1957 model year because sales of two-door wagons were dropping quickly. The Nomad name continued to be used for a few more model years, though.

1955 Biscayne

The Biscayne was a four-passenger, pillarless four-door hardtop described by General Motors as "a superlatively luxurious experimental car that illustrates an entirely new way of thinking about automotive design." The fiberglass-bodied Biscayne had numerous styling cues that were applied to various cars over the next few years. One of them was the side coves, or "indented side panels" as General Motors described them, which would be found on the Corvette beginning the next model year. The side coves of the Biscayne, though, were reversed from the Corvette's and wrapped around the back of its body.

A so-called "Stratospheric" wraparound windshield curved upward into the Biscayne's roof panel. The compound curved windshield was tinted in its upper portion to reduce glare from the sun. A similar windshield was adopted for the 1959 Chevrolet passenger cars. Another feature of this dream car was a touch-type fuel filler cap located just behind the rear window. The taillight and

The front design of the Biscayne included long fairings for the headlights stretching across the hood; they ended just ahead of the inlets for interior ventilation. While the front design was not adopted, Chevrolet did make use of the windshield design four years later. The Biscayne's indented side panels, as Chevrolet described them, did appear in modified form on the following year's Corvette. (Photo Courtesy GM Media Archive)

For 1955, this Chevrolet concept car, dubbed the "Biscayne," was a four-passenger, pillarless four-door hardtop. The rear doors were hinged in back rather than on a pillar post. Doors latched to the body sill. Though Chevrolet introduced a four-door hardtop the following year, it did not make use of this complex pillarless design; that idea was used for a limited-production Cadillac two years later. (Photo Courtesy GM Media Archive)

Swivel front seats to assist occupants with entry and exit represented yet another innovation of the 1955 Biscayne. However, the idea would not be adopted on a Chevrolet until nearly two decades later. (Photo Courtesy GM Media Archive)

rear panel design was similar to what appeared on the 1961–1962 Corvette as well as the later Corvette Sting Ray.

Underneath the hood of the Biscayne was Chevrolet's new small-block "Turbo-Fire" 265 V-8 with a claimed rating of 215 hp reportedly attained through a high-lift camshaft, 4-barrel carburetor, and a dual exhaust system.

Interior features of the Biscayne included thin-shell, swiveling front bucket seats to aid ingress and egress for the driver and front passenger. The bucket-type rear seats were separated by a small console serving as a combination storage compartment and armrest. Chrome-plated brass trim framed the green and white leather-covered seats. The instrument panel with a padded leading edge carried a conventional-looking 110-mph speedometer along with a fuel gauge and clock in round pods underneath. A padded dash became an option for Chevrolet passenger cars the following model year. Eventually the padded dash became standard safety equipment.

1956 Corvette Impala

An unusual Corvette-like dream car graced a turntable at five venues of the 1956 GM Motorama. It was the Corvette Impala, an automobile deliberately styled to give a little sports car "flavoring" to a five-passenger luxury car. The dream car's toothy grille and rounded quarters revealed styling influenced by the newly restyled first-generation Corvette. A special brochure about the Corvette Impala stated the car "incorporates wholly new considerations in fine passenger car design from the standpoint of sleekness, safety, and luxury." The claim was truthful.

The fiberglass experimental car had a 225-hp Super Turbo-Fire V-8 engine coupled to a Powerglide transmission. The V-8 was modified with a 9.25:1 compression ratio and a high-lift camshaft. Spent exhaust exited through a dual set of pipes passing through the driveshaft tunnel and into a transverse-mounted muffler with dual outlets projecting through the lower rear body panel.

Styling of the Corvette Impala foretold that of the Chevrolet Impala that debuted for the 1958 model year. In fact, at one point the toothy grille was proposed for use on the new model, but was abandoned due to cost considerations. Even so, the integral bumper and grille theme was kept. Other styling traits of the Corvette Impala included a tinted Panoramic wraparound windshield curving up into the pale blue–tinted brushed stainless steel roof, a wraparound rear windshield, beltline dip near the reverse-slant C-pillars, and chrome-plated wire wheels with knock-off hubs. All of these, with the exceptions of the wire wheels and the brushed stainless-steel roof, were adopted for the production car. Its nose emblem was close to the production type

The five-passenger 1956 Corvette Impala provided a forecast of styling features of the Impala introduced for 1958 as an upscale member of the Bel Air series. However, the 1958 Impala's styling was not as influenced by the Corvette's styling as the show car. The Corvette Impala's brushed stainless-steel roof did not make production at Chevrolet, but rather was used by Cadillac for its limited-production Eldorado Brougham. (Photo Courtesy GM Media Archive)

used for the 1958–1960 Corvettes but with the name "Corvette Impala" embossed around the crossed flags. Exterior measurements of the Corvette Impala were comprised of a rather low overall height of 53.7 inches, a width of 74.4 inches, an overall length of 202 inches, a wheelbase spanning 116.5 inches, and a road clearance of 6 inches.

Designing safety into the interior of cars was still in its early stages in the 1950s, but the Corvette Impala was certainly advanced in that regard for the era. A unique, air-foil–shaped, padded cornering bar (or strut) emerged from the steering column and angled upward before transitioning into a horizontal component extending across the entire width of the interior. Flush-fitting controls for the heater, defroster, headlights, and windshield wipers were located on the surface of the strut. Nestled above the steering column was the recessed, hooded instrumentation cluster, which consisted of a 120-mph (or possibly 130-mph) speedometer and a speed warning system of 10 circular windows spread across the instrument panel; each would illuminate progressively in more intense shades of red as speed increased. Also included in the interest of safety were seat belts stored in the recesses between the backrests and seat cushion, a steering wheel with a padded single spoke, and a sloped, recessed package shelf along with a padded rear window header. Seat belts, by the way, were optional for the 1956 Chevrolets.

A fixed armrest with power window switches, a courtesy lamp, and an ashtray were mounted on the center of the rear seat. (A fixed rear center armrest was included for the production version of the Impala two years later.) The floor covering material was similar to, if not the same as, that of the 1956 Corvette. Bright metal strips overlaid the carpet in front. The concave section of the door panels was fitted with blue-tinted metal inserts and long armrests for maximum comfort. Other conveniences included a radio and drum clock mounted in the center section of the padded cowl. A drum-type clock would later be included in the front-wheel-drive 1966 Oldsmobile Toronado.

The 1956 Corvette Impala was certainly advanced for the era in regard to safety with its unique air-foil-shaped padded cornering bar (or strut) that emerged from the steering column and angled upward before transitioning into a horizontal component extending across the entire width of the interior. Flush-fitting controls for the heater and defroster, headlights, and windshield wipers were located on the surface of the strut. (Photo Courtesy GM Media Archive)

A fixed armrest with power window switches, a courtesy lamp, and an ash tray was mounted on the center of the rear seat. The rear seat fixed armrest was used exclusively in the 1958 Impala. This is just one of many examples of how the concept cars of the GM Motorama years pushed designers to think of innovations for future Chevrolets. (Photo Courtesy GM Media Archive)

One of the 300 production 1953 Corvettes built at the small Flint assembly plant on Van Slyke Road is shown at the body drop portion of the line. Note the protective wrapping around the hardware lowering the body into place. This view clearly shows the only somewhat protective bumper component in front was the center piece as it was attached to the frame. The outer pieces were bolted to the body. Also apparent is that these cars got quite dirty during assembly. (Photo Courtesy GM Media Archive)

technical problems rapidly. And fourth, they wanted to place all responsibility for parts on one source, and MFG had never done any hand lay-up work.

Morrison told Gormeson that he was willing to totally devote his attention on the Corvette project and "divorce myself from all other business." Furthermore, Morrison mentioned an 80,000-square-foot building in Meadville, Pennsylvania, he had heard about the day before their meeting. Morrison said, "For the next two hours, I sat in Gormeson's office, making phone calls, outlining plans, getting assurances of technical and financial support from material suppliers. . . ." He handled all the objections brought up by Gormeson. There was another meeting scheduled later for that afternoon and Morrison was told if there was a change in plans he would be notified. However, Morrison felt the cause was lost. After another meeting with Kaiser regarding the fiberglass Darrin, Robert Morrison drove home, arriving at 1:30 a.m. Upon entering the house, he was told by his wife to "call a number in Detroit no matter how late." He then spoke with Elmer Gormeson, who told him to proceed with getting the 80,000-square-foot building "because they'd decided to go ahead with me and MFG on the fiberglass plastic body for the Corvette."

The decision to use fiberglass, which almost did not happen, saved millions of dollars in tooling costs and hastened production of the Corvette. Kirksite dies for steel body production would have taken more time to produce, which would have meant that the Corvette would not have been in production in 1953.

GM's Fiberglass Research Begins

After the demonstration by technicians from Naugatuck Chemical of how to make a mold to form a component in fiberglass, Chevrolet's chief body engineer, Ellis Premo, and another engineer flew to three manufacturers (Lunn Laminates in Long Island, New York; Winner Manufacturing in West Trenton, New Jersey; and the Molded Fiberglass Company in Ashtabula, Ohio) to learn more about GRP fabrication techniques. Observed were the hand lay-up method, the vacuum bag molding process, and the matched metal dies system. They reported their findings on the materials and equipment used for each process to GM's upper management as well as Harley Earl and, by November 1951, General Motors was conducting its own research with fiberglass reinforced plastic at the Parts Fabrication Group, which fabricated prototype components.

As explained by the late Steve Koss, a supervisor in the Parts Fabrication Group of General Motors, during an interview by author Noland Adams for *Corvette American Legend: The Beginning*, in the earliest days of experimenting with fiberglass, "We were all show and no go. We knew what fiberglass was. It's the stuff the living room drapes were made of and the attic was insulated with, but we didn't know how to fabricate a roof panel or a hood out of it. During the following six months, we received our first materials, then determined that we could use plaster for our lay-up forms and started making our first resin mixes. We kept a lot of notes, at first mostly of our failures. As the notes piled up, a few badly needed successes started to show up. The reason we liked to use plaster for lay-up forms was that when we had problems parting the laminate from the form, we could destroy the form and save the lay-up. The time was spring 1952 when the bottom line of our notes started to read successes quite often. We were laying up hood outer panels, making inner panel support forms right on top of them without pulling them from the form. We were laying up inner panels which fit perfectly to the outer panels, separating the panels from the lay-up forms without destroying the plaster, and bonding the panels together. These panels were ready to ship to the various departments that were eagerly waiting to test and evaluate them. By July 1952 we were a full-fledged plastics department . . . and we received our first outside order. Fisher Body Engineering ordered a 1952 Chevrolet hood (both inner and outer panels) assembled. Later, Styling sent over a full-sized male plaster of a roof panel. They wanted a five-cloth plastic panel with roof-rail reinforcements bonded in place. These orders were good experience for the Parts Fab Plastics Group and we were off to the 'big league.'"

Entering the big league soon meant Parts Fab was assigned the task of building its first car body of fiberglass. The car was a 1952 Chevrolet convertible. Again, according to Steve Koss, "On August 6, 1952, two brand-new convertibles . . . rolled into the Parts Fabrication shop. One car was set on a full-sized surface plate and the other was covered up and put in storage. It was to be the control car. On August 7, a meeting was called of the Plastic Group. We were told that the car on the plate was to be disassembled panel by panel. Each panel, including the floorpan, was going to be duplicated in fiberglass and set aside until we worked our way down to the chassis. Then, we were to assemble the plastic parts to become a plastic-bodied 1952 Chevrolet convertible."

The group was given a deadline of "ASAP" to complete the project. Now back to the Koss interview:

> The work schedule announced was to be 12 hours a day on weekdays, 10 hours on Saturday, and 8 hours on Sunday. The schedule was to remain in effect until further notice. The 1952 convertible on the surface plate was prepared for disassembly of the body panels . . . All went well on this project as we progressed . . . By October 3, the convertible body was down to the floorpan. The floorpan mold was to be the biggest of all. It kind of made you sweat a little just thinking about handling 15, 100-pound bags of model plaster, almost as much water, and sisal fiber. Once the fiber-reinforced plaster mold is started, it's nonstop for 10 people in the planned two hours or until it's finished. We convinced management that we could get a good lay-up, and save five days, by using the floorpan itself, and eliminate the floorpan mold. Because the floorpan was one of the major structural panels in the car body, it would have to be a five-cloth laminate. The cloth had to fit all the configurations of the floorpan stiffeners, plateaus for the seats, kick-ups over the crossmembers and the rear axle, transmission hump and tunnel section, toe pan, and dash. It was to be a tedious saturation job because of all the irregular surfaces involved. It was decided to compound the resin for a 40-minute kickover reaction. This proved to be about right to allow everyone plenty of time to do a good saturation job, resulting in a bubble-free laminate. It required 16 continuous hours of laminating to do the floorpan lay-up . . . By October 17 the shell was bonded together and the shape of the car body started to take place . . . On October 23 at 8:00 p.m., the plastic-bodied Chevrolet convertible was complete. It was rolled off the plate and was taken on its first test ride . . . After a few miles of stop-and-go driving with six passengers, everything proved satisfactory. The speed was upped and the car driven over public roads. The vehicle was driven back on the surface plate and inspected for loose joints or cracks. None were found, so the Parts Fabrication director declared the car ready, and it was turned over to the engineers for further testing.

About one month later at GM's Milford Proving Grounds, the test driver of the plastic-bodied Chevrolet convertible lost control of the vehicle, resulting in a skid and rollover. The driver was only slightly injured while the car's only major damage was to its convertible top, windshield frame, and one tire. Among the tests to be performed at a later date was a rollover, so the accident simply advanced the test! Body damage was minimal, proving the strength and safety of fiberglass for car bodies.

Back in early September, Styling informed the Parts Fabrication Group that a full-sized male soft plaster of the Opel sports car would be sent to them. Parts Fabrication was told to surface out the plaster, make a full-sized fiberglass mold, and lay-up and assemble two fiberglass bodies in time for the 1953 GM Motorama. Steve Koss elaborated:

> In early November 1952, the all-fiberglass mold for the Opel sports car was finally completed. Because it was all done from scratch, the wood shop had to build a lot of wood models and lay-up forms for the inner panels, lock and hinge pillars, top compartment, floor and toe pans, and dash and instrument panels. On November 18, the floorpan assembly fixture was brought down to the Plastic Department. It was all checked out by the inspection department and stamped as correct per the latest drawings. We could begin assembly of the car as soon as the floorpan lay-up

was complete, cured, pulled from the form, and trimmed. Parts for the Opel sports car were being laid up at a pretty fast pace. On December 6, the hood and deck outer panels, lower nose panel, and the rear end were all laid up and ready to pull and trim. The doors were ready to be hung . . . Because this was going to be a show car getting a show-quality paint job, the body surfaces were to be perfect. Bondo hadn't been invented, so we tried to make our own surfacing putty. First, we tried to use asbestos for a resin filler. It filled the surfaces but contained a lot of entrapped air when it kicked over, resulting in a lot of pinholes. So, we tried a material called Santocel. It was very light, saturated well, did not leave pinholes on the surface when it kicked over, and sanded well. It was the material we used for filling surfaces.

The first show car body was finished by December 12. Styling painted the car at its facility. The assembly buck was returned to Parts Fabrication for construction of the second Opel sports car. Assembly of it went faster, of course.

A few drawbacks were quickly noted with the use of fiberglass for the body of the Corvette. One of them was keeping the surface free of dust due to electrostatic action. William S. Wolfram of the Chevrolet Engineering Department suggested that the component plastic parts of the body be cured in an appropriate electrostatic field so the permanent surface charge would repel dust on the exposed surfaces. Use of electrostatics in industry was already commonplace at the time. Also, since the body was entirely fiberglass rather than steel, there was no shielding from electromagnetic interference produced by the ignition system so that static was broadcast through the radio speaker. A metal shield was added to cover the distributor and spark plugs to reduce such interference.

Despite all the painstaking research and interest in using fiberglass for the Corvette, a December 10, 1952, Chevrolet interorganizational letter to Ed Cole from Mr. Wolfram stated, "The production body will be of steel construction following the basic specifications of the previous plastic body," adding that an experimental steel body was projected to be available July 1, 1953. It also stated production was being planned for 1954 rather than 1953 and that all parts released for 1953 "will be canceled and new releases will be issued for 1954." Replacing the fiberglass bodies of the experimental prototypes with steel ones was also considered. These plans, of course, were soon reversed.

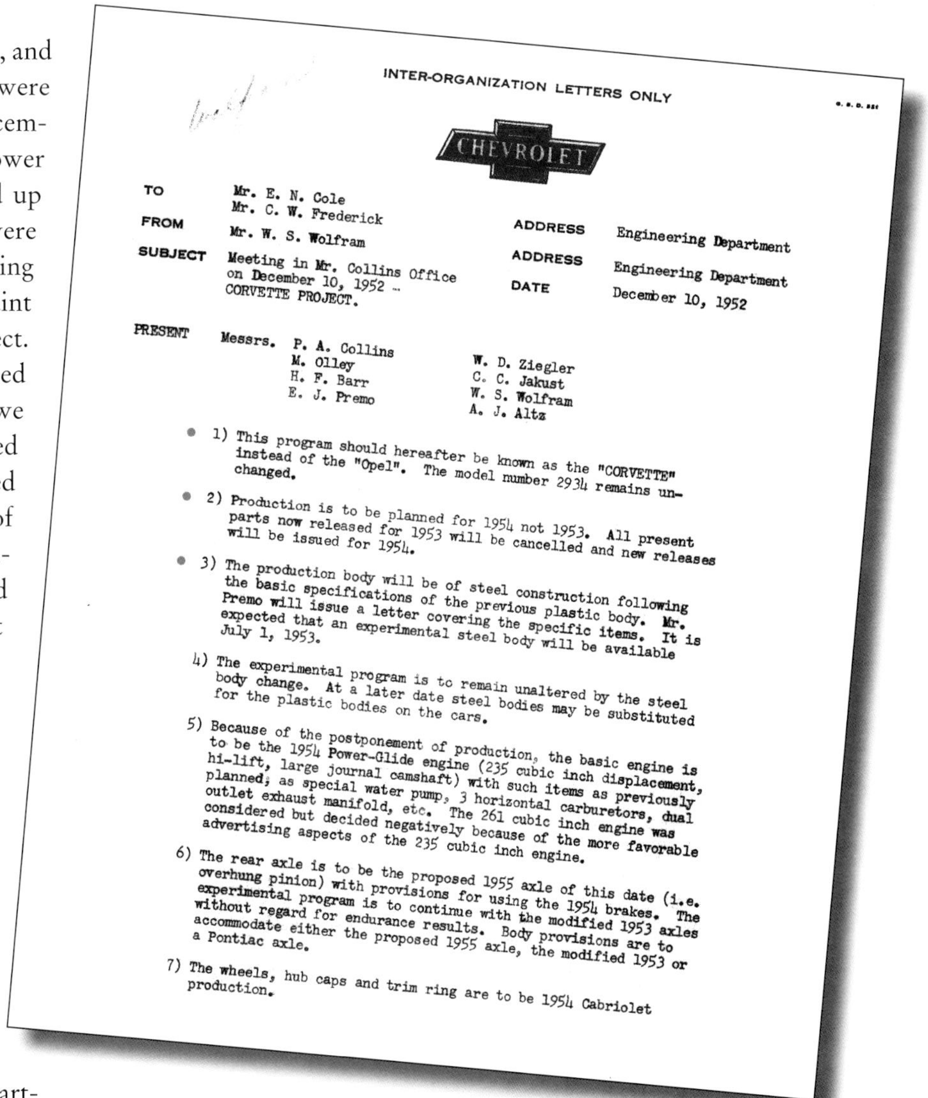
INTER-ORGANIZATION LETTERS ONLY

CHEVROLET

TO Mr. E. N. Cole
Mr. C. W. Frederick
ADDRESS Engineering Department
FROM Mr. W. S. Wolfram
ADDRESS Engineering Department
SUBJECT Meeting in Mr. Collins Office on December 10, 1952 -- CORVETTE PROJECT.
DATE December 10, 1952

PRESENT Messrs. P. A. Collins, M. Olley, H. F. Barr, E. J. Premo, W. D. Ziegler, C. C. Jakust, W. S. Wolfram, A. J. Altz

1) This program should hereafter be known as the "CORVETTE" instead of the "Opel". The model number 2934 remains unchanged.

2) Production is to be planned for 1954 not 1953. All present parts now released for 1953 will be cancelled and new releases will be issued for 1954.

3) The production body will be of steel construction following the basic specifications of the previous plastic body. Mr. Premo will issue a letter covering the specific items. It is expected that an experimental steel body will be available July 1, 1953.

4) The experimental program is to remain unaltered by the steel body change. At a later date steel bodies may be substituted for the plastic bodies on the cars.

5) Because of the postponement of production, the basic engine is to be the 1954 Power-Glide engine (235 cubic inch displacement, hi-lift, large journal camshaft) with such items as previously planned; as special water pump, 3 horizontal carburetors, dual outlet exhaust manifold, etc. The 261 cubic inch engine was considered but decided negatively because of the more favorable advertising aspects of the 235 cubic inch engine.

6) The rear axle is to be the proposed 1955 axle of this date (i.e. overhung pinion) with provisions for using the 1954 brakes. The experimental program is to continue with the modified 1953 axles without regard for endurance results. Body provisions are to accommodate either the proposed 1955 axle, the modified 1953 or a Pontiac axle.

7) The wheels, hub caps and trim ring are to be 1954 Cabriolet production.

This Chevrolet interorganizational letter dated December 10, 1952, details the results of a meeting of Chevrolet engineers and other personnel in which the name "Corvette" was officially chosen for the division's sports car. Also of significance were the two decisions, both of which were later reversed, to postpone production of the car until 1954 and to produce the Corvette body using steel rather than fiberglass. (Photo Courtesy GM Media Archive)

Off-the-Shelf Parts, Styling, and Choosing a Name

What people were willing and able to pay for the Corvette dictated that all-new components needed for the Corvette had to be kept to a minimum. Chevrolet was in the early stages of designing its V-8, so its 6-cylinder would have to be sufficient for a while.

Initial planning called for the Corvette to be powered by the 261-ci inline-6 pickup truck engine. However, the final decision, made during a December 10, 1952, meeting held in the office of Executive Assistant Chief Engineer P. A. Collins,

Fabrication Methods

Fiberglass body fabrication methods changed rather quickly for the Corvette. All of them required that a full-size clay model be built first. The earliest Corvettes, the prototypes and some early production cars, were built using the lay-up method. This involved placing layers of cloth and fiber in a mold to be impregnated with resin. Once this hardened, the component was removed from the mold. The side against the mold was left with a smooth surface. This process was relatively slow and only a couple of parts could be made from a single mold per day. This was certainly not a problem with low-volume production and building prototypes.

With the production rate ramping up a bit during 1953, Corvette bodies began to be made using the bag method. This method, somewhat similar to the lay-up method, was being used to build fiberglass boats. A layer of cloth, fiber, and another layer of cloth were laid in a mold and impregnated with resin. Next, a thin polyvinyl sheet was laid over the mold and the wet cloth-fiber-cloth-resin mix. This was sealed around the edges and a vacuum pump was then used to remove air from under the sheet. This resulted in atmospheric pressure imparting a force on the part being made and caused the inner surface to be smooth, too. Furthermore, the mold was heated with warm water circulating internally to accelerate the curing process. More parts could be made per day with this method.

By the end of the 1953 production run, the matched metal die process was replacing the bag method. The bag method was used for some body components well into 1954 production, but before the end of that model year all the Corvette's body panels were made using the matched metal die, or Kellering, process. While somewhat laborious, it still held an advantage over the dies needed to produce a steel body, which had to be of a higher level of precision and greater in number.

A mahogany die model was made for each of the body sections of the 1953 Corvette prototypes, including this underbody die, from which semi-permanent molds were made. (Photo Courtesy GM Media Archive)

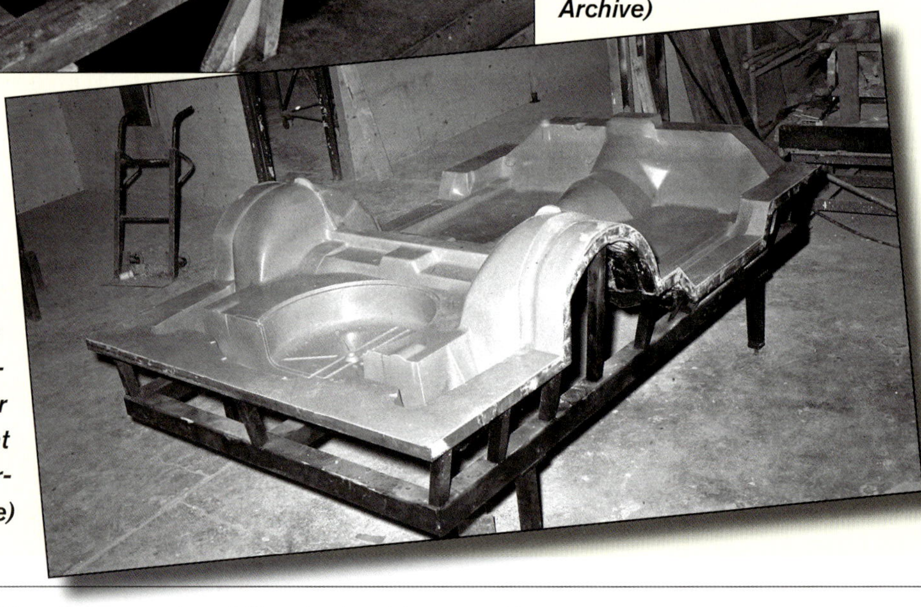

Metal dies like this one for the Corvette's underbody were eventually used for mass production of the fiberglass sports car. Early plans called for steel-bodied Corvettes, but because molds such as this were suitable for the relatively low production of the car helped persuade management to use fiberglass. (Photo Courtesy GM Media Archive)

This process started with a reinforced-plaster female mold taken from the full-size clay. It was then placed in a fixture to be duplicated. A large metal piece was either cast or welded from smaller pieces to produce the female die. While in the duplication fixture, a pickup guide followed the contours within the plaster mold. Another arm with a grinding wheel copied the contours of the surface on the female die. After this step was completed, the female die was left with rows of grooves that were removed by a tool and die maker using a large hand grinder. Once smoothed, the metal die was a mirror image of the original clay model.

Metal dies such as this one for the upper front of the Corvette had to be ground by hand to complete them for use. (Photo Courtesy GM Media Archive)

Next, the male section of the die was produced. The reinforced plaster mold was used again. Sheets of wax were laid in the plaster mold and melted, so the wax would flow into all its contours. When the wax solidified again it was the same thickness as the part to be produced. At this point, another reinforced plaster mold was made from the first plaster mold and wax composite. Another die was produced with the duplicating machine and hand ground to a mirror image of the female die. The dies were placed together, and the part to be made filled in the space between. Fabrication of the part began with a screen, shaped and sized appropriately, placed in a booth. Layers of cloth, fiber, and another cloth were laid on the screen. A blower located behind the booth pulled air through as an air-operated gun applied chopped fiber and resin. After the part was partially cured, it was removed from the screen and sent to the press where the matched metal dies were placed. More resin was poured over the part and the dies were then closed. The temperature was raised in the dies to accelerate the curing process. With this method, at least 50 parts could be produced per day.

Fabrication of the fiberglass body components was contracted to the Molded Fiberglass Company in Ashtabula, Ohio, which had come out ahead in the bidding process, even ahead of GM's Fisher Body Division. However, Lunn Laminates of Long Island, New York, was subcontracted by MFC to produce parts using the bag method until MFC could get the matched metal dies.

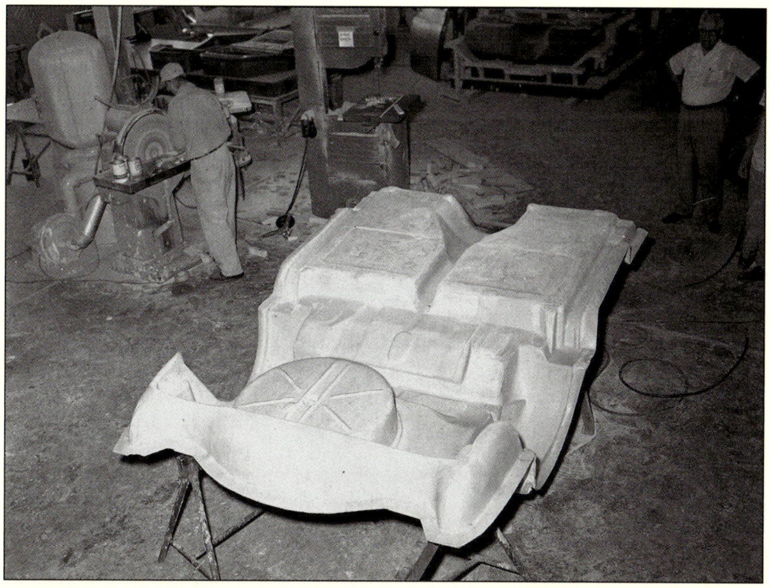

Engineers learned how to fabricate large body components in fiberglass during late 1951 and 1952. Shown is the floor of a 1953 Corvette as it came out of the mold. It required the drilling of about 180 holes of differing sizes before attachment to the upper body panels. The spare tire well is prominent in this view. (Photo Courtesy GM Media Archive)

was to use the 235-ci engine instead. According to the December 10 Chevrolet interorganizational letter prepared just after the meeting, the 235 offered "more favorable advertising aspects." While those more favorable advertising aspects were not specified in the letter, one can reasonably speculate potential buyers of the Corvette may have viewed the use of a "truck engine" in a sports car negatively. The 235 engine received a number of upgrades to improve its performance, including a trio of Carter YF side-draft carburetors, aluminum intake, a higher-lift camshaft with aluminum timing gear, increased compression ratio, and dual exhausts. Modifications pushed the output from 115 hp to 150. McCulloch Motors Corporation proposed to Chevrolet that they offer the company's supercharger as an option to boost performance even more. Ultimately, it was not made available by Chevrolet since the company was more focused on fitting its small-block V-8 into the Corvette for 1955. However, the McCulloch setup was offered as an aftermarket kit and those who bought the supercharger found their 0–60 mph time reduced from near 12 seconds to around 9.

The first-generation Corvette's chassis was a modified version of the passenger car design. As many off-the-shelf components as possible were used to reduce the manufacturing cost of the sports car; hence the use of the "Blue Flame" inline 6-cylinder and Powerglide transmission. (Photo Courtesy GM Media Archive)

Though upgrades to the 6-cylinder were substantive, they were not nearly enough to please Ed Cole, who directed development of high-performance engines and transmissions. Ultimately, further research into getting more from the straight-6 was dropped as the V-8 program advanced. A 4-speed transmission was considered unnecessary and was not produced. The Powerglide became mandatory equipment and was expected to appeal to more potential buyers than would a manually shifted transmission. Interestingly, while the lack of a 4-speed transmission was widely criticized by enthusiasts, some foreign models, such as MG, Delage, Delahaye, and a few others, were equipped with a semi-automatic transmission.

The original specifications for the Corvette called for the 261-ci truck engine, but in the end the decision was made to use the 235. It was upgraded with a trio of Carter YF side-draft carburetors, aluminum intake, higher-lift camshaft with aluminum timing gear, increased compression ratio, and dual exhausts. These modifications pushed the output from 115 hp to 150.

The existing Chevrolet chassis could be modified to reduce costs, with the modified frame to be a welded boxed section. In front, the 1952 Chevrolet suspension was little changed, though it was upgraded with a larger-diameter stabilizer bar, special front coil springs, and a ball bearing for the center arm support for the steering mechanism. Other features included a 16:1 steering ratio with a steering gear similar to the Saginaw type, Hotchkiss drive, four-leaf springs in back placed to the outside of the side rails of the frame, and the same 11-inch brake drums used by the passenger car line, but with the front and rear proportioning changed from 56 percent in front to 53 percent to compensate for the Corvette's nearly 50/50 weight distribution with driver, passenger, full fuel tank, and luggage. Empty it was 53/47. The center of gravity was low at just 18 inches above the ground.

With all of this in mind, the price target was set at $1,850, approximately the cost of a 1952 Chevrolet sedan. How-

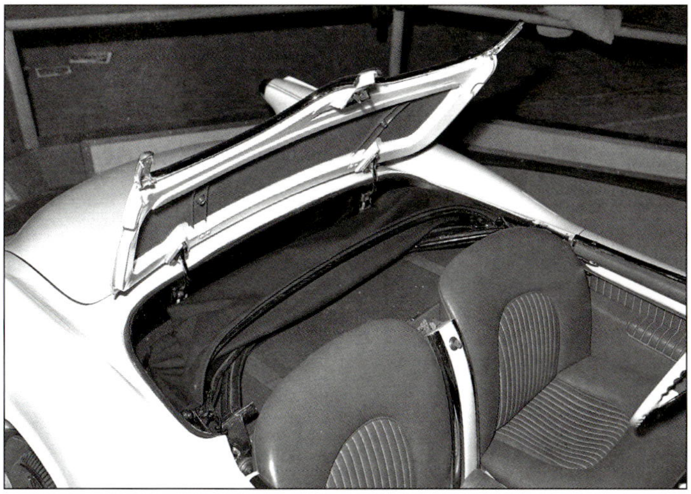

The folded soft top of the Corvette could be stored inside this well, which was covered by a pivoting cover, a concept first demonstrated on Harley Earl's 1938 Buick Y-Job concept car. This photograph shows the stowed soft top of the first 1953 Corvette prototype. (Photo Courtesy GM Media Archive)

The fuel tank for the first generation of Corvettes was installed underneath the well for the folding top. For 1953, the tank capacity was 18 gallons, but this was reduced to 17 gallons for 1954. (Photo Courtesy GM Media Archive)

ever, the low price target was soon found to be impossible to achieve. One factor figured into the original price target was that dies for steel bodies, costing $4.5 million, would not be needed; those for fiberglass would cost only $400,000. However, as explained by author Karl Ludvigsen in *Corvette: America's Star-Spangled Sports Car, the Complete History*, not figured into the price was "the tremendous extra expense incurred . . . with additional shifts and the many provisional molds needed for the temporary vacuum bag installation in Ashtabula." Regardless, Chevrolet was committed to offering the Corvette.

Body design for Project Opel began in a small, enclosed area on the ninth floor of the Argonaut Building where the main Body Development Studio was located. Harley Earl specified that the Corvette receive a wraparound windshield, one of the advanced styling features of his one-off LeSabre, a radically styled experimental car with numerous advanced mechanical systems. Another LeSabre feature passed on to the Corvette, one that had been passed on to the LeSabre from the experimental 1938 Buick Y-Job, was the concealed folding top. Another of Earl's styling specifications was the use of transparent covers over the recessed headlights blending with the shape of the front fenders. Reportedly, laws then in place regulated the placement of anything over the headlights, so in the end, the so-called "fencing mask" grilles were applied.

Even these were objectionable in some states. Earl placed stylist Robert McLean, a graduate of Cal Tech and a sports car enthusiast, in charge of the car's styling. Karl Ludvigsen wrote that McLean was to perform the general layout. The

Narrow band white wall tires and Chevrolet hubcaps with trim rings were originally specified for this prototype. The narrow band white wall tires ultimately were not used and the hubcaps and trim rings were soon replaced with wheel covers closely matching the design later used for production. Also, for a brief time, a set of louvers was intended to be on the front fenders rather than the short spear molding and Chevrolet script ultimately chosen. When this photo was taken of the original prototype show car, it wore "Cougar" script on the front fenders. This was ordered to be removed and the name "Corvette" applied above the grille and on the deck lid. Chevrolet script replaced the Cougar script on the fenders. (Photo Courtesy GM Media Archive)

Norbert Shemansky, an American weight lifter of the era, held up the fiberglass floor assembly of the 1953 Corvette to demonstrate the light weight of a fiberglass body.

standard practice was to start a layout from the firewall and work fore and aft to locate the wheels, engine, and passengers. Instead, McLean began with "the rear axle centerline and started constructing the car from the back to the front." When other stylists saw what he was doing, they collectively told him his method was "impossible," though McLean proved them wrong. He brought the seats as close as he reasonably could to the rear wheelhouses and then drew the occupants seated low and stretched out in the traditional sports car arrangement. From there McLean located the dash line and placed the 6-cylinder engine and gearbox back as much as possible, something considered revolutionary at the time as it was 3 inches lower and 7 inches more rearward than the then-current Chevrolet. The arrangement helped to achieve, as close as possible, the desired 50/50 weight distribution. Lowering the drivetrain lowered the center of gravity for better handling. With all this completed McLean was able to establish the centerline for the front wheels and in so doing arrived at the Corvette's 102-inch wheelbase, the same as that of the Jaguar XK-120.

General Motors purchased at least one XK-120 for dismantling to study its design. McLean's drawing was then converted into a full-scale, detailed, white on black profile drawing by Bill Bloch. Upon completion, Harley Earl viewed it and questioned McLean about the engine placement, "Is that how the Jaguar and MG are?" to which McLean confirmed with a simple "Yes, sir." And with that confirmation, Harley Earl accepted the styling. Within only eight months the new car went from the drawing board to a functional prototype.

At this point, a name for Chevrolet's new sports car had to be selected. A contest was held and many names were suggested. Evidently, one of the suggestions was "Cougar." Two days prior to the December 12 showing of the car to management, there was an order via the Chevrolet interorganizational letter of December 10, 1952, to replace the program

These 10 fiberglass sub-assemblies were combined to make the Corvette's body from 1953 to 1955. This photograph from 1953 was taken at a time when body-forming techniques were being revised periodically as engineers learned the craft of working with fiberglass. (Photo Courtesy GM Media Archive)

name "Opel" with "Corvette." Photographs taken by GM Photographic of the freshly built original prototype, through, show it fitted with Cougar script on the front fender.

Myron Scott, an employee of Chevrolet's advertising department, suggested the name "Corvette" and was declared the winner of the contest. The car's namesake was the British World War II submarine chasers, the corvettes, which were fast and highly maneuverable. Another letter dated December 17, from Chevrolet Chief Engineer E. J. Premo to Executive Assistant Chief Engineer P. A. Collins, ordered the Cougar script be removed from the prototype and replaced with "Corvette" script. With the name finally determined, it appeared on the Corvette as anodized gold script on the nose of the car and above the recessed license plate mounting location on the decklid.

Lessons learned while constructing the original prototype show cars and the test car helped in refining the production version. A small reduction in the thickness of the fiberglass used for the body resulted in a lighter car. The completed production body weighed just 411 pounds, much less than the originally projected 600 pounds. Going to a two-piece (upper and lower) body made the production process easier but also resulted in a seam down the side that had to be concealed with molding. Slightly larger headlight bezels were used and the anodized gold Corvette script was deleted from the hood and deck lid. The wheel cover spinners were also slightly modified.

Since there were so few Corvettes to go around for 1953, the display of one at a dealership offered a special opportunity for interested persons to see one up close. This newspaper ad promoted the first display of the new sports car at a San Francisco–area dealership. Some of those who went to see the Corvette bought another Chevrolet.

Flawed Marketing, Flawed Car, and Mixed Reviews

Approximately 20,000 people had signed with dealers to be included on the waiting list for the new Corvette. However, with only a relative handful of Corvettes to sell, Chevrolet's sales manager at the time, William "Bill" Fish, decided to offer the first Corvettes to VIPs (i.e., town officials, socially prominent people, celebrities, etc.) in the communities of high-volume dealerships rather than on a first come–first serve basis. Word of mouth from such people was expected to help promote the sports car and spur sales when full production was realized for 1954. As examples, an executive of the DuPont Company, which supplied the acrylic lacquer paint used on GM automobiles, received Corvette 5 and Henry DuPont received Corvette number 6. Both executives were major shareholders of GM's stock. According to John Amgwert, a founder of the National Corvette Restorers Society (NCRS), Corvette number 4 went to J. Spencer Weed, head of the Grand Union Grocery Store in Wilmington, Delaware. Mr. Weed was well acquainted with at least one member of the DuPont family. Legendary actor John Wayne received Corvette number 51. Wayne was too tall to sit comfortably in his Corvette and later gave it to actor Ward Bond. Entertainer Arthur Godfrey also got a Corvette as did Chevrolet representative and entertainer Dinah Shore. General Motors retained several others for further testing or promotional use.

When interested members of the public discovered that they could not simply go to the local dealership to purchase a Corvette, they began to lose interest in the car. Several of the early prospects had to be called before Chevrolet found a buyer for one of its sports cars. Moreover, the lack of roll-up windows, no exterior door handles, as well as the lack of other conveniences along with a powertrain of less than stunning performance made the car a disappointment to many of the VIP owners. As for opening the doors, it was simple when the soft top was not in place or at least the side curtains not installed; one merely pulled the inside release to open the door. However, with both installed, one had to push open the vent window and reach through the opening to access the door release, which was not at all convenient, especially when it was raining. Unfortunately, probably as a cost-cutting measure, the push-button external door releases shown on the original prototype did not make production.

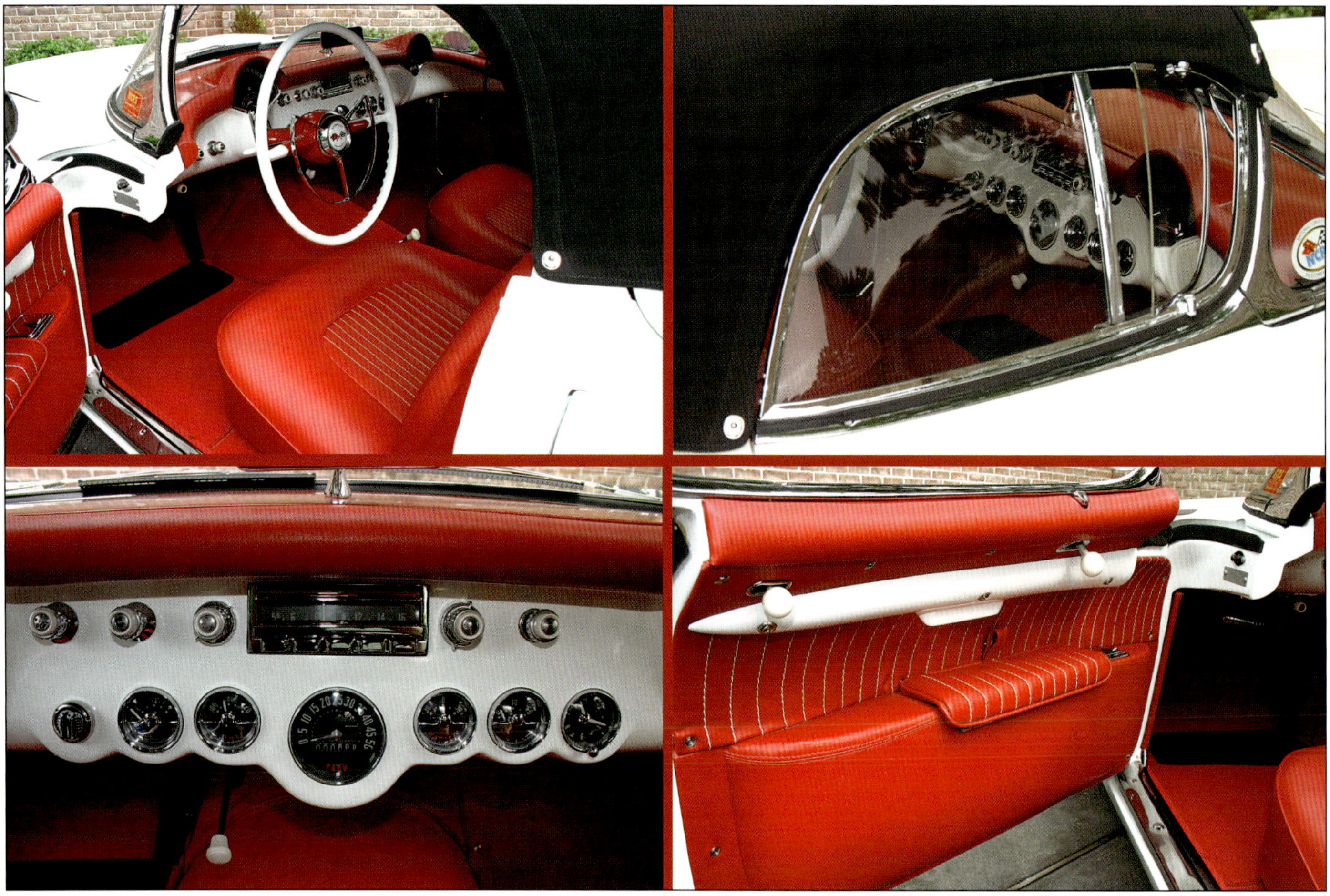

Virtually all 1953 Corvettes left the assembly line with a Polo White exterior, Sportsman Red interior, and a black soft top. (A "no paint, no primer" car went to GM Styling.) White stitching was used for the upholstery, and other white areas included the lower dash, steering column, part of the steering wheel, and a section of the door panels. Snap-in plexiglass side curtains were used instead of roll-up windows until the 1956 Corvette was released. A signal-seeking AM radio was listed as an option, but in practice was a required option.

Curves dominated the styling of the rear of the C1 generation of Corvettes. The short exhaust extensions were lengthened for 1954 to prevent staining of the paint and fumes getting into the interior. Note the red-painted rims and red accents on the wheel covers.

These paired fins on the Corvette were quite conservative compared to those of other GM cars. The Corvette was the first Chevrolet car to have the styling fad.

This photograph conveys the original concept of the Corvette. It was conceived as a car for the country club type such as the avid golfer rather than a true sports car for competition, though the sporting aspect was included in advertising. In the end, the design did not satisfy either type of person. Note the poor fit of the closed door, just one example of the flaws of the first Corvettes. (Photo Courtesy GM Media Archive)

This 1953 Corvette, serial number E53F001014, is reportedly the first Corvette to be sold to the public. It was purchased by newsman Paul Williams of WWJ-TV in Detroit. General Motors retained roughly the first dozen 1953 Corvettes for testing; a few were converted into show cars, some were displayed at dealerships, state fairs, and other venues, and the rest were sold to celebrities and people who were prominent in their community. This marketing scheme ultimately did not serve Chevrolet very well. Corvette number 14, incidentally, still exists and at last report was in a private collection in California. (Photo Courtesy GM Media Archive)

Quality control was another problem with the Corvette. Not only was the panel fit generally poor, stress cracks appeared fairly quickly; the learning curve for fabricating the body with fiberglass was not complete. The Corvette simply was not quite up to the expectations of the American driver.

The price announced by Thomas Kettering, Chevrolet's general sales manager, at the start of production was $3,250, a $1,400 miss from the original target of $1,850. Cost was certainly another factor in the public's declining interest in the Corvette. Worse still, this figure was the *official* base price; in reality the so-called–optional AM radio and heater were each mandatory items, adding more than $200 to the total price. (The radio antenna, by the way, was molded into the Corvette's decklid.) Other standard equipment included windshield washers, whitewall tires, clock, cigarette lighter, outside rearview mirror, and a warning light that glowed red when the parking brake was set. The latter feature was considered innovative at the time.

At the end of the 1953 model year, only 183 of the cars had been sold. At the time, this did not alarm General Motors because so many of the cars were being used for special dealer displays to draw people into showrooms. There remained plenty of confidence in achieving the goal of selling 10,000 Corvettes for the 1954 model year.

Press Reports

The automotive press, at least, usually found a little something mildly positive to say about the Corvette. *Motor Trend* judged the Corvette to be "an exciting car to drive," but noted it would "barely nose out an average [Buick] Century on an unobstructed freeway." The car's top speed was approximately 108 mph. A 0–60 mph run required 11.5 seconds, which was not especially fast but decent for the era. For further comparison, a 1953 Oldsmobile Super 88 could make the run in 12.3 seconds equipped with a Hydra-Matic and even faster with the manual transmission; the Olds' top speed was about 110 mph.

While acceleration was not bad, the Corvette's handling characteristics were less than desirable. Road testers for *Motor Life* reported, "When we tried to break it loose at high speed on a rather severe corner the Corvette . . . showed a definite unwillingness to tuck back in." *Road & Track* noted that "high-speed four-wheel drifts required a certain amount of dexterity." The Corvette fell short in conveniences, quality, acceleration, top speed, and handling. At least it had style, though some did not like the styling either.

However, not everyone thought of the Corvette as a poor example of a sports car. In his book *Corvette: An American Classic*, Michael Lamm wrote about test driving a three-year-old 1954 model that was for sale: "Here was a fantastic handling automobile. My dad's 1954 Hudson Hornet, which in that day represented about the best in passenger-car handling, couldn't lay a hand on the Corvette. The Vette's steering felt light, fast, and precise; hard cornering brought out very close to neutral understeer-oversteer. Even when the rear end started to swing outward, as it did, all I had to do was feed a little more gas to bring it back into line. What a fantastic car I thought." Lamm also commented on the remarks of John R. Bond, the editor of *Road & Track*, in the magazine's June 1954 issue: "He [Bond] said that there had been a lot of talk, especially from diehard owners, that nothing from Detroit could qualify as a true sports car, especially nothing from Chevrolet. 'Furthermore,' said Bond, 'some people seem to feel that no car based on standard family-car components can be much of a sports car.' Nothing could be further from the truth, as can readily be shown by mentioning such famous makes as Mercedes, Porsche, Alfa Romeo, Siata, Lancia, Gordini, Talbot, and Jaguar—all of whom at one time or another built rather successful sports cars using a large proportion of major units from a mass-produced family type car." It is worth noting that Bond had favorable comments about the Corvette as well, saying he was "impressed by the Corvette generally" and "it showed good acceleration, fine road-holding, and a remarkable ride."

Three companies soon began supplying hard tops for the new Corvette: Model Builders of Chicago, Plasticon, and Scott Manufacturing Company. Model Builders offered this one. Chevrolet personnel were interested in researching the matter, evidently, and this 1954 Corvette was fitted with a tinted version. A clear top was also offered.

A Work in Progress

Many people feel that the earliest Corvettes failed to impress and did not live up to the "sports car" billing. More development was needed to make the Corvette a true sports car in the eyes of most enthusiasts. In retrospect, this is not particularly surprising due to the innovative design of the car. Innovative design often requires considerable time to perfect. The Corvette was distinctly different from most American cars both because its body was made of fiberglass and because it was a sports car; Chevrolet, and any other division of General Motors, had no experience from which to draw. Ed Cole confirmed Chevrolet's lack of understanding of the sports car market in Karl Ludvigsen's *Corvette: America's Star-Spangled Sports Car, a Complete History*: "We really didn't know what we wanted. We had no real feeling of the market. Was Corvette for the boulevard driver, or the sports car tiger? We weren't quite sure. But we loved that car. We weren't going to let go."

Thomas Keating clearly explained to journalists that the Corvette was "not a racing car in the accepted sense that a European car is a race car. Rather we have built a sports car in the American tradition. It is intended to satisfy the American conception of beauty, plus comfort, convenience, and performance." The car was intended to combine luxury with sports car design, but those aims were not fully met. Even the term "sports car" was abused for marketing purposes, as evidenced by advertising large, heavy models, such as the 1954 Buick Skylark and the 1954 Oldsmobile Starfire, as "sports cars." Some enthusiasts may not have taken the Corvette very seriously simply because General Motors advertised almost anything as a sports car. Ultimately, the Corvette would be built to order as either a sporty cruiser for the street, an all-out performance car for the track, or something in between. This transformation, though, took a few years.

1954: Still Short of the Mark

Chevrolet's managers were expecting the Corvette to provide at least 10,000 sales for the first full model year of its production. (In fact, Chevrolet had contracted for 12,300 bodies from the Molded Fiberglass Company, 300 of which were for 1953. The remainder were, of course, for 1954 production.)

By about early spring, though, they received a quite unexpected jolt of reality. What put the sports into a sports car was not fully realized in the original version. Even so, sales could have been better (though certainly not up to 10,000) had the list price of $3,498 been affordable for many in the *primary target market*, youthful buyers.

Chevrolet decided to lower the advertised price to $2,774 to boost sales, but there was a catch: The only transmission offered, the Powerglide, was listed as an option, as were the windshield wipers and heater! Many potential buyers were offended by this deception. However, serious sports car fans typically did not care about the price of a sports car if they wanted it. The Corvette was very affordably priced compared to a Nash-Healey, for example, which sold for more than $6,000. The problem with the early Corvette was that Chevrolet was trying to appeal not simply to serious sports car enthusiasts but to a wide range of people. Many of those who were not going to take their Corvette racing could not afford the Corvette, and those who wanted to race did not take the Corvette seriously. Not until 1956 did Chevrolet begin to offer a Corvette that could fit the differing wants of the noncompetition buyer and the serious racer.

Another contributing factor to the poor sales was dealer attitude; some dealers had doubts about trying to sell a "plastic" car built to carry only two people. Dealers, for the most part, also lacked shop staff skilled in repairing fiberglass, so servicing a wrecked Corvette was often problematic. Many Chevrolet dealers were doing well selling the far more conventional Bel Airs, Two-Tens, and the rest of the division's passenger car lineup, and they saw no need to complicate matters by promoting the unusual Corvette. Sales were so slow that a drastic cut in production was needed; indeed, production was periodically stopped for two weeks at a time. In the end, only 3,640 Corvettes were built. Approximately one-third of those remained unsold at the end of the model year.

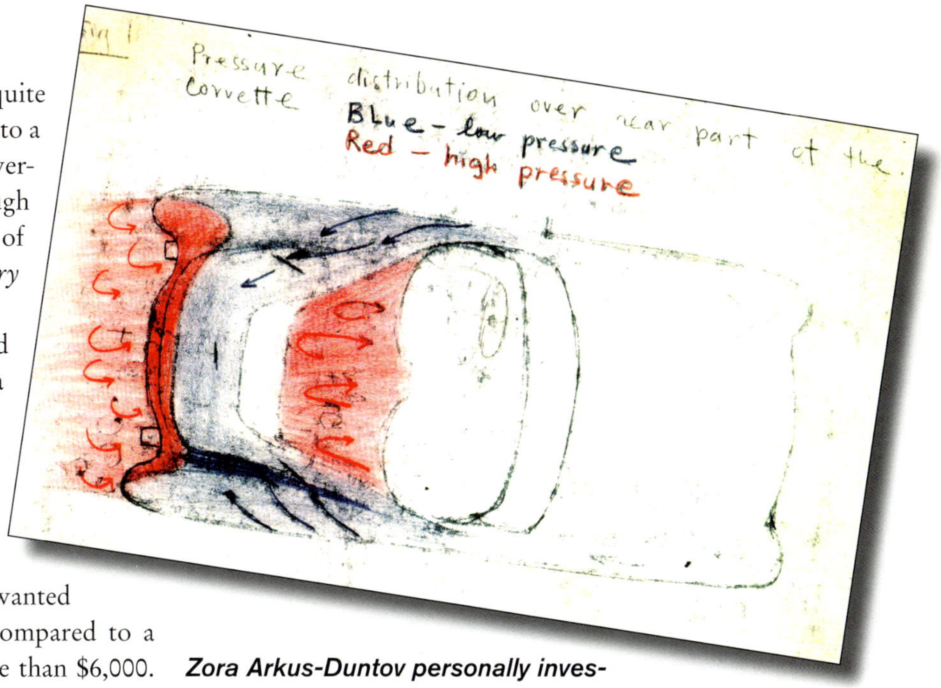

Zora Arkus-Duntov personally investigated the problem of exhaust infiltrating the passenger compartment of the early Corvettes. Since a full-size wind tunnel was not readily available, he applied strips of cloth all over a Corvette then drove it while a photographer following in another car made a movie of the movements of the cloth as the car was driven at varying speeds. Duntov found that the problem was caused by a low-pressure area developing with the top up, the side curtains installed, and the vent window opened to about one-third of maximum travel. Exhaust gases that collected in back due to a stagnant air pocket were drawn ahead to the open vent window because of this low-pressure region. He made this drawing to help illustrate the problem. (Photo Courtesy GM Media Archive)

Minor Changes for 1954

Updates made to the Corvette for this model year were few. As for observable changes, the earliest 1954s had practically none. Not long into the model year, the canvas top and frame color were changed from black to tan.

Another running change was the replacement of the roughly 2-inch-long exhaust extensions with longer units. Customer complaints about exhaust gases staining the surrounding paint and even getting into the passenger compartment led to the change. Zora Arkus-Duntov developed a test procedure to understand the causes of these problems. Since a wind tunnel was not readily available, he applied strips of cloth all over a Corvette then drove it while a photographer following in another car made a movie of the movements of the cloth as the car was driven at varying speeds. Duntov viewed the film and found a stagnant air pocket all around the rear part of the body. Exhaust gases and light road debris got trapped in this region and ultimately stained the paint. Exhaust leaked into the passenger compartment because of a low-pressure area developing with the top up, the side curtains installed, and the vent window opened to about one-third of maximum travel. Exhaust gases that collected in back were drawn ahead to the open vent window because of this low-pressure region. Both problems were largely solved by lengthening the exhaust extensions to about 6 inches long, capping them in back, and including a baffle to direct the exhaust downward through a slot.

Late in the model year, three additional drive lugs were added to the Corvette's Powerglide torque converter for attaching the converter to the engine flywheel. The change provided a more secure means of transmitting the torque

Though black is often listed in various publications about Corvette history as one of the colors offered for 1954 Corvettes, only four or perhaps six were painted this color. The black cars were reportedly built for auto show duty and a few executives. Polo White, Sportsman Red, and Pennant Blue were officially offered. (Photo Courtesy GM Media Archive)

supplied by the Corvette's engine.

Two additional colors, Pennant Blue and Sportsman Red, were listed besides Polo White; though, nearly 89 percent of the 1954 Corvettes were painted Polo White. Interior colors were also changed to coordinate with the new colors, tan with Pennant Blue and either red or tan with Sportsman Red. Another documented variation of the color combination included Pennant Blue with a bright blue interior. A Chevrolet interorganizational letter dated July 22, 1953, listed seven colors authorized for release for 1954. These were listed simply as White, Red, Black, Metallic Beige, Metallic Brown, Metallic Green, and Metallic Blue. However, about one month later H. D. Lund, the assistant national sales promotion manager, expressed the sales department's disagreement with the chosen colors and said they would "be satisfied to continue with Polo White for all Corvettes during the 1954 model year." If additional colors were required, he said, they preferred "a yellow, a red, and possibly a black in addition to the Polo White." Four (perhaps as many as six) Corvettes painted black with a Sportsman Red interior were reportedly prepared for GM executives and the auto show circuit. By now, body panel alignment and surface finish had improved enough that color choices other than Polo White were offered. (The use of only Polo White for the 1953 models helped to partially conceal some of the flaws in the fiberglass body. This practice was also a cost-cutting measure. With production scheduled to ramp up to the expected 10,000 units, additional color selections were economically feasible to offer.) There was still room to improve panel fit, but time and experience were helping improve Chevrolet's fiberglass working skills.

Pennant Blue was the first color added for 1954 and carried forward for part of the following model year. Only 300 of the 3,640 Corvettes built for the 1954 model year were painted Pennant Blue.

Standard interior color with the Pennant Blue exterior was light beige and tan as seen here. As for 1953, instrumentation included a 140-mph speedometer and a tachometer.

Other running changes included replacement of the two-handle hood release with a single-handle mechanism, relocating the fuel and brake lines inboard of the right-side frame rail, moving the choke control from the right to the left of the steering column for convenience of operation, and increasing horsepower by 5 to 155 by means of an improved camshaft. Partway into the model year, the three side-draft carburetors became filtered by twin air cleaners rather than three individual units.

One of the most significant changes made for 1954, though, was relocating the assembly plant from Flint, Michigan,

The upper and lower body were joined together using glue and rivets along the lip on each side. The rivets simply held the body together while the glue cured. Original prototypes, though, had a one-piece body. (Photo Courtesy GM Media Archives)

The first coat of color is being applied on this 1954 Corvette. Next it went to the sanding line followed by the final color coat. Most of the 3,640 1954s built were Polo White. (Photo Courtesy GM Media Archive)

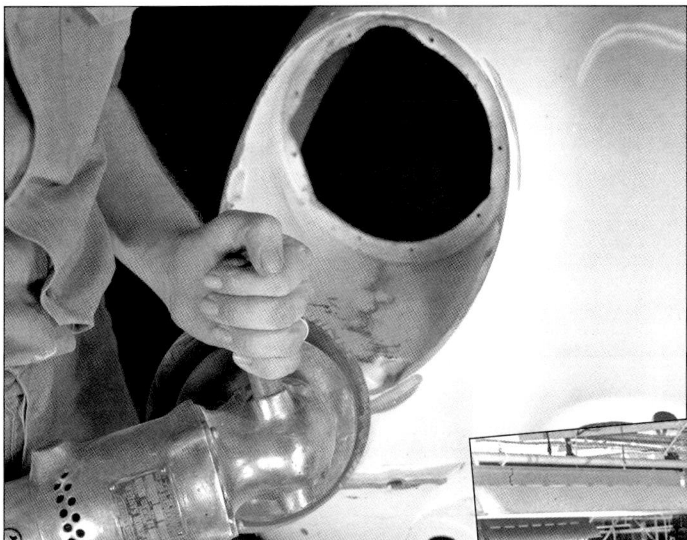

Much finishing by hand was required to complete the Corvette. This need certainly added to the cost to build the car and a price tag that was nearly double the original target. (Photo Courtesy GM Media Archive)

This was the final trim line where the grille, side moldings, and other such pieces were attached. The second car from the front had not had its grille installed at this point. Note that its grille is sitting atop the barrels next to it. Assembly methods are far different today. (Photo Courtesy GM Media Archive)

The body-drop line was near the end of the assembly process. There remained a few more steps to perform such installation of wheel covers and a brief drive around the assembly plant grounds as a final inspection. Note the tires were quite dirty by the end of the assembly line. (Photo Courtesy GM Media Archive)

to St. Louis, Missouri. The last of the 1953 models was built on December 24, 1953, in Flint. Production of 1954 Corvettes commenced at the St. Louis plant just four days later on December 28. The St. Louis facility was far superior to the one used in Flint, which had a line that was six chassis long and where up to six cars per day could be completed. Mass production was never intended there, however. Instead, the Flint line served to test assembly methods for the St. Louis plant. At the much larger facility, 50 cars could be completed in a day. There, the Blue Flame engines were tuned and tested for about 30 minutes on dynamometer stands, and the wheels were balanced on the chassis assembly line. Once the cars were assembled, they were each driven off the line and given a brief drive around the assembly plant grounds as a final inspection.

The Corvette, though, was not passing the most important inspection: that of the American public. It was very likely that it would have been discontinued by the end of the 1954 model year if Ford Motor Company had not released its new Thunderbird, which landed on dealer lots in September 1954. The rivalry between Chevrolet and Ford played a role in saving Harley Earl's sports car from cancellation. Engineer Zora Arkus-Duntov also played an important part in keeping it in production. Chevrolet's legendary engineer and sports car enthusiast wrote a now-famous letter dated October 15, 1954, to engineers Ed Cole and Maurice Olley stating, "By the looks of it, the Corvette is on its way out. I would like to say the following: Dropping the car now will have adverse effect internally and externally. It is an admission of failure. Failure of aggressive thinking in the eyes of the organization, failure to develop a saleable product in the eyes of the outside world . . . Ford enters the field with the Thunderbird, a car of the same class as the Corvette. If Ford makes success where we failed, it may hurt . . . We will leave an opening in which they can hit at will. 'Ford out-engineered, outsold, or ran Chevrolet's pride and joy off the market.'" Evidently the letter was convincing.

Production of the Corvette shifted to the St. Louis plant on December 28, 1953. Somewhere between 12 and 15 cars were completed at St. Louis before the end of the 1953 calendar year. Though the peak assembly rate for the model year was 44 cars per day, up to 50 could be built at the facility in a day, which corresponded to the expected total output for the model year of 10,000 units. The goal proved to be overly optimistic. (Photo Courtesy GM Media Archive)

1955: A V-8 but Still No 4-Speed

The 1955 Corvettes received extremely few styling updates, though major ones were proposed and demonstrated on a modified styling car. Among them were a Ferrari-like grille (which would have given it a "family resemblance" to the all-new 1955 passenger car line) and rear styling similar to the Corvair show car's. However, as sales of the Corvette failed to reach expectations, money for the new tooling required to produce the proposed styling changes was not provided. Furthermore, major styling changes had already been approved for the 1956 model. In the end, the updates amounted to new paint color choices, vinyl-coated canvas top material, tubeless tires, electric windshield wipers, improved body construction, and the inclusion of an anodized gold "V" over the lower case "v" of the Chevrolet script mounted on the sides of the front fenders.

The big "V" signified the presence of a V-8. The big "V" appeared on nearly every one of the Corvettes built for 1955. However, for most of 1955, the 2-speed Powerglide was the only transmission to be had; late in the model year Chevrolet released a Saginaw 3-speed manual transmission for use in the Corvette, but only about 75 Corvettes got it. As with the rest of Chevrolet's lineup for the model year, V-8-powered cars were equipped with a 12-volt electrical system while sixes kept the 6-volt setup. Base price for the V-8-equipped Corvette was listed at $2,909 while those powered by the 6-cylinder (extremely few of which were built) listed again for $2,774.

Color combinations for 1955 included Coppertone Bronze with a dark beige interior and beige top; Gypsy Red (different than Sportsman Red) with a light beige interior, red saddle stitching, tan carpeting, and a beige top; plus Polo White with a red interior and a white top. Pennant Blue was carried over until about the middle of the model year, and then it was replaced by Harvest Gold with a medium green

A yellow and medium green interior was standard issue with the Harvest Gold exterior color that became available for 1955. Other than color revisions, few other changes were made to the interior. Instruments were upgraded to conform to the new 12-V electrical system.

Harvest Gold replaced Pennant Blue early in the 1955 model year. This stunningly restored Corvette is powered with the 265 V-8 and Powerglide transmission. Only 6 of the 700 1955 models are known to have received the Blue Flame six and only 75 had the V-8 with the Saginaw 3-speed transmission, which was made available late in the model year.

and pale yellow interior and a medium green top. A large percentage of the 1954s were Polo White.

During 1954, more than one of the early 1953 Corvettes retained by Chevrolet Engineering was fitted with a test version of the 265-ci small-block. Many miles of testing revealed there were no major problems with a V-8 installation in the Corvette, and, in fact, the modifications needed to make the engine fit were found to be relatively minor.

The Corvette's V-8 was, of course, the new Chevrolet small-block (detailed in the previous chapter), but it received an 8.0:1 compression ratio, a hotter cam, and a Rochester 4-barrel carburetor. In this form, it provided 195 hp at 5,000 rpm and torque of 260 ft-lbs at 3,000 rpm. Redline was 6,500 rpm. With the lighter V-8, weight distribution improved a bit to 52/48. Acceleration and top speed also improved considerably. Furthermore, despite having two more cylinders, fuel consumption dropped by only 2 to 3 miles per gallon compared to Corvettes powered by the Blue Flame 6-cylinder.

The improved Corvette received some praise from the automotive press of the day. The September 1955 issue of *Motor Trend* provided readers with a drive report on the sports car. Test drivers Roger Huntington and Ken Fermoyle found 0–60 mph took only 8.5 seconds, 0–80 mph needed "less than 15 seconds," the standing quarter-mile result was 16.9 seconds "in the neighborhood of 85 mph," and the best top speed attained was 110 mph. While such figures today are not impressive, they were in 1955. The author, Fermoyle, wrote, "The Corvette is an outstanding performer and is a lot of fun to drive. In this sense it's a real sports car, although the purists will argue this point. It is still not quite a serious competition car, although it probably could be modified to give some of the more expensive foreign iron a rough time in road races." He also noted, "It has some flaws—it's not the ideal car for driving in a heavy rain, I found. However, for those interested in a car of this type, the virtues should make up for any minor shortcomings." Fermoyle reported the Powerglide "was not at all bad," but also noted the ideal setup absent a 4-speed would have been the 3-speed with overdrive. As for handling, the author wrote, "the Corvette rates very high. Steering ratio is 16:1 and it's very light. In fact, it's hard to understand why it should require the 3¾ turns lock-to-lock this car is set up for. However, the steering and feel of the car was one of its highlights and was a special joy in these days when power steering is coming to be regarded as almost a necessary accessory." He concluded the article by saying, "the V-8 engine makes this a far more interesting automobile and has upped performance to a point at least as good as anything in its price class. I certainly enjoyed driving it and I'm sure that anyone else who has a chance to do so will feel the same way." Despite the new V-8 and greatly improved performance, Corvette sales totaled only a miniscule 700 for the model year.

Without the influence of Ed Cole and Zora Arkus-Duntov along with competitor Ford releasing its Thunderbird, the Corvette could certainly have been canceled at the end of the 1955 model year. Why did the Corvette fizzle with most sports car enthusiasts? In short, it had an established reputation prior to 1955 of not being a true sports car for enthusiasts. Some of GM's managers reportedly were ready to put an end to the fiberglass sports car, but another group within Chevrolet resisted pressure to give up on the Corvette. With the support and skills of key people within General Motors, such as Zora Arkus-Duntov and Ed Cole, the Corvette began to mature into a genuine sports car.

The appearance of the engine compartment was befitting a V-8-powered Corvette. A 265 rated at 195 hp at 5,000 rpm offered a much-needed improvement for the Corvette. Still, only 700 Corvettes were sold for 1955. Note the sealed Chrome air cleaner that was difficult to clean.

1956: Starting to Get It Right

After extremely slow sales became evident during the 1955 model year, rumors of Corvette's demise circulated in the automotive

Corvette EX-87

Zora Arkus-Duntov became an engineer for Chevrolet not long after viewing the 1953 prototype at the GM Motorama. He wrote to Chevrolet Chief Engineer Ed Cole about his thoughts on how to improve the Corvette and impressed Cole with his knowledge. Duntov helped turn the Corvette into a true sports car respected by enthusiasts. In this photo he is seen sitting in Corvette test car EX-87, fitted with a prototype of Chevrolet's small-block engine. (Photo Courtesy GM Media Archive)

Mauri Rose, a three-time winner of the Indianapolis 500 and Chevrolet engineer, had racing legend Smokey Yunick fit a 1954 Corvette with an experimental V-8. As an experimental Chevrolet, it received an "EX" designation, in this case EX-87. Later, EX-87 (also with the Chevrolet Engineering identification number 5951) was turned over to Chevrolet Engineering where many of its parts, the engine included, were stripped from the car and transferred to Corvette test car 6901, which was driven at Daytona Beach. Car 5951/EX-87 was soon rebuilt.

Prior to making the trip to Daytona, Ed Cole wanted confirmation that the Corvette could top 150 mph. Before test driving EX-87 to get the matter settled for Cole, Duntov first determined how much of the grille he would need to cover to reduce drag yet keep airflow over the radiator as required. He also calculated another 30 hp was needed from the EX-87's V-8. The extra horsepower came from a new solid lifter camshaft design, the Duntov Mark I. Often called a "high-lift" camshaft, in reality it had a lift that was less than the regular production Corvette unit. It provided higher effective flow areas and raised the upper end of the power curve, simultaneously improving the dynamics of the valve gear at high speed, according to Duntov. With the new cam, the engine had an impressive power curve from 5,000 to 6,000 rpm and could run to 6,500 rpm without valve bounce; it easily helped to propel the test car well beyond 150 mph. In fact, it topped out at about 163 mph on GM's Mesa, Arizona, test track, which was certainly fast enough to be confident of reaching 150 mph on the sand at Daytona Beach. The cam was added to GM's parts catalog, thus qualifying it for production-class racing events.

press, but the editors at *Motor Trend* reported, "a very hot version" with a detachable hardtop and roll-up windows was on the way. Perhaps they had inside knowledge of what was happening at Chevrolet since the writer was exactly right.

The introductory comments regarding the new Corvette appearing in the *1956–1957 Chevrolet Corvette Engineering Achievements* manual published by GM's Engineering Product Information Center declared: "The Chevrolet Corvette for 1956 is a new and challenging car, with numerous styling changes as well as many new luxury and convenience features. A more powerful V-8 engine, a new 3-speed transmission, and a new rear axle comprise the power combination." These upgrades were very welcomed, indeed, by sports car enthusiasts, but the Corvette still lacked a 4-speed transmission that wouldn't arrive until 1957.

Styling Changes

Styling for the Corvette was heavily altered for the first time since it became available. The most obvious change was the side cove outlined with a bright molding. This styling innovation was previewed on the 1955 Chevrolet Biscayne concept car exhibited at that year's GM Motorama and other auto shows. The new feature allowed for a two-tone paint option.

The headlight grilles were deleted and the front fenders projected farther forward. The headlight installation was based upon the design of the 1954 Mercedes-Benz 300SL coupe. A new 300SL was purchased by General Motors and brought to the styling studio. In fact, General Motors purchased an example of every new car, domestic and foreign, for study. The Mercedes's hood bumps, labeled by the designers as windsplits, were also carried over into the styling of the new

Dr. Dick Thompson Sizes Up the Corvette

Dr. Dick Thompson, aka the "Flying Dentist," from Washington, DC, won the SCCA championship five times between 1956 and 1962 driving a Corvette. In 1958, he cowrote with Donn Munson *The Corvette Guide*, which detailed the Corvette's transformation from noncompetitor to highly respected sports car. The introductory chapter provided a sports car driver's view of the original Corvette's shortcomings, which led to rejection by serious enthusiasts until 1956.

"The Corvette is a masterpiece of compromise," wrote Thompson of the modern version of the car. He continued: "It is full of stock and slightly modified components which have met with amazing success . . . But it suffices to say here that the original Corvette did not set the sports car world ablaze . . . [It] was greeted with considerable skepticism, much of which was justified. One of the early limitations was the fact that the only engine available was a standard 6-cylinder model. It was great for puttering around town—very durable and economical, but no powerhouse . . . the only transmission available was an automatic transmission trade-named Powerglide. It is fine in passenger cars, but no 4-speed pusher would touch it. Sports car drivers raised on MGs, Jaguars, Alfas, and other European imports turned their noses up at Detroit's offering. [Furthermore] Americans demanded a few more extras than the car afforded. The tried and true I-never-put-the-top-up drivers raised no clamor for side windows but the general public did. Side curtains will be tolerated by the real enthusiast . . . So, the Corvette emerged a loudly heralded thing of beauty, but as far as sports car drivers were concerned, it was a beast."

The early Corvettes, wrote the authors, "remained a comfortable, rather smart street car that quite frankly made a spectacle of itself and its drivers whenever it was placed in fast company on closed circuits. [I]n 1956, only a few weeks before the annual Sebring race, General Motors decided to go all out with a team entry. This decision, perhaps more than any other in the short history of the car, is responsible for creating a true competition vehicle. The men of General Motors who made the decision to face Europe's finest are to be forever credited with advancing the sport in the United States in one gigantic effort . . . The work involved almost every component of the car, but the most extensive was done on the chassis and brakes . . . Brakes never get a rest [at Sebring]."

With every race throughout 1956, Thompson found the deficiencies that needed correcting in the Corvette. Blocking off the heat risers during a race at Fort Worth, for example, would have made a huge difference. Thompson wrote, "I suddenly lost about 20 to 25 horsepower and the car just slowed down . . . but I had enough under the hood to beat the Jags and get a class win." The SCCA did not allow heat risers to be blocked off because it would have been considered an "unannounced" modification. From then on, heat riser plugs were supplied and placed in the glove box if the owner wanted to install them, so they were no longer a modification. With them in place the twin carburetors ran cooler, but without them over a long distance they would get quite hot.

Tire wear was another problem that showed a limited-slip rear end was mandatory for courses like the one at Elkhart Lake. In prior races, Thompson adjusted his driving style, so he felt at the time that he could simply "live without" a limited-slip axle.

In the conclusion of *The Corvette Guide*, the authors wrote, "The record doesn't end at Sebring. It will go on and on as long as Corvettes are manufactured and there are Americans with speed in their hearts to drive them." This sentiment expressed just a few years after the debut of the Corvette stood in stark contrast with the earlier assessment that Chevrolet's sports car was just "a beast."

The Corvette's performance at the 1956 Sebring race and subsequent races helped to persuade Dr. Dick Thompson to drive a Corvette in competition starting in 1957. Previously, he had driven a Mercedes 300SL. Thompson, known as the "Flying Dentist," cowrote the book* The Corvette Guide*, chronicling the Corvette's evolution from being a car that was not taken seriously by enthusiasts to a fine sports car. (Photo Courtesy GM Media Archive)

The clay mockup of the 1953 Corvette was repurposed for the 1956 restyle, the first major styling changes made since the Corvette was first released. Full-scale clay modeling was an innovation Harley Earl brought with him to GM from his days as a custom car builder during the 1910s and 1920s. (Photo Courtesy GM Media Archive)

Corvette. However, there was a functional purpose for them on the 300SL, as they were needed for clearance of the 6-cylinder's single overhead camshaft cover. The ones for the Corvette were simply for the sake of styling. A simulated air scoop placed on the front fenders just ahead of the windshield, a feature of the original 1953 prototype, was finally included.

In back, the fin-like projections were removed and the contour of the quarter panels approximated that of the deck lid. Other changes included revised contours to the front and rear wheel openings, new bumpers, rear license plate relocated to beneath the bumper, exhausts exiting through an opening within the vertical bumperettes located at the end of the quarter panels, and revised wheel covers. Incidentally, locating the exhausts to exit through the bumpers was not simply about styling. It completely solved the problem of exhaust staining and fumes getting into the passenger compartment. Exhaust gases were caught by the moving air stream and carried away from the car. This feature had been one of the changes proposed and rejected for the 1955 Corvette.

Inside revisions included restyled seats and door panels, waffle-pattern upholstery, competition-type steering wheel, and knurled knobs on the instrument panel. Furthermore, the passenger seat was now adjustable in the fore and aft direction.

Performance Upgrades

The Blue Flame 6-cylinder was no longer offered for the Corvette, and its standard engine was the 210-hp 265-ci 4-barrel, which reached its peak horsepower at 5,600 rpm.

Gross torque output was rated at 270 ft-lbs at 3,600 rpm. However, there was a more powerful 265 available equipped with twin 4-barrel carburetors with delayed-action linkage and a cast-aluminum intake. This setup was said to boost output to 225 hp at 5,600 rpm, though this advertised figure was known to be underrated. The use of cast aluminum versus cast iron, incidentally, reduced the weight of the intake by nearly 21 pounds. This option added $172.20 to the base price of $3,467. Also available was the Duntov cam, at a cost of $188.30; it upped the output to 240 hp at 5,600 rpm. A close-ratio 3-speed was now standard issue while the Powerglide was an extra-cost option adding $188.50 to the Corvette's base price. Most buyers, though, did not want the automatic.

This is the fiberglass prototype of the 1956 Corvette. Building a fiberglass prototype was the next step after the final clay modeling had been completed. Note that it was not quite finished (some side trim was not yet installed) at the time this photo was taken. In the background are cars of other manufacturers, which were dismantled for study. (Photo Courtesy GM Media Archive)

New exhaust manifolds with larger passages and heads with a redesigned combustion chamber along with a compression increase from 8.0:1 to 9.25:1 helped to account for the higher performance.

Chevrolet's small-block grew even more powerful for 1956. Offered was a 265 with twin 4-barrel carburetors with delayed-action linkage. The carburetors were mounted on a lightweight cast-aluminum intake. Advertised output was stated as 225 hp at 5,600 rpm. Performance improved even more with the extra-cost Duntov camshaft. (Photo Courtesy GM Media Archive)

Exhaust valves were made of 21-4N high-alloy steel rather than the previous Silchrome XCR steel. This change was said to reduce the possibility of breakage and distortion. Valve faces were aldipped to minimize burning. A nice cosmetic touch was the new die-cast aluminum rocker arm covers. Also giving some decorative function were the two buffed aluminum air cleaners used for the dual-carb engine. Included with either Corvette engine was a full-flow oil filter; the cylinder block casting was revised with a mounting pad for the filter at the rear, left side.

Other upgrades included a new two-breaker distributor for more stable operation at higher engine speeds. Its flatter cam lobes resulted in reduced point bounce and spark scatter, and they increased the durability of the points and rider block. Also included were new spark plugs with ribbed insulators and a new generator mounting to reduce noise and vibration. A new bright metal ignition shield with a channel-like extension on either side housing the spark plug wires was added behind the rear-mounted distributor and coil to reduce electrical interference.

The close-ratio 3-speed transmission had a new clutch with 12 heat-treated coil springs rather than the previously used diaphragm-spring unit. New internal components were the clutch shaft gear, counterbalance gears, and a new second gear. The transmission control lever was relocated to the top of the floor tunnel for this transmission (as well as the Powerglide). Bolted to the left side of the transmission extension was the control assembly, making possible a compact linkage with reduced deflection. This arrangement allowed a more positive shift and added to driver operating ease.

Performance of the 1956 Corvette powered by the 225-hp engine was impressive with a 0–60 mph sprint taking only 7.5 seconds while the quarter-mile could be run in 15.9 seconds at a terminal speed of 91 mph according to a road test published in the May 1956 issue of *Sports Car Illustrated*. The author of the report, Karl Ludvigsen, declared: "In my opinion, the Corvette as it stands is fully as much a dual-purpose machine as the stock Jaguar, Triumph, or Austin-Healey. Without qualification, General Motors is now building a sports car." Writer Tom McCahill noted in the December 1956 issue of *Mechanix Illustrated*, "The Chevrolet Corvette in 1956 astounded more sports car purists with its terrific speed and acceleration than Briggs Cunningham would if he entered Sebring in a rowboat."

Chassis Refinements

Chassis refinements were critical in transforming the Corvette into a genuine sports car. Zora Arkus-Duntov knew European sports cars could perform well in a straight line as well as on curves, and he knew the Corvette would have to be able to do the same to be accepted by American sports car enthusiasts. Duntov began his career at General Motors on May 1, 1953, as the result of a letter he wrote to Ed Cole suggesting ways to improve the Corvette. Both Cole and the number-two man at Chevrolet Engineering, Maurice Olley, were highly impressed with Duntov, who had received a mechanical engineering degree in 1934 while living in Berlin, Germany.

Duntov tested a 1955 model to find the reasons for the car's handling problems. In an article he wrote for *Auto Age* he stated: "The target was to attain such handling characteristics that the driver of some ability could get really high performance safely. The main objects of suspension changes were: increase of high-speed stability, consistency in response to the steering wheel over a wide range of lateral acceleration and speeds, and improvement of power transmission on turns (that is, reduction of unloading of the inside rear wheel)."

Correcting the handling issues of the previous Corvettes were shims installed between the front crossmember and the frame to increase the caster angle to 2 degrees and to alter the angle of the central steering idler arm so that the roll oversteer geometry was removed from the front suspension. Furthermore, changing the rear spring hangers decreased the roll understeer at the rear, so the angle of the springs would be less abrupt. Duntov noted in his article that "the car goes where it is pointed, and does so without hesitation. On turns taken hard, it does not plow or skid, but gets into a drift. If the right amount of power is fed, the drift can be maintained without danger of the rear end getting presumptuous and assuming the position of the front."

A new rear axle very much like the passenger car version came with a 3.55:1 ratio in standard form; however, Corvettes with a manually shifted transmission could be equipped with the 3.27:1 ratio as an extra-cost option. The new rear axle had widely spaced tapered roller bearings to provide rigid support of the hypoid pinion shaft. Also, the differential bearings were larger than those used the previous model year to increase durability and torque capacity and a cast ArmaSteel differential housing replaced the cast malleable iron unit previously employed; the new material offered greater resistance to scoring and increased structural strength. The Corvette's 11-inch drum brakes were little changed other than the use of more fade-resistant lining material.

Betty Skelton at the wheel of Corvette 6903 nears the finish line in what is probably a staged photo op or a practice run. Skelton drove this car to second place in the flying mile with a speed of 137.733 mph and a women's record. (Photo Courtesy GM Media Archive)

Racing Improves the Corvette's Image

As mentioned in the previous chapter, professional racing had a significant impact on automobile sales. The same was, of course, true for the Corvette. Indeed, if not for the successes achieved by Corvette drivers during 1956, the Corvette would surely have been canceled at the end of the model year.

The seriousness of Chevrolet's support for racing is illustrated with the following excerpt from the book by noted Corvette expert and Chevrolet engineer Ken Kayser, *The History of GM's Ramjet Fuel Injection on the Chevrolet V-8 and its Corvette Racing Pedigree*, which offers an exhaustive account of the work on fuel injection and Corvette racing:

> Chevrolet was now emerging in full public view as a major Factory Sponsor in racing! Ed Cole attended as many racing events as his schedule would permit and he was highly visible in the pit and garage areas, which he often frequented with owners and drivers for press photos.
>
> Chevrolet hired Dr. Dick Thompson as a driver for the Corvette team going to the April 22nd Pebble Beach race, and put Chevrolet Engineer Frank Burrell in charge of preparing the cars. Burrell sent special racing suspension and trans-

This publicity photo shows, from left to right, Corvettes 6903, 6901, and 6905 (Chevrolet Engineering identification numbers) prepared for the 1956 Daytona Speed Weeks Time Trials. Seated in the cars, again from left to right, were Betty Skelton, Zora Arkus-Duntov, and John Fitch. Duntov won the two-way flying mile event driving 6901 with a record-setting run average of 147.29 mph in a new class allowing modified engines. After Daytona, the Corvette began to be taken more seriously by sports car enthusiasts. (Photo Courtesy GM Media Archive)

mission parts removed from one of the Sebring Corvettes to Good Chevrolet in Alameda, California, for the Corvette entry in the race and Frank Burrell attended the Pebble Beach race to support their effort.

Dr. Dick Thompson in the #46 Corvette gave the Mercedes-Benz 300-SLs a run for their money finishing first in Class C and second overall giving Corvette its first win on a national SCCA stage!

The now classic, 1956 Corvette advertisement touting the "SR" Corvettes' success at Sebring, proclaiming "Bring on the Hay Bales" [hay bales served as impact barriers] started to favorably change the public's perception of the new Corvette.

In late December 1955, three Corvette test cars with internal identification numbers of 6901, 6903, and 6905 were shipped to Florida for the 1956 Daytona Speed Weeks time trials. Car 6901, a 1955 chassis fitted with a prototype 1956 body, was equipped with the powertrain from the EX-87/5951 test car that reached over 160 mph at GM's Arizona Proving Grounds. Cars 6903 and 6905 were 1956 models, each with a production 265 V-8 and 3-speed transmission. Duntov won the two-way flying mile event driving 6901 with a record-setting run average of 147.29 mph in a new class allowing modified engines.

The other two cars were driven by former Mercedes racer John Fitch, who was then known as America's best road-racing driver, and Betty Skelton, who had achieved fame by setting a number of aviation and racing records, including a land speed record, as well as serving as a spokesperson for Chevrolet's Corvette. Fitch achieved a first place in the Sports Car Class with a 145.543-mph run while Skelton came in second with 137.733 mph. All three cars would have no doubt produced faster results if they had not been hampered by strong winds that day. Duntov's downwind return run reached 156 mph on the beach course.

On March 24, four factory-backed racing Corvettes competed at the Sebring 12-Hour Sports Car Grand Prix of Endurance. Three of the cars finished 9th, 15th, and 23rd and were among the 24 of 60 cars starting the race that were still competing at the end. The race revealed the Corvette's cerametallic (ceramic-metallic) brakes, which held their braking characteristics with a temperature as high as 1,500 degrees, were the solution to the problem of brake fade in earlier races. The Bendix Corporation, which had extensive experience in aircraft brakes, developed the linings for Chevrolet. The linings were combined with thicker cast-iron drums. Corvette's solid axle, instead of an independent rear suspension, showed itself to be less than ideal on a tight road course.

As previously noted, on April 22, Dr. Dick Thompson drove a Chevrolet-prepared Corvette at the 7th annual Pebble Beach National Races, taking Top Honors in Class C Production and a second-place finish overall. Improperly adjusted brakes allowed the driver of a 300SL to overtake Thompson near the end of the race. Barney Clark, the Corvette advertising copywriter for Chevrolet's ad agency, Campbell-Ewald, attended the race. Shortly afterward, Chevrolet advertising promoted the success of the Corvette in competition by asserting, "The 1956 Corvette is proving—in open competition—that it is America's only genuine production sports car."

Thompson again finished behind a 300SL at the Texas National Sports Car Races in Fort Worth held June 3. At Road America held in Elkhart Lake, Wisconsin, on June 9, Corvettes finished 1st and 2nd in Class C Production while two others did not finish. Jerry Earl, the son of Harley Earl, drove his Corvette SR-2 (see sidebar) to a 16th-place finish in Class C Modified competition at Road America. The Corvette had, indeed, become a serious *American* sports car by 1956, needing only further refinement to start finishing in 1st place on a regular basis.

This 1956 Corvette served as the pace car for the races at Daytona Beach. It was later used as the pace car for the Sebring race. Seated in the car was Betty Skelton, who set land speed records at Daytona Speed Weeks, was an accomplished aerobatics pilot, and became an advertising executive in 1956 for Campbell-Ewald, GM's advertiser. (Photo Courtesy GM Media Archive)

Corvette SR and the SR-2 Racers

A very limited number of "SR," or Special Racing, Corvettes were built for 1956. All were equipped with heavy-duty suspension, cerametallic brake linings, special brake drums and braking plates, cooling ducts to the front brakes, rear brake cooling scoops, Halibrand magnesium wheels with knock-off hubs fitted to Firestone Super Sport 170 tires, 37-gallon fuel tank, the Duntov cam, and seat belts. Later a second version, the SR-2, followed. This surviving SR was shown at the 2013 Amelia Island Concours d'Elegance.

In 1956, the Corvette SR (with the letters ostensibly meaning "Sebring Racer," though documentation from Chevrolet Engineering indicates SR denoted "Special Racing") for sanctioned racing events was built in limited quantity. According to Ken Kayser's book *The History of GM's Ramjet Fuel Injection on the Chevrolet V-8 and Its Corvette Racing Pedigree,* "In February 1956, Chevrolet Engineering was totally consumed by the 1956 Special Racing Projects and the 1957 Fuel Injected V-8 Corvette development." Some sources claim that six production SR cars were assembled at the St. Louis plant, reportedly enough to satisfy Sebring racing requirements. However, according to Kayser's book, a work order for "an unknown, but small number of cars" was issued by Chevrolet Engineering. All the cars were equipped with heavy-duty suspension, cerametallic brake linings, special brake drums and braking plates, cooling ducts to the front brakes, rear brake cooling scoops, Halibrand magnesium wheels with knock-off hubs fitted to Firestone Super Sport 170 tires, 37-gallon fuel tank, the Duntov cam, and seat belts. (Incidentally, Halibrand Spot disc brakes were originally planned for the SR, but were not ready in time.) Furthermore, according to Kayser's book, four to six specially built Corvette SR tachometers registering to 7,000 rpm were crafted by GM's AC Spark Plug Division and delivered to Chevrolet Engineering for use in the SRs. The tachs were installed in place of the speedometer. Four of the special cars were raced at Sebring that year.

As for the SR-2 Corvettes, they arose from a rather awkward situation: Jerome Earl, one of the sons of Harley Earl, VP of GM Design, announced he would be driving a Ferrari 250MM instead of a Corvette in competition, and that was not good PR for General Motors. Harley told his son he would build a competition Corvette especially for him if he would give up on the Ferrari. Jerry agreed.

Harley Earl oversaw the styling for the SR-2. A production Corvette was secured for the conversion into what became the first of three SR-2s. During a three-week period beginning in late May 1956 and ending in mid-June, the Corvette was transformed into a full race car with modifications that included a new

The first of the three SR-2s was designed and built for Jerry Earl, son of Harley Earl, GM's vice president of styling. Jerry Earl was at about this time racing with a Ferrari, which was not viewed as an appropriate choice for the son of the head of GM Design. A Corvette built for competition in Sports Car Club of America races was viewed as a much better alternative. GM's styling's Clare "Mac" MacKichan (passenger seat) and GM Styling engineer Ken Pickering (standing at far right) posed with the new SR-2. (Photo Courtesy GM Media Archive)

Corvette SR and the SR-2 Racers continued

lightweight extended nose, a set of windscreens, a central rear fin, modified taillights faired in with the quarter panel, and the SR-type chassis. It was painted a light shade of metallic blue.

The second SR-2, built for Bill Mitchell, differed from the first in having a faired-in headrest and fin similar to that of the EX-87 Corvette, having a large nose emblem akin to that of the later production 1958 Corvette, and being painted bright red. Adding the fairing in back required that the trunk lid be hinged to open backward, something of no concern for a race car. Earl liked the look of the fairing and later retrofitted the original SR-2 with the feature.

The third SR-2 was built for Harlow Curtice, and was really an SR-type in name only as it had the styling of the actual race versions, but was fully street legal. It was equipped with a heater, AM Signal-Seeking radio, parking brake alarm, courtesy lights, windshield washers, whitewall tires, power windows, power soft top, and Dayton wire wheels.

All three SR-2s still exist in private collections.

The second of the three SR-2s built was for Bill Mitchell, an avid fan of sports car racing. Other than the color, his car differed from the original SR-2 in having a faired-in headrest, a feature similar to that of the Jaguar D-Type. A faired-in headrest was later added to the original SR-2. Paul O'Shea and Pete Lovely drove this car to a 16th-place finish at Sebring in 1957. (Photo Courtesy GM Media Archive)

Something else gleaned from the 1956 racing experiences was the toughness of the Corvette's fiberglass body. The October 1956 issue of *Hot Rod* magazine featured an article on the preparations involved in getting the Corvette race-ready. It noted how one Corvette "wiped out the entire side of an Austin-Healey, demolished a 300SL rear fender, and scattered a few hay bales" with the damage to the Corvette amounting to "three small, easily repaired cracks in the body, some chipped paint, and some bent side trim."

Options Revised

Corvette owners finally could have a detachable hardtop as optional equipment. Previously, owners had to rely upon aftermarket manufacturers such as Plasticon of Pasadena, California, to acquire a

This Corvette race car, labeled as the "Real McCoy" in Chevrolet's advertising, was one of two 1956 Corvettes to complete the race at Sebring that year. Sebring was a rugged endurance test lasting 12 hours (from 10 a.m. to 10 p.m.) over a 5.2-mile course. The nearly 200 laps of the race totaled 1,000 miles. About half the cars that started the race failed to finish, and of the four factory-backed Corvette entries, two failed to finish. At the 12-hour mark, this Corvette was the Class B winner having completed 176 laps. Two other Corvettes, one of which was privately entered, took second and third place in Class C. (Photo Courtesy GM Media Archive)

hardtop. A soft top was standard equipment while the hardtop option added $215.20 to the base price. However, buyers could choose to exchange the soft top for the hardtop at no additional charge. Those who chose the hardtop found rearward visibility to be much better than that afforded by the soft top. In fact, glass area was nearly 37 percent greater compared to the window in the 1955 convertible top. A power-assist mechanism for the soft top was also added as an option, but in making room for the mechanism a small amount of space was sacrificed in the already tight-fitting cockpit.

With the introduction of indented side panels, or side coves as they are commonly known, the option of two-tone paint was made possible on the 1956-and-later first-generation Corvettes. This 1957 Polo White car has Metallic Silver coves, an uncommon combination.

Color choices were updated again and were comprised of Artic Blue, Aztec Copper, Cascade Green, Polo White, Onyx Black, and Venetian Red. Soft tops were offered in beige or white with all paint colors except Onyx Black, which could be had with a black or white top. The $19.40 two-tone paint option resulted in the side coves being painted the contrasting color Adobe Beige or Metallic Silver, depending upon the main body color.

Other options included power windows, a new transistorized radio, an outside air–type heater (it replaced the recirculating type shortly after the start of the model year), and competition-type tires. Seat belts were offered as a dealer-installed accessory.

Finally, for 1956 Chevrolet offered an optional hardtop for the Corvette. It could be had for extra cost along with the standard soft top, or the soft top could be deleted in exchange for the hardtop. Roll-up windows were also new for 1956, and they were a much welcome change from the snap-in plexiglass panels. (Photo Courtesy Angelo Van Bogart)

Sales Boost

Production for the 1956 Corvette totaled 3,467 units, a nearly fivefold increase over 1955's output. However, unlike 1954, when nearly one-third of the 3,640 Corvettes built remained unsold at the end of the year, there remained few, if any, unsold cars at the end of the 1956 model year. Furthermore, the 1956 Corvettes had only an 8-month sales year instead of the more typical 11 months. No doubt more Corvettes would have been sold during the 1956 model year had there been more time to do so.

The Corvette was also having a positive impact on the sales of the passenger car line. Dealers found the Corvette to be bringing more customers into their showrooms, many of whom looked at a Corvette then bought a Bel Air, Two-Ten, or another passenger car. Chevrolet now had a performance image that was attracting buyers to not only the Corvette, but to the big cars, as well. The 1956 model year represents a major turning point for the Corvette.

1957: A Full Transition into a Sports Car

The 1957 Corvette improved markedly upon the 1956 version, though visually speaking there were practically no differences between them. Even the paint color offerings were identical except for the addition of Inca Silver, though it was far and away the least selected. Nearly all the changes were mechanical in nature and made a big difference in the Corvette's performance capabilities, which in turn boosted sales.

A 1956 Corvette was fitted with a prototype Rochester fuel-injection unit for testing. Shown here with Zora Arkus-Duntov examining the setup is automotive journalist Tom McCahill, who was well known for his metaphor-filled road test reports. (Photo Courtesy GM Media Archive)

An array of regular production options (RPO) were offered to help transform the Corvette into a serious race car. The body was also more rigid with the introduction of aluminum reinforcements in the dash structure.

The small-block was enlarged to displace 283 ci for 1957. However, Ed Cole, who had been promoted to a GM vice president and to general manager of Chevrolet beginning July 1, 1956, demanded more than additional cubic inches for the small-block. What he had in mind was the fuel-injection unit being developed by Chevrolet Engineering. It would put another spotlight on Chevrolet's ability to offer technical innovations.

More Performance

Chevrolet's small-block received a bore increase of 0.125 inch, bringing its displacement up by 18 ci to 283. While a 265 was still offered in Chevrolet's passenger car and truck lines, it was dropped for use in the Corvette. A 283 4-barrel rated at 220 hp at 4,800 rpm coupled to the close-ratio 3-speed synchromesh transmission was standard equipment.

Powertrain options were highly revised this model year. The 283 with twin 4-barrel carburetors was offered in two states of tune with one delivering 245 hp at 5,800 rpm (RPO-469) and the other, 270 hp at 4,800 rpm (RPO-469C). Well over half of the buyers of this year's Corvette opted for one of the dual-carb engines. Next up the engine options chart were the fuel-injected 283s, of which there were three versions. Corvettes equipped with one of these engines were denoted with "Fuel Injection" script and a crossed-flags emblem mounted on the side coves as well as the script appearing on the decklid.

The mildest version of the fuel-injected engine (RPO-579) with a compression ratio of 9.5:1 and hydraulic lifters was rated at 250 hp at 5,000 rpm. The other engine (RPO-579C or RPO-579D) had a 10.5:1 compression and mechanical lifters rated at 283 hp (1 horsepower per cubic inch) at 6,200 rpm. However, that rating was simply an advertising gimmick, as true output was really 290 hp. Torque specs were 305 ft-lbs at 3,800 rpm and 290 ft-lbs at 4,400 rpm, respectively. Either engine added $484.20 to the $3,176 base price, an approximately 15 percent premium. The racing version (RPO-579D), priced at $726.30, included a column-mounted tachometer and a hand-built cold-air induction system, but getting this option also required the purchase of the Competition Brakes and Suspension option (RPO-684) adding another $780.10 to the cost. A complex set of ducts funneled cool air to the brakes of

Fuel injection was exotic hardware in 1957 and it enhanced the image of the Corvette as a sports car. More than 1,000 of the 1957 Corvettes were ordered with the expensive option.

The Corvette V-8 looked as good as it performed. A 225-hp dual-quad version became available for 1956. The intake manifold was of sand-cast aluminum to reduce weight. It was first released for 1956, and was continued for 1957.

the so-called "Air Box" Corvettes. The radio and heater were deleted from these cars and the hole at the center of the dash where the tachometer was usually installed was filled with a Corvette emblem similar to the one placed on the car's exterior. Only 43 of them are believed to have been built at the St. Louis assembly plant.

The twin fours offered a couple of important advantages over the exotic fuel-injection setup: It was less expensive and it did not require as much maintenance. Fuel injection proved somewhat troublesome; fuel nozzles would clog with dirt deposits and also absorb heat, causing rough idling. Even so, the fuel-injected engine was not intended for those who wanted to drive their Corvette to the golf course on the weekend; it was for those who were serious about competing with other sports car owners.

The aforementioned RPO-684 option consisted of heavy-duty springs, a thicker front anti-sway bar, a limited-slip axle, larger-piston shock absorbers with firmer valving, a faster steering ratio reducing turns lock-to-lock from 3.7 to 2.9, and cerametallic brake linings with finned ventilated drums. These brakes required heavy pedal pressure when they were cold, but as they heated from use they were easier to apply and were highly effective. The limited-slip rear end (RPO-677) was also offered as an option for cars equipped with a manual transmission along with a choice of 3.70, 4.11, and 4.56:1 ratios.

Finally, starting on April 9, a BorgWarner close-ratio 4-speed transmission (RPO-685) priced at $175 was added to the roster of optional equipment. Ratios were 2.2:1 in first, 1.66:1 in second, 1.31:1 in third, and 1:1 in fourth. Because of its late introduction, only 664 of the 1957 models received the 4-speed. The Powerglide remained an option (except with the 270-hp and 283-hp engines), though the vast majority of buyers preferred shifting the gears themselves.

This is one of the 43 so-called "Air Box" Corvettes of 1957. The Air Box cars, essentially factory race cars, were equipped with option code RPO-579D, priced at $726.30, which included a column-mounted tachometer and a hand-built cold-air induction system. This option also required the purchase of RPO-684HD Competition Brakes and Suspension option, adding another $780.10 to the cost. Standard wheel covers did not fit the wider wheels; hence the hubcaps on this car.

In addition, a 5.5-inch wide rim (RPO 276) made by Kelsey-Hayes was offered as a $14 option, but the standard wheel cover would not fit; substituted was the passenger car hubcap. The wider rim was of riveted construction rather than welded like the standard wheel.

The Race for Fuel Injection

Rumors were flying in the mid-1950s that Chrysler Corporation, Ford Motor Company, and even Studebaker-Packard were conducting research into fuel-injection systems. There were good reasons to believe the rumors were largely true. The horsepower race was moving along at a fast pace, of course, and fuel injection fit into the race quite well. Fuel injection, however, offered more than enhanced engine performance.

In 1952, Harlow Curtice directed GM's Engineering staff to begin research into fuel injection. Even then, Curtice knew the federal government would eventually mandate standards for both fuel economy and emissions. Fuel injection offered improvements in both areas. On the other hand, Ed Cole certainly had more interest in the performance edge offered by a reliable fuel-injection setup metering fuel to Chevrolet's small-block. He was a strong proponent of getting fuel injection as an option for Chevrolet's sports car. One of the Corvette's strongest rivals at the time was the Mercedes-Benz 300SL equipped with a Bosch mechanical fuel-injection system, a modified version of the company's diesel engine. Designing a system for the Corvette would help level the playing field and give the Corvette much more credibility as a true sporting automobile. In the end, the fuel-injection engine was offered for the passenger car line, too, just as the 225-hp dual-quad Corvette engine released for 1956 was also made an option for the rest of the passenger car line that year.

The arrival of fuel injection brought even greater credibility to the Corvette as a real sports car. Two versions of the fuel-injected 283 were offered, one with hydraulic lifters producing 250 hp and the other with solid lifters officially rated at 283 hp for marketing purposes (1 horsepower per cubic inch), though in reality output was a bit higher at 290 hp. (Photo Courtesy GM Media Archive)

Chevrolet was not the only car division of General Motors eyeing fuel injection; indeed, in the beginning all five of GM's car divisions were expected to have fuel-injection engines listed as an option. Ultimately, only Chevrolet and Pontiac made it available. As for the competition, Ford chose to offer a couple of supercharged versions of its 312-ci V-8 for 1957, Rambler announced they would offer Bendix Aviation's electronic fuel injection for 1957, but ultimately backed out, while Chrysler briefly offered the highly complex Bendix unit for 1958. All of the Chrysler products with fuel injection were ultimately recalled to be converted to conventional carburetion. Pontiac offered fuel injection through 1958, while Chevrolet retained it through 1965.

Research and Development of Fuel Injection

GM's Engineering staff purchased two new Mercedes-Benz 300SL "Gullwing" sports cars to study during their early research. The 300SL's Bosch fuel injection used in the Gullwing was known for its reliability and was an ideal unit for analysis. John Dolza was in charge of the fuel-injection project, which after about two years of research evolved into System A and System B. The former was a continuous flow injection unit and the latter a timed speed density arrangement.

System A's continuous flow injection system did not have mechanical injectors timed to the engine; therefore, it offered relative simplicity of design. As the name implies, fuel was sprayed constantly into the intake port of each cylinder, and the fuel-air mixture entered a cylinder with the opening of the intake valve on the intake stroke. Fuel flow was carefully balanced to each cylinder and well atomized by the fuel injectors. Timed speed density fuel injection had been in use on aircraft and was more complicated. It required a device that very accurately sensed absolute temperature and pressure and correlated them to the control of the mixture strength.

System B required fuel supplied in an equal amount per cycle, which in turn required a uniform flow pump capable of maintaining an exacting flow and pressure. The exacting requirements of this system meant it was naturally more costly.

System A was intended for Chevrolet, Pontiac, and Oldsmobile, while the "B" setup was to go to Cadillac followed by Buick. Early in the planning, Harlow Curtice intended for Cadillac to get the hardware first, a move befitting the division that was promoted as "The Standard of the World." However, Cadillac's general manager, Don Ahrens, was not comfortable with the more complex System B fuel injection, nor was Buick's general manager, Ivan Wiles. In the end, System A was given the okay for production with only Chevrolet and Pontiac opting to offer fuel injection. GM's Rochester Division in New York was assigned to produce the fuel-injection units.

The engineers knew cost would be among the many design considerations. To that end, a low-pressure fuel pump delivering 0.75 pound of pressure at idle speed of 900 rpm was chosen over a more expensive, yet better, high-pressure system like that used by the Mercedes-Benz 300SL. Also understood was the fact that over time as more units were sold, the price would gradually decline, resulting in more and more sales. Indeed, this reasoning was sound. By 1965, the final year of availability of the fuel-injection engine in the Corvette, until 1982, the option was priced at just $292.70.

Corvettes again showed up at the Sebring, Florida, road course for the 1957 endurance race. The #4 Corvette was entered by John Fitch and driven by Gaston Andrey and Dr. Dick Thompson, also known as the "Flying Dentist," who made the switch from the Mercedes 300SL to Chevrolet's sports car this year. They co-drove the car to a 12th-place finish overall and won the GT class. (Photo Courtesy GM Media Archive)

Stunning Performance

Performance of the Corvette with the fuel-injected engine was remarkable. A road test report in the June 1957 issue of *Motor Life* reported its 283-hp test car with a 3-speed manual transmission and 3.55:1 rear end was capable of 0–60 mph in just 6.35 seconds. The *Road & Track* staff established that with the 4-speed attached to the fuel-injected engine, the 0–60 mph time was cut to 5.7 seconds and the standing-start quarter-mile required just 14.3 seconds, reaching 96 mph in the process. Top speed was determined to be 132 mph. Figures such as these were truly the right ones for a sports car. Some of the conclusions reached in testing the fuel-injection engine included:

> Praise and criticism are both to be found . . . and should not be interpreted to mean that the injector is either perfect or a failure. One thing is certain: driving a car that will reach 100 mph in the length of time it formerly took (a few years ago) to reach 60 mph left everyone who drove it in a high state of excitement.
>
> Basically, the Chevy injector system is quite thoroughly planned. A great deal of thought was apparently given to all the conditions that had to be met. The numerous control and compensating devices incorporated in the unit indicate that a strong effort was made to design something that was more than just a substitute [for the carburetor].

This 1957 Corvette has had one owner for the past 56 years and was raced by its owner, Tom Felton, for a few years. He joined the Long Island Corvette Association in 1963; then he began competing in the slalom rally and high-speed events at Bridgehampton and Lime Rock Park. Drag racing was quickly added to his racing schedule. At West Hampton, Felton drove his car through the quarter-mile in 13 seconds flat at 101 mph. (Photo Courtesy Tom Felton)

One of the advantages of the fuel-injected engine to racers was that it avoided the power loss associated with the carburetor in tight turns. The G-load developed in such turns forced the fuel to one side of the fuel bowl, temporarily starving the engine of fuel just when the driver needed power to maintain control of the car. With fuel injection, this power loss was eliminated even in the tightest of turns. It also offered instant throttle response since the fuel was under pressure at all times.

For those who took their Corvette to the track, the cost of the fuel-injected engine was worth the extra maintenance required. For those who did not compete in sanctioned events, the choice of dual-quads made more sense.

This is one of the 9,168 1958 Corvettes built receiving its final color coat at the St. Louis assembly plant. Each year since 1956 the Corvette neared the 10,000-built goal that had been set in 1954. (Photo Courtesy GM Media Archive)

Evident in this high-angle view of a virtually completed 1958 Corvette at the end of the St. Louis Assembly Plant are the controversial styling elements, quad headlights, and the louvered hood. The latter was most objectionable among the critics, thus the louvers were eliminated for 1959. Despite the objections expressed by the automotive press regarding the car's styling, the 1958 sold in record-setting numbers. (Photo Courtesy GM Media Archive)

This 1957 Corvette was formerly part of the Reggie Jackson collection. Ed Welburn, who was the VP of GM Global Design for 13 years, currently owns it. Not only does it wear the least-ordered color offered, Inca Silver, it is also equipped with the fuel-injected 283 and 4-speed transmission. It was photographed on the turntable on the 11th floor of the former Argonaut Building, where GM Styling was originally located and where this car's styling was developed under the leadership of Harley Earl, founder of GM's styling department.

The interior for the 1957 Corvette was the same as that of 1956. Note the radio-delete plate and 4-speed shifter on this fuel-injected car.

Chevrolet quickly began to proudly advertise its Corvette once the race victories began to occur on a regular basis. This illustration is from the 1957 Chevrolet dealer's showroom album and refers to the Corvette as "America's Own Sports Car."

The bright red interior of this 1957 Corvette combines quite well with the Inca Silver exterior. Only 65 of the 6,336 Corvettes built for this model year were painted this color. Seat belts were a dealer-installed accessory, and finally became standard equipment two years later. This car also has the optional hardtop, but no soft top.

A 225-hp 283-ci small-block with a pair of 4-barrel carburetors powers this Venetian Red and Beige 1957 Corvette. The engine is coupled to the 3-speed non-synchromesh transmission.

In total, 1,040 Corvettes were purchased with a fuel-injected engine, about 16 percent of total production. The cost of this option could have been a factor in this relatively low number. Another factor in the low sales of the Ram Jet option may well have been the instances of head and piston damage to the fuel-injected engines on Corvettes built prior to March of 1957. Improvements helped to alleviate these problems. Of course, some simply preferred other sports cars.

A Complaint

In the previously mentioned *Motor Life* article, Tom McCahill wrote: "If Chevy had adopted the adjustable steering wheel of its closest competitor, the comfort and safety factors would have shot way up. As it is, the steering column cannot be moved in or out to fit the driver. Tie this up with shallow, small seats and you have a car that is suitable for men on the smallish side only."

Despite its drawbacks, sales of the 1957 Corvette rose to 6,339, a new high by a vast margin; this record, though, was (gladly for Chevrolet's executives) a short-lived one!

1958–1959: Getting Closer to the 10,000 Mark

Once again, styling for the Corvette was heavily altered,

GM's Early Corvette Race Program

In 1956, Zora Arkus-Duntov's quest to see General Motors fund the construction of a Corvette race car came to fruition. He strongly believed that a Corvette designed and built to racing standards would bring favorable publicity for the Corvettes built for the street. Duntov had witnessed the impact the Porsche 550 Spyder had on sales of the typical Porsche and the racing version of the Mercedes-Benz 300SL's impact on Mercedes-Benz as unarguable evidence for his conviction. Less than three years earlier, on September 28, 1953, Duntov had spoken to members of the Mid-Michigan Chapter of the SAE in Lansing, Michigan, on the topic of the sports car. He noted, "Even if the vast majority of sports car buyers do not intend to race them, and most likely will never drive flat out, the potential performance of the car, or the recognized and publicized performance of its sister—the racing sports car—is of primordial value to its owner. The owner of such a car can peacefully let everybody pass him, still feeling like the proud king of the road, his ego and pride of ownership being inflated by racing glory."

According to *Corvette: America's Star-Spangled Sports Car,* by Karl Ludvigsen, "Duntov's philosophy was given added credibility by the 1956 Sebring event. Watching the race, it didn't take Ed Cole long to realize that no modified version of the stock Corvette would ever be able to challenge for the outright lead against the specialized sports-racing cars; Jaguar and Ferrari were the chief protagonists that year. He began to come around to the view that a special Corvette would be needed, one that bore the same pace-setting relationship to the stock Corvette as the Corvette itself did for the Chevrolet production models."

Harley Earl evidently saw the matter the same way. Earl purchased the D-Type Jaguar that was driven to a third-place finish at Sebring in 1956. Soon after that race, the car's engine was damaged beyond repair and was removed. The Jaguar was received at Styling, where it was to be fitted with a Corvette engine. It was also ordered to be converted from right-hand drive to left-hand as well as have its body extensively modified to resemble a Corvette. Once the alterations were completed, it was to be raced as an experimental Corvette. However, engineers found attaching a Corvette engine onto the D-Type Jag chassis to be highly problematic. Chevrolet's chief engineer, Harry Barr, contacted Duntov regarding the problem. Duntov expressed his reservations about the swap and ultimately determined the difficulties were so serious that an alternative was needed. The Jaguar D-Type went back to its former owner and the XP-64 Corvette SS was born. The Jag highly influenced its styling, though.

The Corvette SS had a chrome-molybdenum space frame that was a reverse-engineered version of the one for the Mercedes-Benz 300SL. It also made use of a DeDion-type rear axle, a type of semi-independent suspension with a chassis-mounted differential and driveshafts typically located by various links. It offers a significant reduction in the unsprung weight of the suspension and keeps the wheels parallel under hard use. The DeDion axle and the fuel-injected Chevrolet small-block can both be clearly seen in this photo of the chassis surrounded by technicians. (Photo Courtesy GM Media Archive)

Three fully functional cars were to be built with their bodies constructed from sheet magnesium and their exhaust systems of titanium. Cast-magnesium wheels with knock-off hubs for quick tire changes were also included. These cars were designed to be lightweight to help achieve a high horsepower-to-weight ratio. A "mule" test car was built with a fiberglass body as was another fiberglass body for wind tunnel testing. With manpower and time in impossibly short supply, the order for three racing cars was cut to one.

The 1957 Corvette SS racer might have been a major force in competition if company president Harlow Curtice had not imposed the conditions of the AMA ban on performance promotion and racing. However, the ban did not come before the car was raced at Sebring. Early testing revealed some problems with the car's brakes and overheating of the engine. The latter was an easy problem to solve: Simply removing the grille "teeth" allowed for better airflow over the radiator. (Photo Courtesy GM Media Archive)

The body of the Corvette SS, featuring partially enclosed wheel openings and a circular cross-section headrest with an aerodynamic fairing concealing a roll bar, was mounted on a 180-pound chrome-molybdenum space frame, a reverse-engineered version of the one for the Mercedes-Benz 300SL. The independent front suspension had nonparallel control arms linked by coil spring–surrounded shock absorbers to provide excellent corning stability and positive control. Brakes were similar to Chrysler's center-plane units, which used two wheel cylinders per brake. A mercury switch sensitive to deceleration was coupled to the inboard rear brakes to limit rear wheel braking to a predetermined amount. Cerametallic linings were, not surprisingly, also included. In back, a DeDion-type axle was installed (a semi-independent suspension axle type with a chassis-mounted differential, and driveshafts typically located by various links). It offers a significant reduction in the unsprung weight of the suspension and keeps the wheels parallel under hard use.

Zora Arkus-Duntov drove the 1957 Corvette SS on the newly opened Daytona Speedway at a speed of 155 mph. He later drove it to a top speed of 183 mph at GM's Mesa, Arizona, Proving Grounds. A pair of NASCAR 1959 Chevrolets can be seen in the background. (Photo Courtesy GM Media Archive)

A more powerful fuel-injected 283 powered the SS; output was rated at 315 hp at 6,800 rpm. Aluminum cylinder heads were tried at first, but soon warped and had to be replaced with cast-iron units. The fuel-injection unit was nearly the same as those used on production Chevrolets except that the air metering valve was relocated away from the injector plenum chamber and was fed by a duct from the front grille. Other special features included aluminum clutch housing, water pump, and radiator core; engine oil cooler; a magnesium oil pan; plastic 43-gallon fuel tank; two electric fuel pumps; an overall steering ratio of 12:1; and an aircraft-type 12-volt generator. Engine weight per horsepower was approximately 1.5 pounds.

Helping to provide a Corvette identity were the car's grille and side coves. A competition windscreen was part of the design, but an auxiliary plastic canopy was also included to abide by the SCCA rule requiring sports cars to have a top. The final product was a work of art. Performance was excellent, but the car's first outing at Sebring came to a rather quick end due to overheating, erratic braking from the rear brakes, and improperly installed bushings for the chassis. All of that was fixable. However, the AMA agreement to ban factory-sponsored racing put an end to further development of the Corvette SS. All components of the SS were ordered to be scrapped except the car itself. The ban and subsequent end of SS development were major disappointments to Duntov and others, such as Briggs Cunningham who was scheduled to drive the car at Le Mans.

A couple of years later, Duntov drove the SS on the newly opened Daytona Speedway at a speed of 155 mph. He then tested it at GM's Mesa, Arizona, proving grounds where he reached 183 mph. Even without the AMA ban on factory racing promotion (detailed in chapter 3), the SS would soon have been disqualified from SCCA Class D competition. A rule change cut the allowed maximum engine displacement to 3 liters, or approximately 183 ci.

1959 Stingray: Prelude to the C2

In late 1957, work got under way on the XP-87, which ultimately became the original Sting Ray racer, a car that served as the basis for the second-generation Corvette, the *Stingray*. As envisioned at the start, the XP-87 prototype was to be developed as a new Corvette for release as a 1960 model.

Among the members of the design team, who in the early stages of the project worked in Research Studio B, was a very young junior designer, Pete Brock. Brock, who began his career in the automotive industry at age 19, had an audacious task ahead of him with the Sting Ray project. The XP-87 originated with Brock's boss, Bill Mitchell, who would soon ascend to the position of head of GM Design. In its original form, the XP-87 was a coupe, later dubbed the "Q-Corvette" to distinguish it from the car that eventually emerged. It was designed for racing even though company president Harlow Curtice had forbidden racing projects.

Mitchell reviewed sketches of the new car by Brock and the others through an informal competition. These sketches were tacked up on a wall for Mitchell to evaluate, and, according to Brock, "Mitchell came in, looked them all over and immediately picked my car and said, 'this approach to the theme has some possibilities. Your goal is to expand on this.'" Design inspiration had come from European models, the Alfa Romeo Disco Valante, Bertone-designed Abarth 750 Streamliner, and the Boano-designed Abarth A 207. Later, Mitchell explained to his designers that the basic dimensions and internal architecture of the 1957 Corvette SS would be the basis for the design of the XP-87. Mitchell had purchased (with his own money) the Sebring "mule" version of the car along with the SS test chassis to be used for study. Bill Mitchell believed that enforcement of the AMA ban would diminish over a relatively short time. His assumption was almost correct; more time than expected was required for the ban to fade away and then only for a short while.

The lines of the Stingray racer were clearly used in the design of the second-generation Corvette of 1963–1967. Bill Mitchell personally hired Dr. Dick Thompson and others to race the Stingray to distance the car from General Motors to comply with official company policy banning performance promotion and driver support. (Photo Courtesy GM Media Archive)

Bill Mitchell, posed with the Stingray in this photo, also drove the one-off car as personal transportation from time to time. It must have been an especially surprising experience for motorists to see this car on public roads! (Photo Courtesy GM Media Archive)

As the design advanced, a straight line around the body appeared. It would prove to be a point of disagreement between Mitchell and Brock. Brock, who had an awareness of the importance of aerodynamics at high speed, saw a need to raise the rear of the car for improved airflow over the car, more specifically to reduce lift as air flowed over the body. Pete Brock approached his boss

The Stingray was restored several years ago after having fallen into a state of disrepair over the decades. It is now a part of the GM Heritage Center collection in Sterling Heights, Michigan, not far from the GM Tech Center in Warren.

about this matter more than once, but finally Mitchell put his arm on Brock's shoulder and insistently said, "Do it my way." As far as Mitchell was concerned, the aesthetics were more important because, as he expressed it, most owners would not drive their Corvette past 90 mph. The Sting Ray was a different matter, though, as it would far exceed 90 mph. Brock was later vindicated; lift at high-speed was a problem with the Stingray. Regardless, Mitchell's design edict looked spectacular. At the time, most American designers simply did not fully realize the significance of considering aerodynamics in the design of automobiles.

Brock said once the sketches were refined to the point of proceeding with the crafting of its fiberglass body the project went upstairs to the so-called "Hammer Room." The name for the studio was a facade of Mitchell's done as a means of building the Stingray in secret. The reason it was taken out of the Research B Studio was the need for absolute secrecy. Taking it to the Chevrolet Studio was clearly not an option. Executives could go in there at any time and often did. With Curtice's edict concerning racing activities, Bill Mitchell hid the project from him and virtually everyone else.

The sign on the door said "Hammer Room" and when anyone went inside, they saw various tools. However, Mitchell had put a false front in, and behind that was the studio complete with a surface plate where Larry Shinoda, Tony Lapine, and Gene Garfinkle worked on the car. Studio X, as it was known to them, was where the Sting Ray was turned into hardware. In having Studio X, Mitchell was taking "quite a risk with his career," said Brock. In his book, *Corvette Sting Ray: Genesis of an American Icon,* he wrote, "Poor sales and skepticism over its [the Corvette's] value as a technical production experiment made it a risky financial proposition. The AMA ban, too, had created a menacing shadow that should have easily killed off the Corvette, but Mitchell wasn't about to give up on the car he felt had the best chance of being a vital, fresh aesthetic lead for GM's future."

Among the ideas considered for the original XP-87 were a transaxle, four-wheel independent suspension, and disc brakes. Better weight distribution would be achieved with the transaxle. Even the starter was to be mounted on it for better weight distribution. The coupe, which by the way featured a split rear window, was put on the back burner while an easier-to-design roadster version was developed, the car that became the first Sting Ray. Mitchell knew a Corvette with a transaxle would not be put into production anyway and considered Duntov's engineering proposals to be nothing more than fantasy. When the Stingray was completed, it wore no Chevrolet identification—just the name "Stingray." Mitchell personally hired Dr. Dick Thompson and others to race the Stingray, a move that distanced it from General Motors. Bill Mitchell also drove it as his personal car from time to time.

While the proportions and general look of the coupe version were used for the roadster, exotic features such as the transaxle and even the disc brakes envisioned for the coupe were not included. Drum brakes with cerametallic linings were used and proved to be insufficient with the 140-plus-mph capability of the Stingray. Lift was also a major problem. In the early 1960s, General Motors used the Stingray as a show car and it became a star on the auto show circuit. Its lines as well as those of the abandoned coupe design strongly influenced the look of the XP-720 Corvette that led directly to the 1963–1967 Sting Ray.

The XP-87 Stingray was restored a number of years ago and is now part of the automobile collection of the GM Heritage Center.

though the 1958 model was largely the same underneath its fiberglass skin. This restyle was carried forward with few changes through 1960. The Corvette proved to be more popular than ever, as sales continued to approach the coveted 10,000 mark despite the fact that the new styling was not universally praised.

The C1 Continues

For a while, a C2-generation Corvette was in the works for introduction as a 1958 model. Its styling was based mostly upon the 1956 Oldsmobile concept car dubbed the *Golden Rocket*. The *Golden Rocket* featured a split rear windshield with a sloping roofline and modest fins. In the end, the split backlight would have to wait for 1963 when the C2 was finally introduced. The *Golden Rocket* design was dropped because of a lack of manpower to complete the engineering chores; efforts had to be focused on the all-new 1958 Chevrolet passenger car and truck line. Fortunately, a backup plan based on the C1 had also been under way.

One feature from the *Golden Rocket*–inspired proposal that was carried over to the 1958 Corvette was its quad headlight layout. The setup in which the low and high beam functions were split into individual seamed beam units became legal in all states by then, so auto manufacturers took advantage of the additional styling concepts offered by the arrangement. The choice of quad headlights for the Corvette was certainly an inevitable one.

The basic grille design, dating back to 1953, but with fewer teeth, continued to be used. Flanking it, though, were nonfunctional air inlets split horizontally by thin wraparound bumpers. However, the fake air inlets were converted to functional with the purchase of the Special Equipment heavy-duty chassis (RPO-684). Ductwork from the inlets carried cooling air to the front brakes through openings in the special backing plates as well as through the rocker panels to the rear brakes.

Windsplits still appeared on the hood but were peaked, and in between was a set of 18 simulated louvers, which was a one-year only feature that was criticized by some. The hood design was virtually identical to that of the 1956 SR-2, though the latter had functional louvers. Another set of windsplits, but as bolt-on bright moldings rather than molded into the fiberglass skin, ran along the decklid. As with the fake hood louvers, this was also a one-time feature. Bumpers this time were attached to the frame rather than the body, improving their protective function. The thin wraparound bumpers in back continued to feature exhaust ports at the optimum location for carrying exhaust gases away from the car, but this time the openings were oval-shaped. Side coves continued to be included in the styling, but this time simulated engine compartment air extractors were placed at the front of them immediately behind the front wheels. Three thin horizontal moldings extended several inches behind the fake air outlets.

A newly designed instrument panel for 1958 brought a tachometer within easy sight of the driver to the relief of most buyers that year; about three out of four 1958 Corvettes were ordered with either a 4-speed or had the standard 3-speed manual transmission. This car has the 6,000-rpm tachometer, but those with the fuel-injected engine were equipped with an 8,000-rpm tachometer.

This latest revision of the first-generation Corvette resulted in a heavier looking car; it was no illusion. The Corvette was 3 inches wider, 10 inches longer, and about 200 pounds heavier. Not all the weight gain was simply due to the increased dimensions. Improvements to the fiberglass and additional support along the rocker panels also contributed to the extra pounds. The aluminum reinforcements to the dash structure introduced for 1957 were extended back under the door openings for 1958, so some portion of the extra weight served to strengthen the car's body. The standard 283 4-barrel

Styling of the 1958 Corvette was somewhat controversial at the time. Many objected to the louvered hood, and it did not return for 1959. Quad headlights were another new feature for this model year. Despite some harsh judging of the styling as "over the top," sales of the 1958 Corvette reached their highest total to date.

The passenger's side of the 1958 Corvette's dash was deeply curved and fitted with a brushed aluminum panel. Spanning this area was a padded grab bar, inside of which was a 0.06-inch steel rod with sponge rubber padding and covered with leatherette to help a passenger stay in place during high-performance driving.

gained a little more horsepower; it was now rated at 230 at 4,800 rpm, which helped move the extra weight.

A more user-friendly instrument panel was designed for the latest Corvette. Instrumentation was grouped directly ahead of the driver's position and included a 6,000-rpm tachometer (8,000 rpm for the fuel-injected engine). While the tach had improved placement, some complained that its relatively small size made it somewhat difficult to read, an important matter considering the purpose of a tach is to aid drivers in making precise shifts. The passenger's side of the dash was deeply curved and decorated with a brushed aluminum molding. Spanning the area was a grab bar of 0.06-inch steel rod padded with sponge rubber and covered with leatherette to help a passenger stay in place during high-performance driving. A center console housed the clock, optional radio, and controls for the optional heater. Upholstery and door panel patterns were also revised.

This time, the top-performing fuel-injected engine received the more accurate rating of 290 hp. Improvements to the fuel-injection system's nozzles and metering controls permitted more control over the fuel-air ratio. The revisions included eliminating the starting bypass fuel-line, switch, and solenoid; use of a single line system to the main control diaphragm; the addition of a cranking signal valve for additional starting enrichment; and a replaceable spill plunger and sleeve. Combined production of fuel-injected Corvettes this model year totaled 1,511 with the 290-hp version outselling the 250-hp engine by nearly 2 to 1. Those who bought a Corvette with the 290 fuel-injected engine were made aware by Chevrolet that the car was not intended for normal street driving. By now, Chevrolet was officially out of factory-sponsored racing activities, but it continued to offer the equipment racers wanted.

Chevrolet advertising claimed its 1958 sports car was the "Sweetest Two-Seater Going." Though its exterior styling was criticized as over-the-top by some, sales still reached a new high of 9,168 units, and this was achieved during a recession year in which overall sales were substantially down for all auto manufacturers. Reportedly, this was also the first model year in which the Corvette was profitable for Chevrolet.

Options

Options offered for 1958 were little changed from 1957. In addition to the 250-hp and 290-hp fuel-injected 283s were again the optional 245-hp and 270-hp engines with twin 4-barrel carburetors. More than half of the total Corvette production for 1958 had one of these optional engines. Other extra-cost equipment included the 4-speed synchromesh transmission, Powerglide, Posi-Traction axle, power top, power windows, and Signal-Seeking AM radio.

The heavy-duty brakes and suspension, or "Special Equipment" option, available with the fuel-injected engine consisted of larger shock absorbers with an 88-percent-larger working area, a 40-percent-stiffer front stabilizer bar, fast steering linkage giving a 16.3:1 overall ratio and less than three turns lock-to-lock, finned cast-iron brake drums with cerametallic linings, vented flange plates with air scoops, limited-slip differential, and heavy-duty front and rear springs. The front coil springs had a 13.5 percent higher spring rate and the rear leaf springs had an extra leaf along with a 9.5 percent higher rate. Cars equipped with the Special Equipment option were delivered to the customer with a placard on the windshield stating, "This car is not for street use."

Color choices numbered eight this time and included Inca Silver, Panama Yellow, Tuxedo Black, Regal Turquoise, Signet Red, Charcoal Metallic, Silver Blue, and Snowcrest White. Two-tone paint was again offered for an extra $16.15 more than the $3,591 base price; side coves could be painted Snow-

Many consumers did not care for the bright metal windsplits along the trunk lid, and like the hood louvers, they did not return for 1959. Regal Turquoise was not a particularly common color for the 1958 Corvettes, with only 510 painted this color, though more than one-third of the total production had the $16.15 two-tone paint option.

This 1958 Corvette, dubbed* Fancy Free*, is the only known surviving car created by the "Damsels of Design." They were a group of female designers hired by Harley Earl to introduce a woman's touch to the automobile. Ruth Glennie was responsible for the changes made to this 1958 Corvette, which include "Silver Olive" paint with matching interior, slip-on seat covers corresponding to each of the seasons, color-coordinated instrument faces, white phosphorescent gauge numerals and needles, brushed aluminum appliqués for the instrument panel, leather-wrapped tray for purse storage, glove box storage bin, floor-mounted waste receptacle, contoured seats, and others. The contoured seats were similar to those of 1959.

crest White or Inca Silver. Well over one-third of the Corvettes built for 1958 had this option.

Road Tests

The January 1958 issue of *Sports Car Illustrated* gave an account of its test drive of a 1958 Corvette driven at GM's Milford Proving Grounds. They found its test car to handle quite well: "Whether on fast bends or slow, when you reach the limits of adhesion, the back starts to come in a calm, unhurried manner that leaves you plenty of time to get off the throttle a bit. On a really rough surface, it is rather more ruffled, for the rear axle is a heavy item of unsprung weight. After finishing the tests we were told that the car we had been driving was not equipped with the HD suspension options. We were suitably impressed."

Acceleration tests with a fuel-injected car by *Sports Car Illustrated* showed 0–60 mph took 7.6 seconds, 0–80 mph 12.2 seconds, and 0–100 mph needed 21.4 seconds. Maximum speed in first gear was 56 mph, second gear 72 mph, third 93 mph, and fourth gear 125 mph. Fuel consumption was remarkably good with "touring speeds" resulting in 22.5 mpg and "high speeds" giving 18.4 mpg.

The writers for *Road & Track* seem to have disliked the styling, but they did appreciate the mechanical improvements: "This month's cover car has been the subject of sundry improvements, as well as the *corrosive* [emphasis author's] influence of the 'stylists.' It can stand firmly on its still-15-inch wheels without the assistance of copywriters' ecstatic groans, from which we have gleaned the following facts: Chevrolet has gone further than ever before in attempting to please, via the option route, all potential Corvette buyers. Those who want a real sports car will lean toward the dual 4-barrel carburetors or the fuel-injected engine, with or without the special camshaft . . . The cockpit . . . is a highly satisfactory job of pleasing buyers with different tastes. The most glaring fault of previous models, the too-small tachometer placed low in the center, has been rectified. It is now in front of the driver, where it belongs, though it is still too small."

The Corvette Culture Emerges

Significant milestones involving the Corvette occurred during 1958 when the "Corvette Club of America" was formed in Los Angeles, California, and soon more than two dozen chapters of the club had formed all over the country. Chevrolet also began publishing *Corvette News* in 1958 to keep owners informed on such topics as rallies across the country and technical matters. A "Corvette culture" had begun. Furthermore, the 1958 Corvette took a first-in-class award at that year's Pebble Beach Concours d'Elegance.

The Corvette had made great gains over the past five years and had earned respect from many sports car enthusiasts. It had reached a high level of maturity as a true *American* sports car just as Harley Earl had envisioned.

Refinements for 1959

Styling changes for 1959 were few but evident. The hood lost its louvers, the decklid was without the bright windsplit moldings, and wheel color was changed from silver to black. Color choices totaled seven: Classic Cream, Crown Sapphire, Inca Silver, Frost Blue, Roman Red, and Tuxedo Black. A practical option priced at $10.80 was a set of sun visors; while the uncluttered windshield frame provided a clean look, this was at the cost of driver fatigue when driving into direct sunlight over long distances. Base price for the Corvette climbed to $3,875.

Engine choices remained the same as they had been the previous two model years, but orders for the fuel-injected types dropped by a whopping margin of nearly 40 percent from 1,511 the previous year to 920. Orders for one of the twin-quad setups held nearly steady. The fuel-injection setup received more improvements. Compared with the original setup offered for 1957, the fuel-injected engines operated on a leaner mixture, air leaks around the nozzle anchorages were sealed, each injector nozzle received filter screens, and a simpler manifold vacuum–operated valve replaced the complex arrangement of a solenoid for cold starts and a micro-switch to bypass the solenoid for hot starts.

Advanced research into using aluminum for various components that began with the Corvette SS led to using aluminum clutch housings on the manual transmission, reducing the weight of the 1959-model Corvettes with the manual setup by

Bill Mitchell's 1958 XP-700

The Corvette XP-700, a modified 1958 Corvette, was developed as a personal car for Bill Mitchell, who became the VP of GM Design upon the retirement of Harley Earl at the end of 1958. Its body was restyled with a long, low front overhang and extended rear end that was later adapted to the 1961 Corvette. Other special features included Lucas Flame Thrower headlights, Dayton wire wheels with knock-off hubs, front brake cooling ducts with the inlets below the headlights, angled louvers along the front of the scoops on the body side coves, twin outlet side exhaust pipes along with ribbed mufflers, and brake cooling scoops for the rear wheels. The car's styling was heavily influenced by Grand Prix race cars of the era.

Mitchell drove the car for about one year before the XP-700 was modified with a longer and smaller oval grille and a double-bubble plexiglass canopy coated with vaporized aluminum to help reduce heat buildup within the interior. Also included was a periscope-type rearview mirror. It then made the rounds of the auto show circuit for a while.

A 1958 Corvette was turned into the Corvette XP-700 as a personal car for Bill Mitchell. Mitchell extended the front end with the design being influenced by Grand Prix race cars of the era. Other features included Dayton wire wheels with knock-off hubs, Lucas Flame Thrower headlights, and front brake cooling ducts. (Photo Courtesy GM Media Archive)

The extended rear end of the 1958 Corvette XP-700 was later adapted to the 1961 Corvette. A double-bubble plexiglass canopy coated with vaporized aluminum to help reduce heat buildup within the interior was added about one year after the car was built. (Photo Courtesy GM Media Archive)

18 pounds. Incidentally, after further research with aluminum heads seemed to be going well, Chevrolet decided to announce that they would be available for the fuel-injected engines beginning the following model year, but casting problems caused the option to be canceled. If successful, the lighter heads would have shaved another 53 pounds from fuel-injected Corvettes. The goal of the research, though, was to be able to manufacture and offer an all-aluminum V-8, something that Chevrolet would not offer until the release in 1997 of the high-performance LS1 small-block. The March 1957 issue of *Speed Age* in an article titled "Engines Go Aluminum," speculated that such an engine would be available possibly as early as 1958. They noted that an aluminum-block V-8 could be as much as 230 pounds lighter than a conventional iron core, cheaper to produce because of the higher level of precision made possible with cast aluminum (thus less machining), and offer superior heat dissipation compared to cast iron.

Cerametallic brake linings could be had without buying the Special Equipment chassis option; this option was listed as RPO-686 and sold for $26.90. However, the ducted cooling system was not included, and therefore the base backing plates were still installed. The base drums were also used, but were honed to a finer finish. Larger, heat-resistant pull-back springs were required with RPO-686.

Stronger front wheel hubs, redesigned brake drums, radius rods added to the rear suspension for greater handling stability and traction, and shocks with a nitrogen-filled plastic sleeve to prevent aeration of the shock fluid were also new features of the 1959 Corvette. Another new feature was the positive lock-out for the reverse gear. It consisted of a pull handle on the gearshift lever that was easily activated by the first two fingers of the right hand when resting on the gearshift knob.

At about midyear, a 24-gallon fiberglass fuel tank, LPO-1625A (limited-production option) was made available at

The 1959 Corvette was further refined and brought praise from the automotive press of the day.* Motor Trend *may have provided the most interesting of all reports on the 1959 Corvette in its April issue by comparing it to a Porsche. This was far removed from its comments on the original Corvette.

a cost of $161.40. It offered an additional 8 gallons of capacity over the standard fuel tank.

The seat structure was redesigned for 1959, much to the delight of enthusiasts. Improvements to the seat design resulted not only in more comfort, but also helped to hold the driver and passenger in place during all but the most extreme maneuvers. However, some were highly critical of the change made to the passenger's side dash in which the glove box was replaced with a package tray. It was noted for being potentially hazardous to a passenger's knees. In the interest of safety, though, the Corvette was now fitted with seat belts as standard equipment. Also, the door armrests were relocated to provide more elbowroom when cornering.

The Automotive Press Reviews

The January 1959 issue of *Road & Track* provided a more enthusiastic review of the Corvette than its report on the previous model. In it, writers noted just how far the Corvette had come since its introduction. In comparison, they asserted the original version was "rather prosaic and had little to offer with the exception of being different from the other U.S.-built cars. Powered by a 6-cylinder engine that was essentially the same as the one introduced in the 1937 Chevrolet, the Corvette offered neither performance nor exceptional appearance." In contrast, the writer concluded, "Taking everything into consideration, the Corvette is a pretty good car. It probably has more performance per dollar than anything you could buy and parts are obtainable without sending to Italy, Germany, or England."

The author of the *Road & Track* test report heartily approved of the styling changes: "The appearance of the 1959 Corvette has been improved by the simple expedient of removing the phony hood louvers and the useless chrome bars from the deck lid." However, there was still resistance to the quad headlight setup that was "inflicted" by the "commercial artists."

As for the way the 1959 Corvette performed, *Road & Track* called the 4-speed "one of the smoothest working units it has been our pleasure to use. The lever is placed at just the right location for driver convenience and shifts, either up or down, can be made quickly and easily at any speed within engine limits . . . Weight distribution of the car had shown 53 percent of the weight to be on the front wheels with one person in the car, but in spite of the nose-heavy attitude there was a marked tendency to oversteer. It was found with a little practice that a drift, once set up, could be maintained with little effort by dexterous manipulation of the throttle and steering wheel. The abundance of horsepower at the driver's command and adequately quick steering helped somewhat, too."

The magazine's test car was equipped with a fuel-injected engine, 4-speed, and the Special Equipment option. The testing affirmed their belief in the advantages of fuel injection over carburetors. While some enthusiasts believed the dual carburetors offered an advantage at the top end, *R&T* found "fuel-injection has it all over carburetors for throttle response and lack of sensitivity to motion. There is no flooding or starving on hard cornering with fuel-injection." The cerametallic brake linings were noted for not being as effective when cold as they were when hot, and they squeaked after their tests were completed. "In spite of these minor annoyances," wrote the author, "the brake kit is to be recommended for anyone contemplating fast driving with a Corvette and is an absolute necessity for competition work."

Road & Track performed the usual standing starts to 30 mph up to 100 mph as well as the quarter-mile test. Acceleration to 60 mph took 6.6 seconds, to 80 mph was 10 seconds flat, and reaching 100 mph needed only 15.5 seconds. As for the quarter-mile, the result was 14.5 seconds at 96 mph. Another interesting stat provided to its readers was the weight-to-horsepower ratio of just 11.62:1 for its car with a test weight of 3,370 pounds.

Motor Trend may have provided the most interesting of all reports on the 1959 Corvette in its April issue. It compared the Corvette to a Porsche. "On the surface they would seem to defy comparison. But dig a little and see how much alike they really are," argued *Motor Trend*. They compared such matters as assembly quality, city driving, open country driving and high-speed handling, fuel economy, and others.

Comments by *Motor Trend* revealed a vast improvement over the early Corvettes regarding fit and finish. "If you have definite feelings against fiberglass, consider revising your views," the writer declared. "Corvette's glass work is smooth and every bit as functional as steel . . . Panels match properly, doors close in a satisfying fashion; it is a carefully constructed automobile." As for the Porsche, it "is a masterpiece of precision fitting and close tolerances in its body construction."

In city driving conditions, *Motor Trend* gave a slight edge to the Porsche "because quicker, lighter steering makes moving through tight traffic less of a chore." As for the Corvette, "Torque from the Corvette is so fierce that the engine can loaf along in fourth, say at 20 mph, and pull away smoothly."

Comparison driving on the open road also gave the advantage to the Porsche in some situations: "Match the two cars on a tight mountain road where the Corvette's torque and acceleration can't be utilized and you'll probably get there quicker in the Porsche. It just hangs on better in the turns. If this mountain should be downhill, the Porsche's brakes will outlast the Corvette's." The Corvette's brakes, though, were said to be more than adequate for normal driving, but the optional cerametallic brakes were "a must" for hard use and competition. The Corvette was said to ride "harshly with a substantial amount of pitch and chop on rough roads. The same routes are gobbled up by the Porsche's four-wheel independent suspension with a minimum amount of shock transmitted to driver and passenger." However, their overall view was that choosing between the two for a cross-country trip "would be difficult. Both of them are capable of speeds far in excess of any legal speed limit . . . The Corvette will handle. It corners flat and can be jockeyed through a hot turn with surprising ease."

In terms of fuel economy, the comparison was not even remotely close. The 4-cylinder engine of the Porsche delivered 35 mpg on the open road and 24.5 mpg in congested areas. The Corvette managed just 14.9 mpg on the open road and 14.3 in stop-and-go driving. The latter was noted as "not bad for 283 cubic inches constantly begging to be opened up."

A comparison of 0–60 mph times gave the advantage to the Corvette by a huge margin: 7.8 seconds versus 15.2 for the Porsche. The quarter-mile was equally disproportionate: 15.7 seconds at 90 mph for the Corvette and 19.9 at 67.5 for the Porsche. On the Riverside Raceway, the Corvette also showed itself to be faster with a time of 2 minutes, 32 seconds with an average speed of 78.5 mph through the course; the Porsche required 2 minutes, 47 seconds with an average speed of 71 mph.

The September 1959 issue of *Motor Life* had high praise for the Corvette's 4-speed transmission, which was fitted to the 245-hp dual-carburetor engine of its test car. Other pluses included the engine's dual-point distributor, the full set of instrumentation, and comfortable seats. They noted the car's light weight made brake fade of the standard brakes less of a problem compared to full-size models. However, they were not especially impressed with its test car's handling with the standard suspension: "The test car didn't display outstanding handling characteristics as those expected from a sports car. In fact, it is entirely possible that there are a couple of sporty production sedans that will corner better." (The writer was likely referring to Chrysler's 300-E and Plymouth's Fury, which the automotive press proclaimed to have handling characteristics similar to that of a sports car.) Other criticisms levied against the Corvette were the lack of adjustment to the steering wheel and too many turns lock-to-lock. In conclusion the writer noted, "The Corvette, with very few exceptions, can be whatever its owner wants it to be. Powered with five different engines, ranging from the conservative 230-hp model to the 290-hp fuel-injected hot rod, it is one of the most versatile cars offered today."

A sidebar appearing in the *Motor Life* article titled, "Evolution of a Dream Car," served to illustrate how the Corvette had evolved in a short time. Among the brief year-by-year commentary taken from previous reviews were these:

> *1954*: Hurrah for the true American sports car. Chevrolet took up the European challenge and the result is proof that a "compromise" car can be built. We'd be much happier with a wider choice of transmissions and engines.
>
> *1956*: New, more graceful lines make the Corvette much racier looking. New 3-speed stick-shift gear box is the best one Chevrolet has ever had.
>
> *1957*: It will reach 100 mph in the length of time it formerly took to reach 60 mph.
>
> *1958*: From the small changes that continue to be made to the Corvette there is proof that the car's designers have been listening to the critics.

The sidebar concluded, "Thus the story of Corvette's sensible evolution continues. It has established a design philosophy that might well be copied by other manufacturers."

Conclusion

Production of the Corvette finally cracked the 10,000 mark during the 1960 model year. The Corvette with its 315-hp fuel-injected engine ran impressively at Le Mans that year, giving Chevrolet's sports car greater credibility as the real thing. By 1962, the Corvette was dominating in SCCA racing. Because of the vision of Harley Earl and Bill Mitchell along with the determination and mechanical expertise of Zora Arkus-Duntov and Ed Cole, the Corvette became an iconic part of American car culture.

In 2014, the C7 generation emerged, and a C8 version will be in production soon. When this book was being written, a C8, nicknamed "Zora," was reported to be a mid-engine car with expected availability in mid-2018 as a 2019 model. Harley Earl and Zora Arkus-Duntov would surely be pleased with the evolution of this American sports car.

CHAPTER 5

TRANSFORMATION OF THE TRUCK

1950–1959

From the time pickup trucks began to be produced and onward into the 1930s, they were viewed simply as utility vehicles for hauling cargo from the farm to the marketplace. Styling for pickups was given about the same level of thought as passenger cars, but the largely utilitarian approach underwent some change during the 1930s. Eventually, comfort and convenience for pickups began to approach that of the passenger car.

The 1957 Cameo Carrier received the same styling changes as the rest of the pickup truck line. It featured twin hood ornaments like the passenger cars. Sales of the Cameo Carrier, which had been low all along, dropped even more after Ford and Dodge released their own high-style pickups to counter Chevrolet's.

Arguably the most stylish pickups of the 1950s were the Chevrolet Cameo Carrier (as well as the nearly identical GMC Suburban Carrier) of 1955 to mid-1958. The most notable features of these pickups were their fiberglass bed and tailgate and concealed tailgate hinges. The side panels were flush-fitting with the cab, which brought the cargo box to the same width as the cab. The Cameo Carrier was expensive and relatively few were sold, but it served its purpose of drawing people to Chevrolet dealerships, where they often purchased a more affordable vehicle. (Photo Courtesy GM Media Archive)

GM Styling, under the direction of its vice president, Harley Earl, was instrumental to Chevrolet's success. Earl firmly believed styling was an essential part of automotive design. Clearly, he was right; by the 1950s, General Motors had half the automobile market. Of course, other factors played a part in GM's success, such as modern V-8 engines and automatic transmissions, both of which were ultimately offered for the company's pickup trucks.

The "halo model" pickup emerged in the mid-1950s. Just as cars like Chevrolet's Nomad station wagon and Buick's Skylark convertible were low-production models meant to entice people into GM dealer's showrooms, Chevrolet (as well as GMC) offered a high-style, specialty pickup with fiberglass components in back and flush-fitting rear side panels.

Design of the pickup truck certainly advanced in the decade of the 1950s and today such vehicles offer virtually the same level of comfort as any full-size car. More miles of paved roads helped to spur along better trucks. Those living on farms with dirt roads, often marred with ruts, needed ruggedness as well as cargo capacity in their pickup trucks, but with the improved roads of the postwar era, building trucks that were stylish and more comfortable became practical and of interest to a larger number of drivers. In 1956, President Eisenhower authorized the interstate highway network across the United States, resulting in even more miles of paved roadways.

A Brief History of Chevrolet Trucks

Chevrolet introduced its first light trucks in 1918 with two types, a 1/2-ton and a 1-ton model. The 1/2-ton version's chassis was based on the Model 490 passenger car, but with stronger rear springs, while the 1-ton variant, strangely dubbed the "Model T," had its own chassis. (Interestingly, Ford Motor Company, which had been building the Model T since 1909, evidently did not object to Chevrolet's use of the name.) Both had only forward sheet metal. The new owner of either model had the chassis fitted with a body built by a body company, oftentimes the Martin Perry Company, along with a wide variety of cargo-carrying setups. By 1921, Chevrolet contracted body companies to deliver its light trucks directly to the assembly line already fitted with a body. Also, a 3/4-ton truck, the Model G with a longer wheelbase (at 120 inches), was introduced.

Two model years later, the Commercial 490 was replaced with a light-truck version of the Superior Series cars. The Superior B had a longer wheelbase than the Model 490 and a more modern appearance with its taller hood. The 1-ton Model T was replaced with the Model D and the 3/4-ton Model G was dropped. However, the Model D 1-ton had the same 120-inch wheelbase as the G. For the rest of the 1920s, Chevrolet's light truck chassis would be based on the current passenger car type. Frontal styling would also largely match that of the car line.

In 1928, Chevrolet introduced its Sedan Delivery, a passenger car–based cargo-carrying vehicle for commercial use. It had side panels in lieu of side windows, a single seat (though a passenger seat was an option), and a cargo door in back. The Sedan Delivery remained in production through 1960, and was generally used by upscale businesses wanting to present a more sophisticated image to customers. Also new for this model year was a new 1-ton model, the LP, with four-wheel brakes

Chevrolet introduced the Sedan Delivery, a passenger car–based cargo-carrying vehicle for commercial use, in 1928. It had side panels in lieu of side windows, a single seat (though a passenger seat was an option), and a cargo door in back. The Sedan Delivery remained in production through 1960. and was generally used by upscale businesses wanting to present a more sophisticated image to customers. Shown here is a 1950 model. (Photo Courtesy GM Media Archive)

The need for the Sedan Delivery was on the wane throughout the 1950s, but Chevrolet continued to offer the model through 1960. This 1955 model was based on the One-Fifty Handyman station wagon. A total of 8,255 were built for the model year. (Photo Courtesy GM Media Archive)

and 4-speed transmission. A more powerful 6-cylinder engine gave the new 1929 LQ Series trucks a $1\frac{1}{2}$-ton rating.

The car-based International AC Series roadster pickup appeared in the Chevrolet lineup for 1930. For 1931, Chevrolet offered a pickup much more similar to the one of today in that it offered a higher-capacity bed instead of a utility box fitted to the rear chassis. Also, at this point Chevrolet's trucks began to take on a stylish appearance more like the cars upon which they were based. A stronger structure utilizing an all-metal cowl emerged for Chevrolet's trucks at this time, unlike the passenger cars, which were still constructed on a wood framework with the sheet metal tacked onto it. The doors were hinged to metal instead of a wooden post as well.

An all-new light-truck lineup, the DB Series, was released for 1934; the deluxe version came with a chrome-plated grille and headlight buckets. A Suburban Carryall was a new addition for 1935 in what was now the EB Series, which included a front bumper as standard equipment. The Suburban Carryall, a panel truck–based station wagon with more windows and seats, was an all-metal vehicle serving a variety of purposes, such as carrying guests to resort-type hotels.

In 1936, Chevrolet continued offering the essentially unchanged 1935 models until about the midpoint of the model year when the second series truck line was released. The truly

This businessman needed a fleet of sedan delivery trucks. Shown is the 1956 Chevrolet Sedan Delivery, which was based upon the One-Fifty Handyman station wagon. (Photo Courtesy GM Media Archive)

Completely redesigned trucks were released for sale in June 1947 and were marketed as the "Advance Design" trucks. This design was carried through about the midportion of 1955. The 1947 models reflected a realization that appearance, as for passenger cars, was a major consideration in the purchase of a pickup. Furthermore, the design was based on extensive interviews of truck owners regarding their expectations of a pickup. Among the improvements desired were increased cabin space, wider seats, and more glass area for improved visibility. To accommodate the wants of the public, the cab was 7 inches longer and 8 inches wider than that of the previous model and the seat allowed for up to three people to sit in reasonable comfort. The all-steel cab was made wider by allowing the sides to hang over the side rails of the frame. This, in turn, pushed the doors outward, allowing for the wider seat. The seat cushion, by the way, could easily be removed for access to a toolbox located under the floor. Glass area was increased, especially with the new five-window Deluxe Cab Package, which offered a three-piece virtually panoramic rear window. The three-piece rear window had curved side pieces and was marketed as "Nu-Vue." Interior ventilation was improved through the use of a vent on top of the cowl along with a set of vents inside.

In addition to all the new advancements, Chevrolet stopped using a basic single design for both the light- and heavy-duty truck lines. The result of the change was the issuance of two truck lines, the Thriftmaster and the Loadmaster. While they shared the same cab and major styling characteristics to maintain a family resemblance, they were distinctly different trucks. Seats and door panels were now covered in rich Naugahyde (while leather remained an option) and more chrome accents were added.

Chevrolet's 1/2-ton, 3/4-ton, and 1-ton Advance Design Series 3000 trucks offered greater payload space and came with a bed measuring 78 inches, 87 inches, and 108 inches, respectively. In addition to the light- and heavy-duty ($1^1/_2$-ton and up) trucks, Chevrolet continued to offer the panel truck. It was comprised of three types using two different wheelbases.

new second series was lower in height and offered the major advance of hydraulic brakes. Though stylish on the outside, the interior remained about as utilitarian as ever with simple upholstery, rubber floor mat, and a cardboard headliner interrupting the otherwise all-metal surroundings. The dash and door panels, at least, had a crackle finish for some degree of decoration. A stake body pickup was added for 1937.

A significant change took place with the 1939 Chevrolet trucks in that they were no longer based on the forward sheet metal and chassis of the passenger car line. The so-called "turret top," an all-steel roof minus the fabric insert of the past, came to the pickup truck just as it had for the passenger cars. Styling became more impressive, too, especially the 1941 models with their art deco–inspired grille work. The 1941 model year was extremely good for sales of Chevrolet trucks.

Soon after America's entry into World War II, civilian truck production came to an end. However, a need emerged by 1944 for civilian pickups, so the U.S. government authorized Chevrolet to produce a small number of pickups in 1944 and 1945, which were essentially copies of the 1942 models with 6.50 x 16 tires and a 4-speed transmission.

Full-scale production resumed in August 1945. The 1946 models offered several improvements, including better sealing for glass, longer-wearing seat upholstery, 6-ply tires, and more durable water pump. Even leather upholstery became an option.

Throughout the 1950s, Chevrolet offered a truck in every weight class, though not for every imaginable purpose. Owners could customize what the company offered, a truck with a cab and chassis, with the type of cargo-carrying design they needed, whether that be for carrying special equipment, hauling furniture, serving as a fuel truck, or any number of duties. (Photo Courtesy GM Media Archive)

The Panel Delivery truck was essentially the same in concept as the Sedan Delivery except the Panel Delivery was based on the truck design rather than the passenger car. As a truck-based vehicle it offered greater cargo carrying capacity. This is a 1953 Series 3100 version. (Photo Courtesy GM Media Archive)

Improvements to it were similar to those offered in the pickup truck line.

As the 1950s began, Chevrolet resolved most of the shortcomings of its trucks, such as too much frame twist in front leading to the cracking of the radiator after traveling many miles on rough roads. Standard equipment was reduced; the tool kit and rear bumper were no longer included. While a couple of items were dropped from the standard equipment list, those buying a 1951 model got a more durable and wider "double-decker" seat using two layers of springs. The seat adjuster functioned more smoothly with a combination of roller and ball bearings instead of double rollers on a central shaft. Furthermore, self-energizing Bendix brakes, similar to those of Chevrolet's passenger cars, were used. The rotation of the brake drums provided some of the energy that forced the shoes outward against the drums, resulting in reduced brake pedal effort for the driver. Additional improvements included a stronger bed and a swing-down spare tire support placed underneath the rear of the pickup bed.

Only very minor changes differentiated Chevrolet trucks through 1953.

1954: Even More Advanced

With the 1954 model year, Chevrolet introduced the most significant changes to its truck line since 1947. Changes included a new grille, a one-piece curved windshield, and a load box that was 2 inches lower to ease the loading and unloading of cargo. A revised instrument panel featured recessed instruments to minimize reflections as well as a defroster opening extending the full width of the windshield. Increased comfort was provided with a new, optional Ride-Control seat, a standard feature of Chevrolet's cab-over engine trucks. The Ride-Control seat cushion and back was built as an integral unit and, therefore, flexed as a unit. An air valve located in the bottom of the seat restricted sudden movements resulting from intense road shocks. The seat was mounted on an inclined track and was adjustable. A companion, two-passenger conventional seat was installed to the right when the option was ordered.

Other upgrades included two-tone interiors for Deluxe pickups and panel trucks and an optional chrome-plated grille. Eleven single-tone exterior paint colors were offered at no extra cost in addition to the standard Juniper Cream. Two-tone schemes were also offered as an extra-cost option. The new "Comfortmaster Deluxe Cab" provided bright metal trim reveal moldings, rear corner windows (three-piece rear window), dual-note horns, right-hand sunshade, driver armrest, and cigar lighter.

Of greater significance was the availability of the Hydra-Matic automatic transmission as an extra-cost option for all light-duty truck models powered by either the 6-cylinder or the V-8. The Hydra-Matic was released for the 1940 model year and was the first mass-produced fully automatic transmission and had been an option for Pontiac, Oldsmobile, and Cadillac prior to America's entry into World War II. It was used extensively in Cadillac-powered tanks during this war. The Hydra-Matic used a fluid coupling and a torus rather than a torque converter, to transfer power instead of the conventional friction clutch and three planetary gear sets to give four forward speeds. The final drive ratio was 1.0:1. A parking pawl locked the drive wheels when the engine was off.

The use of the Hydra-Matic in the war greatly bolstered its image with the public. Indeed, it was advertised as "battle tested," certainly a truthful claim. The transmission was so

THE CANOPY EXPRESS

The Canopy Express was sold by Chevrolet from 1947 to 1955 and was offered in 1/2-ton and 1-ton versions. It was essentially a light-duty cargo van based upon the chassis of its panel truck, but with an open display area in back ("weather-proof" side curtains were provided for protection against inclement weather). Types of commercial uses included the selling of vegetables and fruit and deliveries requiring easy access. Pictured here is a 1950 Series 3100 1/2-ton model. (Photo Courtesy GM Media Archive)

Chevrolet sold the Advance Design commercial vehicle, Canopy Express, from 1947 to 1955. It was of all-steel construction with a plywood floor and steel skid strips. Offered in 1/2-ton (model 3107) and 1-ton versions (model 3807), the Canopy Express was essentially a light-duty cargo van based on the chassis of the panel truck, but with an open display area in back (though "weather-proof" side curtains were provided for protection against inclement weather). Types of commercial uses included the selling of vegetables and fruit, as well as for deliveries requiring easy access, such as newspapers, tools, and radio equipment. Other manufacturers, such as International Harvester and Dodge, produced this type of vehicle as well.

The Canopy Express trucks evolved from the pickup version first produced by Chevrolet in 1920, which had an open canopy installed over the pickup bed.

As Americans moved closer to cities after the end of World War II, sales of Canopy Express vehicles began to fall sharply. As a result, Chevrolet discontinued the model with the end of the 1955 model year.

successful that even some of GM's competition, namely, Hudson, Nash, Kaiser, Willys, and Lincoln, contracted with General Motors to supply it for its line of cars. Unfortunately, a catastrophic fire, the largest in industrial history at the time, in the Hydra-Matic plant on August 12, 1953, interrupted production. General Motors could no longer supply other auto manufacturers with the Hydra-Matic and its passenger car divisions had to adopt either Buick's Dynaflow or Chevrolet's Powerglide until Hydra-Matic production could resume nine weeks later using the large Willow Run plant where B-24s had been built during the war. By the start of the 1954 model year, production of the Hydra-Matic had returned to its normal rate.

The standard-issue 3-speed synchromesh manual transmission was upgraded with strengthened helical gear teeth and was given a more durable positive diaphragm spring clutch with an 11-inch disc. A heavy-duty version was offered as an option for the 3000 Series as was a 4-speed manual transmission. The 112-hp 235-ci "Thriftmaster" with a new cylinder head was said to be more durable and operate more quietly. Chrome-plated top rings were standard on the 235 "Loadmaster" and the 135-hp 261-ci "Jobmaster" engines. The latter's output was boosted with a new high-lift cast-iron camshaft. Both the Loadmaster and Jobmaster engines benefited from more durable exhaust valves made of steel with a high-alloy content. All versions of Chevrolet's inline-6 received a more efficient cooling system, a full-flow oil lubrication system, and

Chevrolet introduced the most significant changes to its truck line since 1947 with the release of the 1954 model truck line. New features included an open radiator grille with a massive crossbar, a one-piece curved windshield, and a load box that was 2 inches lower to make loading and unloading cargo a little easier. This 1954 Series 3100 1/2-ton model was equipped with the optional Deluxe Cab option featuring rear corner windows, a two-tone interior, stainless steel windshield and side window reveals, two-note horn, and passenger-side sun visor and armrest. The Hydra-Matic automatic transmission became an option for Chevrolet pickups this model year. (Photo Courtesy GM Media Archive)

Heavy-duty Chevrolet trucks of 1954 included the Series 5100 shown in this photograph pulling trailers in elaborate livery used for hauling the concept cars, production cars, and other equipment for that year's GM Motorama. (Photo Courtesy GM Media Archive)

more rigid drop-forged steel connecting rods and crankshaft.

Heavy-duty–class trucks, Series 5000 and 6000, were upgraded with a stronger frame as well as stronger front and rear axles. A more durable 2-speed rear axle with ranges from 6.13–8.1:1 and 6.7–8.86:1 was yet another improvement. While Chevrolet had maintained the lead over Ford in truck sales, its lead had narrowed by 1954. Ford had introduced a new truck the prior model year that proved to be very popular. The all-new 1955 Chevrolet "Task Force" trucks, though, would again give Chevrolet a comfortable lead over Ford.

1955–1957: Task Force Trucks and the High-Style Cameo Carrier

The all-new 1955 truck line with "Work-Style Beauty" was intended to be released at the same time as the new passenger car line, but the engineering demands of designing the latter along with fulfillment of government contracts to support the war in Korea delayed their release until March 25, 1955. Up to that point, a lightly altered 1954 model served as an interim offering. Like the passenger cars, this first series 1955 pickup did receive a Hotchkiss open driveline, replacing the closed torque-tube type used since the 1930s. The change allowed owners of a 1/2-ton model to add the aftermarket four-wheel-drive conversion by Northern Auto Parts Company, commonly known as NAPCO, when desired. Chevrolet dealers performed the conversion at a cost of approximately $1,200.

The 1/2-ton line was subdivided into Commercial Model H Series 3100, Commercial Cameo Model H Series 3100, Commercial Model M Series 3200, and Dubl-Duti Model F Series 3400. The Model M Series 3200 had the longer-wheelbase chassis of the 3/4-ton models with a longer cargo box. The latter Dubl-Duti type was a Forward Control Chassis with a 104-inch wheelbase. It could be supplied with a walk-in delivery truck body from a variety of factory-approved sources or the buyer could have a truck body supplied

The second series 1955 Chevrolet trucks released in March of that year took styling cues from the passenger car line, including the Ferrari-inspired grille, hooded headlights, and wraparound windshield. Chevrolet and GMC were the first to offer the wraparound windshield for a pickup, which provided roughly one-third more glass area. The new front bumper wrapped around the fenders, offering better protection for the sheet metal. A 12-volt electrical system was also a welcome upgrade. This light-duty model is a Series 3100 1/2-ton. (Photo Courtesy GM Media Archive)

Chevrolet provided a 172-inch wheelbase chassis, dual rear wheels, and front-end sheet metal upon which school bus bodies could be installed. Shown is a second series 1955 Series 10800. It could be configured to transport 41 to 50 passengers. (Photo Courtesy GM Media Archive)

from another source. Furthermore, the 3/4-ton models were divided into Dubl-Duti Series 3500 Model 3542, 3600 Model J, and the 3700 Model K. The Series 3500 was like the 1/2-ton Forward Control Chassis, but with a longer, 125-inch wheelbase. The sole 1-ton variant was the Series 3800 Medium-Duty Commercial Model L. The lettered model designations were altered for 1956 and 1957 for the 1/2-ton and 3/4-ton lineups, however. For example, the 1956 Cameo Carrier became Model 3B56, then for 1957 and 1958 it was simply the Model 3B.

Other than simply being virtually all-new, the second series 1955 Chevrolet trucks also could be had with four new options: the small-block V-8 Trademaster, overdrive, power brakes, and power steering. The 265 available for the light-duty pickups was not as performance-oriented as those for the passenger car line. Instead, the optional small-block was rated at 145 hp.

More new features included a more powerful 6-cylinder at 123 hp (up from 112), larger radiators, angle-mounted double-acting shock absorbers, 4-ply tubeless tires (for 1/2-ton models), 12-volt electrical system, a new parking brake with propeller shaft band, higher-capacity rear axles, improved leaf springs, a wider track, and a new ladder frame. The redesigned "Flite-Ride" cabs came in Deluxe and Custom styles with the former being equipped with an improved ventilation system, Finger-Tip Control Panel, an oak-bark textured plastic and

This medium-duty 1955 Series 5400 truck cab and chassis was outfitted to carry combustible liquids, in this case perhaps aviation gasoline. (Photo Courtesy GM Media Archive)

rayon seat cover, embossed beige metal door panel inserts, black headliner, and black rubber floor mat. With the Custom Cab came a foam-rubber seat cushion covered with dotted nylon and vinyl upholstery, beige headliner, beige rubber floor mat, textured brown paint for the door panel inserts, and a "Full-View" wraparound rear window that more than doubled the glass area provided by the small window of the Deluxe Cab. A foam-padded seat, by the way, was available at extra cost for the Deluxe version of the pickup. Both cabs were fitted with forward-leaning roof pillars, wraparound windshield, and concealed running boards. The redesigned V-shaped gauge cluster was based on that of the 1953–1955 Corvette.

As in the past, a plethora of styles was offered to fit any need. For 1955, the range ran from the typical light-duty pickup to the Carryall Suburban to the Stake-type, four chassis platforms, the Forward Control Chassis (essentially a cargo van) to school bus chassis on up to the heavy-duty cab-over engine variety.

Also available for the 1955 pickups were several additional extra-cost options. Among them was a chrome package consisting of a plated grille and headlight bezels. These were painted in standard trim. Chrome-plated bumpers (a separate option), hood ornament, backup lights, grille guard, wheel covers, two-tone paint, heater, dual fog lamps, external sun shade, turn signals, heavy-duty rear springs, heavy-duty clutch, high-output generator, electric wipers, and windshield washer were among the many options offered. As mentioned earlier, power steering was a newly added option. It was an add-on unit with its hydraulic pump bolted to the rear of the generator.

The all-new 1955 Chevrolet trucks sold very well and gave the division a 31-percent share of the truck market with Ford trailing by a wide margin.

1956–1957

Only modest changes differentiated the 1956 Chevrolet trucks. Reworked fenders, hood, and grille were the most obvious ones. More noteworthy was that the 1956 Chevrolet trucks offered more power. A compression boost from 7.5 to 8.0:1 generated another 17 hp out of the 235-ci 6-cylinder pushing its rating to 140 while the optional V-8 was now advertised as producing a maximum of 155 hp. While the passenger-car 205-hp version of the small-block was not offered for the pickup line, that did not stop Smokey Yunick from getting high performance out of the 265 powering the Cameo Carrier he drove on the beach at the 1956 Daytona Speed Weeks. With the modified vehicle, Yunick set a record in Class 5 standing-mile acceleration with a run of 89.524 mph and took top honors in the flying mile. Strangely, there seems to be no surviving record of the speed he attained

The panel truck was among the Series 3100 Task Force Trucks offered by Chevrolet for 1956; it had a base price of $1,968. Ambulance-style doors offered versatility of use. The standard interior vinyl upholstery colors were limited to gray and black, though an extra-cost option allowed the customer to have synthetic fabric in blue, green, charcoal, and gray. Cargo floor was wood.

Only modest changes to the all-new 1955 truck design were made for the 1956 model year. This front end is shown undergoing finishing touches before installation. (Photo Courtesy GM Media Archive)

Starting with the 1957 model year, Chevrolet offered its own four-wheel-drive setup with a 4-speed gearbox and a 2-speed transfer case for its pickup trucks. Previously, Chevrolet used the four-wheel-drive conversion made by the Northern Auto Parts Company, commonly known as NAPCO. (Photo Courtesy GM Media Archive)

in the flying mile. A special milestone was achieved for Chevrolet during the 1956 model year when the division's 4-millionth *postwar* truck was assembled. More important, Chevrolet gained slightly in the truck market share, increasing to 32 percent.

Heavy-duty Chevrolet trucks for 1956 got a new automatic transmission, the "Powermatic," built by GM's Allison Division. Drive was through a torque converter to a hydraulically controlled planetary gearbox with six forward gears and one reverse.

Chevrolet's pickup trucks for 1957 received more changes than the 1956 models. Styling alterations included a busier trapezoidal grille, dual hood windsplits akin to those of the passenger car line, new side badging, and a new large rear window, which became standard for all light-duty pickups. Also, Chevrolet now offered its own four-wheel-drive setup with a 4-speed gearbox and a 2-speed transfer case. The control lever for the 2-speed system was mounted to the right of the transmission tunnel, and with it, the driver could select direct drive or underdrive. Underdrive gave a 1.87:1 ratio and provided eight forward and two reverse speeds. The front drive axle could be engaged with this lever for direct drive only. Constant velocity joints were installed in the front axle, but other than that it was virtually identical to the rear axle.

Late in the model year, Chevrolet's four-wheel-drive option became available for all light-duty truck models as well as the Suburban series.

Despite the improvements, Chevrolet barely edged out Ford in truck sales with only a 14,000-unit margin for the 1957 model year. Ford had all-new 1957 models to go up against Chevrolet's third-year designs.

Standard interior features of the 1957 Cameo included two-toned nylon-faced pattern-cloth and vinyl upholstery, a foam-padded seat, interior garnish moldings, red waffle-pattern headliner, color-coordinated rubber floor mat, chrome-plated control knobs, cigarette lighter, armrests on both doors, two sun visors, pine bed, and all the features of the Custom Cab option.

The Cameo Carrier

Among the roughly 1,000 people working within GM Styling (renamed GM Design in 1956 with the opening of the Tech Center) in the early 1950s was Charles M. "Chuck" Jordan. He began his 43-year career at General Motors in 1949, just after graduating from the Massachusetts Institute of Technology. However, his career at General Motors was interrupted in 1952 when he was called to active duty for a one-year stint in the U.S. Air Force. Upon his return to General Motors, Jordan served as assistant chief designer in Luther Stier's Chevrolet truck studio, where he developed the stylish Chevrolet Cameo Carrier and its companion GMC Suburban Carrier, both of which went into production for the 1955 model year.

In the October 1999 issue of *Collectible Automobile* magazine article detailing the 1955–1957 Chevrolet trucks, Jordan said, "I was happy to go into the truck studio . . . Nobody else was interested in going into trucks back then because, after all, trucks normally didn't change very often. And even when they did, they still looked like workhorses. But not to me." Several years earlier in the December 1991 issue of *Collectible Automobile* Jordan explained that inspiration for the Cameo/Suburban Carrier came from his time in the U.S. Air Force: "We weren't very busy, so all the free time I had I worked on the 1955 Chevy truck program . . . I found my own niche . . . when I was in Cape Canaveral in 1952, and I found the art department . . . I used to design various charts on the job, and in-between times I would design trucks . . . But timing in this world is everything. We were doing a new truck [the 1955 Chevy], and I said, 'Let's do it on this truck.' You know, the cab and the front of the sheet metal was on the sketch. Let's just tie the whole thing in." Jordan brought his sketches to General Motors while on leave, and the ideas on those sketches evolved into the production 1955 Cameo Carrier pickup.

Chevrolet's 235-ci inline-6 was the standard engine for the Cameo, but this 1957 model received the extra-cost 265 V-8. It also had a heater.

The earlier designs for the Cameo Carrier integrated the cab and bed as a single unit. However, body flex issues put an end to the idea. Instead, the gap between the cab and bed was largely hidden by a wide, bright metal molding. The most notable special feature of these pickups, though, was its fiberglass bed and tailgate along with concealed tailgate hinges. These fiberglass panels were supplied by Molded Fiberglass Company of Ashtabula, Ohio, the same company that supplied the panels for the Corvette. Flush-fitting side panels brought the exterior width of the box out to that of the cab. Chrome-plated corner bumperettes in back flanked a fold-down panel behind which was the spare tire. This feature was lifted from several of GM's concept cars shown during the 1954 GM Motorama.

Standard equipment for this top-of-the-line pickup included the Thriftmaster 235, 3-speed synchromesh transmission; chrome plating for the grille, bumpers, and headlight bezels; red nylon-faced pattern-cloth and beige vinyl upholstery covering a foam-padded seat; red fabric-covered door panel inserts; red interior garnish moldings; red waffle-pattern headliner; red rubber floor mat; chrome-plated control knobs (instead of black); cigarette lighter; armrests on both doors; sun visors; pine bed; and all the features of the Custom Cab. The exterior color scheme was limited to Bombay Ivory with Chevrolet Commercial Red accents, which included the finish for the inner bed walls and the 15-inch wheels. Incidentally, the NAPCO four-wheel drive chassis was not offered for the Cameo Carrier.

For 1956, the Cameo Carrier could be had in any of eight choices of eye-popping two-tone paint schemes, such as Jet Black with Golden Yellow, Ivory with Ocean Green, and Car dinal Red with Sand Beige. Interior color selections were also expanded.

The 1957 Cameo Carrier had a wide horizontal band with the Chevrolet bowtie emblem located at the leading edge on the pickup box side panels. Furthermore, the model had twin hood ornaments along the forward end of the hood windsplits that mimicked the look of the passenger car line. Sales of the Cameo Carrier and the GMC Suburban Carrier had slumped to the point that these specialty models were terminated prior to the end of the 1958 model year. The price tag was one factor discouraging high-volume sales, the other was the modern-looking pickups offered by the competition. Ford's F-100 received a wraparound windshield for the 1956 model year, Dodge released its D-100 Sweptside featuring a finned pickup box and two-tone paint, and International offered a 50th anniversary special model, the A100 Custom.

Total sales of the 1955–1958 Cameo Carrier pickups amounted to just 10,321 with the figures breaking down to 5,220 for the first year, 1,452 for 1956, 2,244 for 1957, and 1,405 units for the final model year of production. During February 1958, General Motors ceased production of the Cameo and GMC Suburban Carrier pickups.

As stylish as the Cameo was, it did not sell in high numbers because the price tag was about $500, or 30 percent, above that of the standard pickup. However, they were not really meant for high-volume sales, but served their purpose as an image enhancer for General Motors. Chevrolet replaced the Cameo Carrier with the lower-cost Apache Fleetside model featuring steel, flush-fitting box side panels.

The Suburban Carryall

The Suburban Carryall was first introduced to the Chevrolet truck line as a 1935 model. Twenty years later, it was still in production. This 1/2-ton model had little competition in the marketplace. GMC offered its nearly identical model, simply called Suburban; International had the Travelall starting in 1952; and in 1956 Dodge released the Town Wagon. These were the only others of the type to be manufactured. The Suburban Carryall could be equipped with either ambulance-style doors or a pickup-style tailgate, giving it some versatility. It could also be fitted with the NAPCO four-wheel-drive setup at Chevrolet dealerships.

The Advance Design models released in June 1947 were equipped with twin cowl-mounted windshield wipers, concealed door hinges, chrome-plated grille, and two-toned green

The Cameo Carrier was discontinued during the 1958 model year, but carried the same vibrant two-tone color options and level of luxury as past versions. It also benefited from the mechanical upgrades received by the rest of the 1958 pickup line, which included a more powerful inline-6 and the 283 V-8 as an option. (Photo Courtesy GM Media Archive)

Chevrolet unveiled the Suburban Carryall and added it to the truck line as a 1935 model. For 1950, it was offered with a choice of ambulance-style doors, as seen here, or a pickup-style tailgate, giving it some versatility. (Photo Courtesy GM Media Archive)

paint. Second- and third-row passengers had sliding side windows.

In 1954, the last full model year of the Advance Design trucks, the Suburban Carryall came standard with the Thriftmaster 6-cylinder, 3-speed manual transmission, driver's door armrest, two sun visors, and maroon and gray upholstery. It also received the same styling updates as the rest of the 1954 pickup line, including the single-piece curved windshield.

The Task Force Truck line beginning in March 1955 included the all-new Suburban Carryall. It continued as such until the Task Force Truck design was replaced with another all-new truck for 1960. As did the pickups, the Carryall had concealed running boards called "Safety Steps" that were said by Chevrolet ads to be "a big improvement over the old-fashioned exposed running boards still used on some competitive trucks. Located inside the door, they stay clear of snow, mud, and ice, and give you firmer, safer footing."

The drawback of the panel truck design not mentioned in the ads, though, was that the eight-passenger vehicle had only two entry doors, making access to the rear seats a bit awkward for passengers. At least the front seat was split 2/3–1/3 with the latter moving forward to aid in passenger entry and exit. The Suburban Carryall's most serious competitor, the International Travelall, had a second door on the passenger side, making entry and exit much easier for passengers. Even so, Chevrolet did not see a need to add a third door until 1967. However, another plus offered by the Carryall was the fact the middle and rear seat could be removed for additional cargo capacity.

1958–1959: Task Force Truck's Final Years

Chevrolet's 1958 truck line featured an all-new look and the new trend in styling for 1958, quad headlights, was included, too. This was the first full model year in which the quad setup was legal in all states. Low-beam visibility was claimed to be 50 feet farther than that of the previous setup. The new styling, dubbed "Massive Functional Styling" by the marketing people, was simply another facelift of the second series 1955 design with the sheet metal ahead of the cowl accounting for most of the cosmetic changes.

Three new series nameplates were applied to the 1958 models, though they were still marketed as "Task Force Trucks." Light-duty trucks were labeled "Apache" while medium- and heavy-duty models were called "Viking" and "Spartan," respectively.

Mechanical upgrades for this model year included raising the output of the 235 from 140 to 145 hp and finally offering the 283 version of the small-block that had been released for the passenger car line the previous model year. It was rated at 160 hp.

Chevrolet's medium-duty trucks starting in 1958 wore the name "Viking"; the truck shown is a Viking 60 stake truck. This model was offered in several wheelbases. The Viking was powered by Chevrolet's inline-6 connected to a manual transmission and a 2-speed rear end. (Photo Courtesy GM Media Archive)

Fins never made it to Chevrolet's pickups, but they were considered as shown by this mid-1956 photo of a clay mockup named "Daytona." Note that the rear bumper design is similar to that of the Cameo Carrier. (Photo Courtesy GM Media Archive)

Chevrolet's 1958 truck line received new designations, such as "Apache" for light-duty models. The Apache Fleetline (shown) replaced the Cameo Carrier around mid–model year. It was less expensive than the Cameo. The term "Fleetline" referred to the bed panels' flush fit with the cab, a Cameo feature made with steel rather than fiberglass. Bright two-tone paint schemes were offered, and the Fleetside could be equipped with either a standard or "long box" version with respective wheelbases of 114 inches and 123.25 inches. (Photo Courtesy GM Media Archive)

The new 1958 "Task Force" Chevrolet pickups offered buyers more rounded styling (dubbed "Massive Functional Styling"), a new grille, quad headlights, trim, and mechanical changes. Shown is a Model 3100 Stepside 1/2-ton model with a base price of $1,884. (Photo Courtesy GM Media Archive)

Starting with the 1954 model year, Chevrolet pickup trucks became more car-like and continued to offer more comfort as the decade progressed. This photograph shows the interior of a 1958 Apache. Note the V-shaped speedometer housing, a feature similar to earlier Chevrolet passenger cars, as well as the combination vinyl and pattern-cloth upholstery, dual sun visors, and headliner. (Photo Courtesy GM Media Archive)

The Apache Fleetside essentially replaced the canceled Cameo Carrier in February 1958 and featured a cargo box as wide as the cab due to its flush-fitting body side panels. Cargo boxes were of double-wall steel construction with a hardwood floor and steel skid strips. Chevrolet said the use of hardwood allowed for easier replacement of damaged portions of the floor compared to the solid steel floor used in Ford's competing Styleside pickup. Compared to the Chevrolet Stepside pickups, the Fleetside cargo box offered 50 percent more width and more than 9 percent more depth. It measured 50 inches across between the wheelwells and 75 inches wide overall.

A dealer-installed "Cool-Pak" air-conditioning became available at about midyear. It featured an electric blower and evaporator mounted on the floor of the cab along with a belt-driven compressor placed ahead of the radiator. Another option newly added was Posi-Traction rear axle. Later, zinc-coated mufflers were phased-in, nearly doubling the life of the muffler. The change was needed because exhaust from the combustion of ever-higher-octane fuel was causing mufflers to corrode faster than in the past.

The 1959 Chevrolet pickups were little changed from 1958. This 1959 Apache Fleetside wore the livery of Nickey Chevrolet of Chicago, Illinois, one of the most well-known Chevrolet dealerships among enthusiasts today. It began operations in 1925. From 1957 to 1977, Nickey Chevrolet catered to performance enthusiasts by specializing in engine swaps, building cars to customers' specifications, and offering speed parts. (Photo Courtesy GM Media Archive)

For 1959, the Task Force Truck design was in its final year of production. Very little was changed to differentiate the 1959s from the 1958 models. Changes included altered ornamentation and a shuffling of the color schemes offered. The impact of the recession that took a firm hold of the economy during 1958 was addressed with a more economical 235. A change to the camshaft resulted in more low-end torque at the expense of high-end performance. However, the revision provided an improvement in fuel consumption. Another mechanical upgrade was larger rear brakes for the Series 31 and 32 models; the shoes and linings were .25 inch wider, providing an additional 10.5 square inches of lining area.

The 1959 models sold well and kept Chevrolet in the lead in truck sales for the 23rd consecutive year.

El Camino

Chevrolet countered Ford's car-based pickup, the Ranchero released in 1957, two model years later with the El Camino. However, a 1955 version made it as far as the Chevrolet Studio drawing board but was rejected for production. Even earlier than that was a design based on the then-upcoming 1952 Chevrolet. Harley Earl discussed the idea with designers in the Chevrolet truck studio. An article in the February 2004 issue of *Collectible Automobile*, written by Michael Lamm, provides Chuck Jordan's account of the story: "No one came to give us instructions. Everyone pretty much left us alone. But there was one time when Harley Earl did come in. It was on a Saturday . . . He walked into the studio . . . He said, 'Fellas I g-g-got an idea,' the way he stuttered, and he sat down in front of the [full-sized] board . . . and we're all standing behind him, wondering what was happening. He said, 'Now here's what I want to do,' and he described an early version of an El Camino pickup." Earl then spent several hours in the studio giving instructions of the styling, and, said Jordan, "It seemed like a great idea and it excited everyone in [Luther] Stier's studio. But Earl later lost interest in the project." No one ever knew the reasons for that.

The concept of the car-based pickup was not an especially new one in 1950. Since the 1930s, General Motors as well as Ford and some other auto manufacturers produced coupe-pickup models for the Australian market. Known as "Utes," short for utility, in the land down under, these vehicles combined the styling of a coupe body with an integrated pickup truck box.

While Chevrolet could have beaten Ford to the market with its El Camino as early as 1952 or at least in 1955, for whatever reasons it chose not to do so until after Ford began production of its 1957 Ranchero. The earliest practical model year to offer the Chevrolet counterpart was the 1959 model year. Ford dropped the Ranchero based on the full-sized body after the 1959 model year and Chevrolet ceased production of the El Camino altogether at the end of the 1960 model year.

Features

The 1959 El Camino body, which was based on the two-door sedan station wagon, sat on essentially the same "Safety-Girder" X-frame with a coil spring suspension front and rear as used for the passenger car line, though with different spring rates. Ostensibly, any engine offered for the passenger cars could be had for the El Camino including the 250-hp and 290-hp fuel-injected 283s, though none are known to have been built with either engine. However, any of the 348s offered were definitely available for the El Camino. (More information about the 348 V-8 is provided in chapter 6, which details the Chevrolet passenger cars of 1958 and 1959.) The February 1959 issue of *Hot Rod* magazine provided a comparison report of the Ranchero versus the El Camino; the latter was powered by the 315-hp version, the highest-performing 348 available at the time, fed fuel through a trio of 2-barrel carburetors, and coupled to a 4-speed transmission. It could propel the car-based truck from 0 – 60 mph in just 7 seconds. Its predicted top speed was 130 mph and its quarter-mile run was estimated to be about 14 seconds at 100 mph with the right axle ratio. The El Camino did lean plenty in a hard turn because of its

Chevrolet could have beaten Ford to the car-based pickup for 1955 if it had chosen to put this design into production. In fact, the idea was briefly considered for 1952. Instead, Ford released its version, the Ranchero, for 1957 while Chevrolet had to wait until 1959 with its El Camino. (Photo Courtesy GM Media Archive)

Chevrolet countered Ford's car-based pickup, the Ranchero released in 1957, two model years later with the El Camino. Its body was based on the two-door station wagon, though its roof was a shortened version of the so-called "flying wing" roof used for the Sport Sedan four-door hardtop. This restored Aspen Green and Snowcrest White 1959 El Camino is among the impressive automobile collection of the GM Heritage Center.

soft springing, yet it still "managed to negotiate curves as well as the Ranchero," according to the report.

The coil spring suspension of the El Camino was set up to provide a level profile when unloaded. However, a heavy load resulted in a very noticeable rear end squat, or negative rake. Ford's Ranchero, with leaf springs in back, was just the opposite: It sat higher in back when its cargo box was empty, but it sat level with a heavy load.

Six-cylinder and V-8-powered El Caminos were given separate model numbers; those with the 235 were designated as Model 1180, while those with any of the V-8s offered received the designation Model 1280. The base price for the Model 1180 was $2,352 and for the Model 1280, which came with the 195-hp 283, was $2,470. Regardless of the model number, the El Camino came standard with the 3-speed column-shifted synchromesh transmission; Biscayne-Brookwood level trim including leather-grained vinyl with pattern-fabric upholstery in either gray, green, or blue; black vinyl floor covering with colored flecks matching the upholstery; tapered body side molding with a white-painted recess; chromed bumpers, hubcaps, and bright moldings along the roof edge, around the wraparound windshield and rear window, as well as outlining the pickup box. Any single-tone paint color or optional two-tone scheme offered for the passenger car line was available for the El Camino. With the latter the roof, roof pillars, window frames, and the area above the box outline molding were painted the contrasting color.

The roof of the El Camino was essentially a shortened version of the so-called "flying wing" roof used for the Sport Sedan, a four-door hardtop that shared its wraparound rear window with the El Camino. Total glass area was immense at 4,121 square inches and was said to provide "control-tower visibility" in an introductory GM press release.

A corrugated steel floor insert was used rather than wood for the El Camino. It was bolted over the floorpan used for the Brookwood two-door station wagon; even the footwells of the Brookwood floor were still in place. In all, nearly 33 cubic feet of cargo space was provided with the El Camino's box. To take full advantage of the cargo space, the spare tire was stowed in the empty space behind the passenger's side of the bench seat.

The tailgate opened level with the box floor, extending the cargo box's carrying capability. When open it allowed for up to 91 inches of load length. The license plate mount located on the tailgate was hinged to allow it to pivot down when the tailgate was open, so the license plate showed when the gate was down.

Sales

The El Camino created some excitement when it debuted. According to an article in the February 2003 issue of *Collectible Automobile*, GM Design employee Arthur Jones said the 1959 El Camino was "so admired by designers that some of them ordered one in lieu of the Corvette they typically drove." The story went on to note the model was popular with hot rodders and customizers, especially in California.

Sales of the new El Camino were reasonably good with 22,246 being sold. This figure exceeded that of the first-year Ranchero by a little more than 500 units. However, sales took a major tumble, down about a third, the following year. Ford's Falcon-based Ranchero brought slightly more than 21,000 sales, a sales level it maintained for the next couple of years. Chevrolet later gave its El Camino a conceptual rethink leading to the Chevelle-based El Camino four years later.

CHAPTER

6

THE CURTAIN CLOSES ON A PROLIFIC DECADE

1958–1959

For nearly 30 years, Harley Earl and his staff helped lead Chevrolet to first place in sales with innovative styling. The engineering and marketing departments played major roles, too. During the 1950s, styling was the number one factor (other than cost of course) in the purchase of a car. Considerations that followed were the V-8 engine and the automatic transmission. Chevrolet offered a superior combination of styling and mechanical systems at affordable prices in the eyes of buyers, making the division virtually impossible to beat.

The 1958 Impala convertible was a popular model, accounting for 55,989 sales. This example was painted Glen Green, one of 15 single-tone colors offered that model year. (Photo Courtesy GM Media Archive)

This 1958 Chevrolet and another were fitted with an experimental self-driving system developed by RCA (Radio Corporation of America). Tests were carried out on a specially prepared new intersection on the outskirts of Lincoln, Nebraska. The system comprised radio receivers and audible and visual warning devices that could operate the steering mechanism, accelerator, and brakes. Special "detector" circuits were buried into the road by the Nebraska Department of Roads. A series of lights along the edge of the road provided the data needed to determine the location and speed of the vehicles and transmitted radio impulses to guide the cars. The system actually worked well. (Photo Courtesy GM Media Archive)

However, by the end of Harley Earl's career many of his stylists thought he had lost his way. The only engineer to work at GM Design under Harley Earl, Ken Pickering, said, "as powerful as Earl was during most of his career, his magic touch failed him near the end of his time as vice president. Younger designers were changing the rules and beating Earl at his own game. In the past, when his designs were setting the trend and others were starting to follow, Earl would always say, 'It's time to cross 'em up.'" Earl's strategy worked well until near the end of his career at General Motors. Unfortunately, not all the 1958 models were well-received by the public and the stylists working on the earliest designs for the 1959 models (based upon the 1958s) firmly believed the public would find the styling highly objectionable.

While not all the divisions of General Motors during the 1958 model year fared well, the Chevrolet lineup was well-accepted by the public. It included a new model within the Bel Air line: the upscale Impala, which was

A 1958 Chevrolet Impala convertible was fitted with a "Unicontrol" system for driver control of steering, acceleration, and braking. It was operated with a swivel stick. A forward push or a backward push caused the car to accelerate or brake, respectively. A relatively small rotation of the handle in either direction engaged reverse and a much larger rotation in either direction engaged park. Pushing it left or right steered the car. Three analog computers engaged servos to control the movements of the swivel stick, and it compensated for too much driver input, such as a sudden turn at high speed. The system was also tested on the experimental 1958 GM Firebird III turbine car. Note this car was fitted with bucket-style front seats. (Photo Courtesy Media Archive)

offered in two-door hardtop and convertible body styles only. Its namesake, the medium-sized antelope, was chosen to convey the image of grace and speed. Also new for the model year were the 348 big-block V-8, a new "Safety-Girder" X-frame chassis with four coil springs, and the extra-cost "Level-Air" air suspension. Wheelbase grew from 115 inches to 117.5. Interiors for all models were upgraded with more sophisticated patterns, even for the low-cost Delray and Yeoman station wagon.

The introduction to the *1958 Chevrolet Engineering Features* guidebook written by Chief Engineer Harry Barr began, "The 1958 passenger car represents the most extensive engineering development program in Chevrolet's history. A full-coil suspension, an optional Level-Air ride, the new Turbo-Thrust V-8, and an advanced concept in automotive styling testify to the scope of product progress." The work done on the 1958 models was said to exceed even that performed for 1955!

Chevrolet Engineering also spent time and money conducting advanced research on self-driving cars (thus proving once and for all time there is nothing new under the sun) and a system dubbed "Unicontrol," which made use of a swivel stick to control the automobile. Though these systems worked, the former is only just now being seriously considered.

While some mechanical systems were carried forward for 1959, the body design was completely new, owing to a directive from top management for more extensive use of body sharing among the divisions. Unlike the 1958 Chevrolets, the styling was somewhat controversial. Indeed, Ford closed the sales gap with its longtime rival by taking some sales away from Chevrolet, but in the end the company fell a little short of surpassing Chevrolet in model-year sales.

The 185-hp 283 Turbo-Fire V-8 was an option for the 1958 Chevrolet passenger cars. A single exhaust was standard with this engine, though dual exhaust was offered at extra-cost. This one powers a 1958 Impala Sport Coupe. Note this car also has power steering; the power steering pump reservoir bolted to the back end of the generator.

For 1958, the 3-speed synchromesh transmission gained various engineering improvements to optimize performance and increase durability. Overdrive was an option and was engaged with this control located under the dash.

Powertrain Choices

Chevrolet's passenger car line could be had with a vast array of engine options, though several were carried over from 1957 with mild modifications. In addition to these there was the new 348 available in three states of tune. The carried-over engines included the inline 235-ci 6-cylinder with a quarter-point compression boost to 8.25:1, the Turbo-Fire 283 2-barrel, and the Super Turbo-Fire 283 4-barrel. Both the 235 and 283 4-barrel received an output boost, with the 6-cylinder going from 140 hp at 4,200 rpm to 145 hp while the Super Turbo-Fire rose from 220 hp at 4,800 rpm to 230 hp at the same revs. Both the 2- and 4-barrel versions of the 283 came standard with a single exhaust, though a dual system could be had at extra-cost. Also, the 250-hp Ram Jet fuel-injected 283 was retained, but with upgrades to increase reliability. Its lofty price tag and the availability of powerful 348s at a much lower cost resulted in very few 1958 passenger cars being ordered with the Ram Jet setup. Two of the three 348s, the 250-hp "Turbo-Thrust" with a 4-barrel carburetor and the 280-hp "Super Turbo-Thrust" with a trio of 2-barrel carburetors were offered at the start of the model year. These were followed later in the model year by another tri-carb type rated at 315 hp. When the optional V-8 was chosen, a V-shaped emblem was placed on the hood and decklid signifying its presence.

Transmission choices were similar to those offered for 1957. The Super Turbo-Fire, Ram Jet, and Turbo-Thrust engines could be had with a close-ratio 3-speed while the Super Turbo-Thrust came with a close-ratio 3-speed as standard equipment. When either Turbo-Thrust engine was coupled with the 3-speed transmission, it had a coil spring clutch similar to the one used on the Corvette, but with a 10.5-inch drive

This 1958 Chevrolet Delray must have been ordered new by a hotrodder. It is equipped with the 315-hp Special Super Turbo-Thrust 348 coupled to a 4-speed transmission. The 4-speed for the big Chevrolets arrived at about the middle of the model year as option code RPO 685. The economy model Utility Sedan had fixed quarter windows, no passenger-side sun visor, and no armrests. (Photo Courtesy Phil Aubrey)

Option code RPO 685 was evidently not widely advertised as it is almost unknown today. When the option was ordered for this 1958 Delray the owner received a 4-speed in place of the much more common 3-speed coupled to the car's 315-hp 348-ci V-8. Note the radio delete and the original vinyl-coated floor mat, something that has rarely survived over the decades. (Photo Courtesy Phil Aubrey)

plate rather than the 10-inch plate. The synchromesh transmission was improved for better cooling and smoother engagement via the use of only 12 fingers in the diaphragm spring rather than 18. This diaphragm spring also had a decrease in crown. Conforming to the decreased travel of the pressure plate, a thinner friction surface was used on the driven plate to prevent dragging. The greater mechanical advantage in the linkage achieved through decreased release travel brought the further advantage of reduced clutch pedal effort.

The Powerglide could also be coupled to the Turbo-Thrust engine while the Turboglide was offered as an option for all V-8s, with the supposed exceptions of the fuel-injected engine and the 315-hp 348. However, the November 1957 issue of

A Posi-Traction rear axle was again an option for the Chevrolet passenger cars. This 1958 Impala convertible is equipped with the feature and has the fact noted on the glove box door. Posi-Traction axles had a "P" cast adjacent to the casting number on the left side of the carrier housing. Later in the model year, a circular caution tag was added to the filler plug reading, "Use Limited Slip Differential Lubrication Only" to help prevent the wrong lubricant from being used during servicing operations. The electric clock on the far right side of the dash was standard equipment for the Impala and all other members of the Bel Air line.

Chevrolet Service News stated the Turboglide transmission was available with the fuel-injected engine.

Research by Vintage Chevrolet Club of America member Phil Aubrey revealed that a 4-speed for the big Chevrolets arrived at about the middle of the model year. Those equipped with the 4-speed were first built on the assembly line with the 3-speed unit then moved to another location where the 4-speed conversion was made. The 3-speed components within the steering column were left in place, but they were secured to prevent the parts from rattling. Somehow the 4-speed, listed as option code RPO 685, did not get much publicity; therefore, it was seldom ordered. Its availability was likely for the purpose of making it legal under NASCAR rules; yet it was not publicized to give the appearance of adhering to the AMA agreement banning factory support for racing activities. Most racers who competed with a Chevrolet continued driving their 1957 models, which were lighter than the 1958s.

The performance enthusiast could still obtain the optional "Posi-Traction" limited-slip rear axle. Inclusion of this axle was noted with an emblem mounted on the glove box door.

The Unconventional 348

Preliminary design work on the 348 began in 1955. Chevrolet's engineers saw a need for engines of increased displacement to provide optimum low-speed and midrange vehicle performance to go with the increasing demand for automatic transmissions. A larger engine with good low-speed torque was judged to make an exceptionally good pairing with the Turboglide transmission under development at the time. In 1956, demand for Chevrolet's small-block V-8 was outpacing demand for its inline 6-cylinder by an even greater margin than in 1955. Management forecast a need for more lines for V-8 engine production by the 1958 model year. The cost of expansion was not increased greatly by creating a new engine to build on the new lines. Furthermore, the same basic engine could be used for the higher gross-vehicle-weight truck models Chevrolet was planning to build. Management considered these facts and authorized the development of the proposed new V-8.

The 348 was, indeed, a virtually all-new engine with a very limited number of interchangeable parts between it and the 283 small-block. This large bore, short stroke big-block design, which produced good low-end torque, was initially designed for Chevrolet's medium- and heavy-duty trucks. The layout of the exhaust and intake valves of this big-block formed the shape of the letter W; hence, it was labeled the "W Series." The 348 continued to be used in passenger cars through 1961 and in trucks through 1965. The W-series engine was modified for 1961 to become the legendary 409 and yet again for 1963 to become the "Z11" 427 racing engine.

Two of the 348s, offered from the start of the 1958 model year, were officially rated at 250 hp at 4,400 rpm and 280 hp at 4,800 rpm. Their respective torque outputs were listed as 355 ft-lbs at 2,800 rpm and 355 ft-lbs at 3,200 rpm. As previously noted, the 280-hp engine had a 3x2-barrel carburetor setup. Both engines had a compression ratio of 9.5:1 and a dual exhaust system. A full-flow oil filter was optional and was upgraded with a 10-pound bypass spring, replacing the previous 5-pound type. The 315-hp Special Super Turbo-Thrust released about the last quarter of the model year reached its peak horsepower at 5,600 rpm; its torque output was listed as 353 ft-lbs at 3,600 rpm. Its additional performance came from the Duntov cam, 11.0:1 compression ratio, solid lifters, and its trio of Rochester 2-barrel carburetors. A "Police Special" had virtually identical performance ratings; its torque was rated marginally higher at 356 ft-lbs at 3,600 rpm.

According to the *1958 Chevrolet Engineering Features* manual, the 348 was "designed primarily around a new combustion chamber. Improved induction and exhaust systems, together with the combustion chambers, combine to provide high volumetric efficiency and top performance throughout the entire operating range." Its combustion chamber differed from others of the era. As explained in the engineering features book, "The main volume of the combustion chamber, located within the cylinder block, is bounded by the walls of the cylinder bore, the flat bottom face of the cylinder head, and one-half the top of the piston which is peaked. In the conventional cylinder block, the top faces are perpendicular to the cylinders, but in the new block, the top faces are inclined 16 degrees from this typical position. As a result, the elliptical-shaped opening of the top of each bore allows the use of larger valves." The valve ports were large and, with the relatively unshrouded position of the valves in the flat face of the head, allowed good flow of gases through both intake and exhaust valves. Spark plugs were positioned near the center of the combustion chamber.

Though the 348 provided excellent performance for the era, it was almost as optimized as it could be when it was engineered. It did not lend itself to continuous modifications like the small-block offered. The W-series engine was, therefore, comparatively short-lived.

315 hp: Exhilarating, Thrilling, and Amazing

With the 1959 model year already well under way, the January 1959 issue of *Sports Cars Illustrated* featured an unusually late report on a 1958 Delray two-door sedan equipped with the 315-hp engine. The motivation for this report arose from a subscriber's response to a test report on a Ferrari Superfast published in an earlier issue. Basically, his response amounted to, "Look what I got for a lot less expense." The editors said they were "intrigued" and, in an unusual move, tested

Chevrolet released the 348 big-block for the 1958 model year. In its highest-output form it offered 315 hp at 5,600 rpm. Dubbed the "Super Turbo-Thrust," this version of the 348 had a trio of 2-barrel carburetors and a compression ratio of 11.0:1 that demanded the use of premium fuel. (Photos Courtesy Phil Aubrey)

the subscriber's car. To say the test driver of the Delray was impressed would be an understatement. He wrote, "For sheer straightaway performance the car is exhilarating, thrilling, and amazing." The writer went on to elaborate, "It's a most unprecedented feeling to be in a big, soft-sprung Detroiter that rushes out to 100 mph like Col. Stapp's rocket sled." (This was a reference to Colonel John Stapp, a U.S. Air Force flight surgeon who investigated the effects of acceleration forces on the human body via a series of acceleration tests performed with a rocket-powered sled at Holloman Air Force Base in which up to 40 times the force of gravity was briefly experienced.) When the writer called Frank Milne, a racing expert of the era working with Harry Mann Chevrolet in Los Angeles, California, a dealership specializing in Corvettes, to tell him of the just 7.2 seconds needed to go from 0–60, Milne was a bit stunned. Milne then recalled another owner of a 315-hp Delray telling him of "waxing stock Corvettes consistently at the drag strips and turning elapsed times in the high 14s." He said he didn't believe him at the time, but reconsidered, saying, "Now I guess I'd better."

Cornering was said to be "incomparably better than the '57 Chev while still retaining a very buoyant ride." However, this was balanced by the comment, "This is a stock Chev suspension and, as good as it is, it does not represent Detroit's best. Both front and rear wheels hop unpleasantly when bumps are encountered on a curve." The writer also noted that "its stock Chev brakes are miserable." A switch to 15-inch wheels and Chevrolet racing drums with wider Pontiac or Olds brake shoes in front was strongly recommended.

Turboglide Modifications

The Turboglide was modified for 1958 to increase its torque capacity and to meet the requirements of the new chassis. Among the changes was a new multiple-disc neutral clutch, a redesign of all other clutches, revised vacuum modulation, and a new transmission housing extension and output shaft.

The neutral clutch, which was a cone design in its original form, now had a six-plate active-face clutch. (A multi-plate clutch has a greater capacity to transmit power because of the greater frictional area offered by multiple plates.) All the other clutches were very similar to the earlier types, but were changed to increase torque capacity. The grade retarder's multiple-disc clutch increased from four to six active faces and total area increased by 50 percent. Forward and reverse cone clutch angles were reduced by 4 degrees to 13, which increased the effective application force from a given piston force. The nonmetallic facings were removed from the steel cones, so the cones would bear directly on the aluminum rings. These rings were knurled to maximize their oil shearing and holding capability as well as durability. Revisions to the vacuum modulator assembly kept transmission main line oil pressure more proportionate with the engine's output. The new chassis design resulted in the need to shorten the transmission housing and output shaft.

The Safety-Girder X-Frame

Chevrolet's sales literature stated its new 1958 models were "lower and longer, wider and stronger." Its claim was based

This photograph provides a comparison between Chevrolet's previous frame and its new 1958 X-frame. Later, some would argue the X-frame design was not safe even though the body was designed to be strong enough to account for the less rigid frame. The cowl was double-walled, the underbody crossmembers with frame mounts were larger and more rigid, and the rocker panels were larger and extended up the toe pan to the dash panel. (Photo Courtesy GM Media Archive)

upon the new "Safety-Girder" X-frame. Chevrolet's X-frame was similar to the one Cadillac began using for 1957. While an X-design had been used many times in the past, those earlier types were simply an X-member inside a ladder-type frame. Such an arrangement was often used to strengthen a frame for a convertible. According to the *1958 Chevrolet Engineering Features* manual, "The structural efficiency and strength of the body and chassis supplement each other to create an effective integrated combination. The result is a union that dramatically reduces the height of the new models and produces the rigidity essential to a quality automobile." In conjunction with a new two-piece driveshaft, it did allow for the lowering of the floor wells, which in turn made possible a lower overall height of the body without any sacrifice in headroom or impeding easy entrance and exit for rear-seat occupants. According to Chevrolet's sales literature, the X-frame had 30 percent more torsional rigidity than older designs. The frame for the convertible was strengthened with steel plates welded to the top and bottom side members and center beam of the frame.

The two-piece driveshaft contained a third universal joint and bearing in the midsection of the assembly. It permitted the shaft to dip in the middle and assume an angle permitting space for lowering the car's underbody tunnel. Of course, it also resulted in increased maintenance since this bearing and U-joint eventually required replacement.

Despite what was believed at the time, the new X-frame with three crossmembers and a center tube may not have been one of Chevrolet's best design choices, but it continued to be used through 1964. To make up for the lack of strengthening side rails, the cowl, underbody, and rocker panels were made stronger. The cowl was double-walled, the underbody crossmembers with frame mounts were larger and more rigid, and the rocker panels were larger and extended up from the toe pan to the dash panel. Even with the stronger body components, the X-frame design began to be perceived as weak; my father witnessed firsthand the aftermath of a collision at a downtown Little Rock, Arkansas, intersection circa 1960 in which a 1958 Chevrolet had been cut in two! Indeed, other accidents suggested an inherent weakness in the design leading to lawsuits. Furthermore, the rocker panels were prone to collecting debris and moisture. As a result, over a relatively brief time they were vulnerable to serious corrosion that reduced their strength and negated engineers' attempts to provide a strong body-frame assembly. Even the frame itself was prone to corrosion.

The infamous book by safety advocate Ralph Nader, *Unsafe at Any Speed*, first published in 1965, noted the Chevrolet X-frame: "In the fall of 1959, a photograph of a Chevrolet Impala that was broken in half after striking a tree broadside was widely circulated in the newspapers throughout the country. The frame had severed at the intersection of the X. The report of the General Motors investigators who rushed to the scene attributed the severance of the frame to the semi-airborne position of the car as it struck the tree. This had apparently allowed the engine mass to act as the head of a sledgehammer. At the General Motors engineering center in Michigan the conclusion was that 'automobiles are not designed to withstand such tremendous lateral forces' . . . General Motors spokesmen continued to defend the cruciform type frame as offering substantial resistance to side impacts because of the rocker panel and floor pan underbracing members." (Incidentally, despite the controversy at the time, Buick chose the cruciform frame for its new Riviera, which debuted for the 1963 model year.) Ford Motor Company took advantage of the matter in the early 1960s by advertising its perimeter frame as "providing all around protection" through "a rugged ring of steel."

New Suspension

The new four-link, coil spring suspension was designed to improve ride quality and vertical control in starting and stopping. To achieve this goal, specific assignments were given to the new components, and, because of this, the new components were less compromised and more effective.

The term, "four-link," described the means in which the axle was linked to the frame at four points. Lower control arms were attached to the frame brackets at their forward

This 1958 Chevrolet body was placed on hydraulic jacks designed to simulate driving conditions. The test setup, known as the Ride Simulator, was in the 638,000 square foot Chevrolet Engineering Center. (Photo Courtesy GM Media Archive)

ends and to the axle housing brackets at their opposite ends while the upper control arms were also anchored at their forward ends to frame brackets. However, the upper control arms connected to the axle housing at a single point on the axle housing banjo. All these mounting points pivoted through compressed rubber and, therefore, did not require lubrication.

Nearly all driving and braking forces to the rear axle were absorbed by the control arms, leaving the coil springs to simply perform the singular function of ride cushioning. Shock absorber action also benefited from the four-link design. In the past, the shock absorber upper ends were attached to the chassis underbody, resulting in erratic damping characteristics when under mild suspension movements. This method of anchoring the upper part of the shocks was replaced with short cantilever brackets welded to the frame side members for more rigid mounting points.

The four-link coil spring suspension was better than the former leaf spring arrangement at restraining the natural tendency of the rear axle to rotate during acceleration. As explained in the *1958 Chevrolet Engineering Features* guide, "During acceleration, the shift of the car weight toward the rear tends to compress the rear springs. Control arm geometry is designed, however, so that in order for the springs to compress, the control arms must force the axle housing to rotate in a counterclockwise direction. Thus, a torque reaction is created to oppose the clockwise engine torque reaction on the housing . . . The result is that driving torque is utilized to produce a slight lift, rather than the conventional squat of the rear end of the car during acceleration." As for braking action, "forces counteract each other in the same way due to a similar but opposite relationship so that the rear end rise is minimized on rapid deceleration."

The upper control arms maintained lateral stability. Lateral thrust placed one upper control arm in tension while the opposite one was in compression. These forces were cushioned by the rubber pivot bushings. The central pivot on the axle housing for the upper control arms contributed to balanced handling.

Level-Air Suspension

With coil springs all around, improved shocks, and a four-link-type rear suspension with short and long arms, the ride was softer than in the past. An attempt to make the ride even smoother was made with the optional air suspension setup, marketed as Level-Air, which added $124 to the base price. Level-Air was available only with a V-8, with the exception of the fuel-injected engine in which space limitations under the hood made the setup impractical to install. It was similar to the version used on the Eldorado Brougham. When equipped with the option, "Level Air" script appeared on the decklid underneath the V-shaped emblem used to identify V-8-equipped models.

Level-Air (as was the Cadillac system) was derived from the suspension used by GMC Coach. Much of the equipment for it was underneath the hood and consisted of an air compressor, high-pressure reservoir, and an outside air intake with an anti-icing alcohol bottle along with low- and high-pressure lines. The leveling valves were inside the air bellows (one on each side in front) and one was in back mounted in the left rear air spring though operating both sides. All four of the standard coil springs were replaced with air bellows.

Advantages offered by the air bellow were a variable deflection rate and oscillation dampening characteristics. The air bellows would react like soft springs to light impact forces and like increasingly firm springs to stronger impact forces. Their self-dampening properties kept the

An X-frame chassis was developed for the 1958 Chevrolet passenger cars. It was used through 1964. This chassis is fitted with the 348 4-barrel Turoglide and the "Level-Air" air suspension. (Photo Courtesy GM Media Archive)

This 1958 Bel Air Sport Sedan is still equipped with the rare Level-Air option. Note the Level-Air script on the car's decklid. Most cars fitted with the troublesome setup were converted to conventional coil springs. (Photo Courtesy Collectible Automobile)

A 283 4-barrel powers this 1958 Bel Air Sport Sedan with the Level-Air option. Note the compression for the air suspension system. Level-Air was available on all V-8-powered passenger cars with the exception of the fuel-injected V-8. (Photo Courtesy Collectible Automobile)

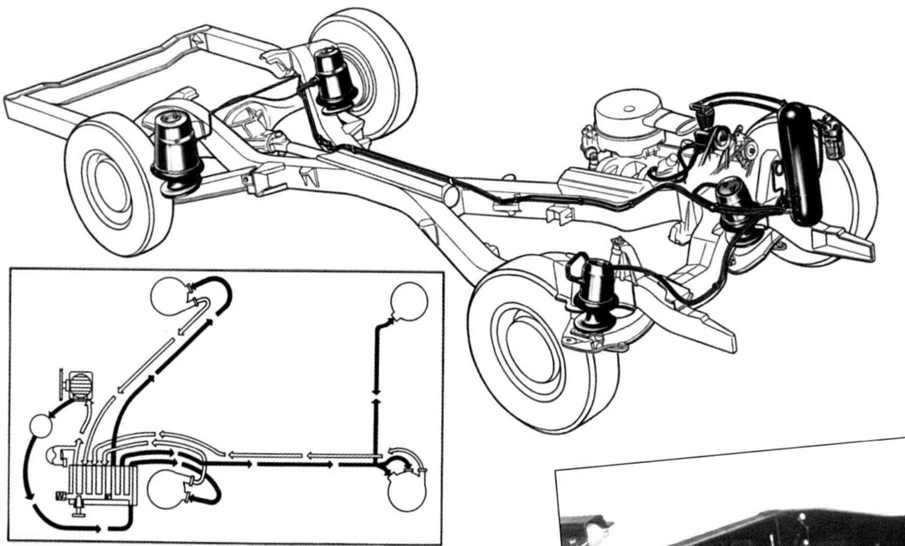

This diagram shows the major components of the Level-Air system. The system was comprised of an air compressor, high-pressure reservoir, and an outside air intake with an anti-icing alcohol bottle along with low- and high-pressure lines. All four of the standard coil springs were replaced with air bellows. (Photo Courtesy GM Media Archive)

Rubber air bellows as part of the "Level-Air" air suspension system replaced all four of the conventional coil springs. Despite improvements to various components throughout 1958 and 1959, it remained unreliable. (Photo Courtesy GM Media Archive)

wheels in constant contact with the pavement, reducing the workload on the shock absorbers. The system was designed to maintain a constant level regardless of whether the car was fully loaded or occupied only by the driver.

This self-leveling property resulted in the optimum suspension travel and consistent handling qualities. That was how Level-Air was supposed to work and it did work well when it was working. The January 1958 issue of *Motor Life* provided readers with a road test of a 1958 Impala equipped with the optional air suspension and judged it to provide an excellent ride. Among their comments was, "Extensive cornering checks brought out the fact that the Impala has excellent roadability for such a soft-riding automobile. It might be a shade behind steel sprung 1958 Chevrolets, in this respect, but the slight loss in handling is compensated by improved ride . . . The most impressive single advantage of air suspension is that rebounding after a bump is completely eliminated."

Attempts to improve the system were made during the model year. Unfortunately, problems with leaks in the valves were not fully resolved. Most of the few cars equipped with the setup were converted to standard coil springs. Chevrolet did not quit trying to make it work, though. Refinements were made during the model year and the option returned for the 1959 model year.

Additional Changes for 1958

The Frigidaire air-conditioning system received significant revisions for 1958. One of them was the inclusion of a center outlet just underneath the dash in addition to the two side outlets. Another change was in the refrigeration unit. The thermostatically operated clutch for starting and stopping the refrigeration compressor was replaced with a hot gas valve for temperature regulation. With this setup, the compressor ran continuously when the air conditioner was in use. This method was said to permit closer regulation of the temperature with less fluctuation of temperature inside the car. It also resulted in less wear on the electromagnetic compressor clutch and the compressor itself since there was no stopping and restarting of the compressor when it was operating. The compressor had a larger capacity at 12.2 cubic inches whereas the previous one had a 9.28 cubic inch capacity. Furthermore, the condenser was larger to reduce compressor head and line pressures.

A new steering mechanism replaced the previous symmetrical, relay linkage of the past. The steering gear and linkage were placed ahead of the centerline of the front wheels and a new two-piece steering shaft was employed. This arrangement was said to provide faster, more responsive action with no increase in steering effort and to better isolate road shocks and vibrations from the driver's hands. The steering ratio was reduced from 25.7:1 to 23.0:1 due to changes in the pitman arm and the steering arm lengths. Low-friction nylon bushings on the idler arm kept steering effort from being noticeably effected by the new steering design. Chevrolet passenger cars equipped with a V-8 received a front sway bar.

In addition, durability of the front suspension was increased through the use of higher-capacity wheel bearings, improved spherical ball joints, and softer ride rates.

A power brake unit manufactured by Moraine Products Division was intermixed with the previously used Treadle-Vac unit in the power brake option.

A new radiator core, smaller in size, provided better cooling of the engine. Previously, a ribbon-cellular type was used. It was replaced with a tube-on-center core with water passages of brass tubing. Running transversely to these tubes were air passageways formed by a corrugated copper fin soldered to the water tubes. The stronger structure of the core allowed for the increase from a 7-pound pressure cap to a 13-pound type. A ring-shaped shroud was used with V-8 engines to direct cooling air to the fan.

Because of the increased electrical loads imposed by the quad headlight setup, additional taillights, and a larger heater blower motor, the standard passenger car generator capacity was increased from 25 ampere to 30. When air-conditioning and power steering options were installed, a 35-ampere generator was used. The latter generator could also be had as a separate option.

A new voltage and current regulator with better weatherproofing and better internal construction was another improvement for 1958. Its revised internal design eliminated relay "chatter" when the generator went in and out of engagement.

Revised Model Lineup

Chevrolet's 1958 passenger car line consisted of the Bel Air, Biscayne, and Delray. The new Impala was not a separate series, but rather an upscale part of the Bel Air series; thus, technically it was a Bel Air Impala. "Biscayne" was a new model name and it replaced the previous Two-Ten series. The name "Delray" was not a new one, having formerly been a part of the Two-Ten lineup, but it was now consigned to the low end of the model hierarchy.

The station wagon lineup, which was considered a separate series by Chevrolet, paralleled the rest of the passenger car line with the Nomad positioned at the top of the hierarchy, the Brookwood in the middle, and the Yeoman at the bottom. Each shared the same trim levels with their respective counterparts (i.e., the Nomad and Bel Air shared the same trim level).

The Bel Air, Biscayne, and Delray lines were given series designations 1800, 1600, and 1200 when equipped with one of the V-8s, or designated 1700, 1500, and 1100 when powered by the inline 6-cylinder.

Exterior Styling: New and Inspired

Other than its wraparound glass and front bumper incorporating the grille surround, the sculptured styling of the 1958 Chevrolet passenger cars appeared nothing like Chevrolets of the past. Design work for the 1958 Chevrolets began in June

Placing exhaust ports in the lower rear quarter panel was an early idea presented on this full-scale clay model of a proposed design for a 1958 Bel Air. (Photo Courtesy GM Media Archive)

This looping quarter panel molding was considered for the 1958 Chevrolet. Note the simulated vents in the leading edge of the molding. It would have offered a division line for two-tone paint as shown. (Photo Courtesy GM Media Archive)

The one-off 1958 Impala convertible, the "Martinique," featured fitted luggage and a pair of storage pockets sewn into the upholstered inner decklid. Neither of these innovative features was adopted for production. (Photo Courtesy GM Media Archive)

The 1958 Bel Air and Delray models had paired taillamps while the Impala had a trio of lights on each side with a central backup light as standard. If backup lights were ordered for a Bel Air or Delray, they took the place of the inboard taillights.

1955 with a meeting between Clare MacKichan of the Chevrolet Studio and Paul Gillan of the Pontiac Studio (since Pontiac shared the body with Chevrolet) along with the GM body design committee.

Parking lamp shape was inspired by the engine nacelles of two of the U.S. Air Force's bombers, the B-47 and the long-range B-52, which had just entered service. Finlike ornaments on the top of each front fender were standard for all Bel Air and Nomad models and optional for others. All members of the Bel Air series had a 1954 Fiat V-8 coupe–inspired body-side spear and all series had gullwing fenders. Common to all series of Chevrolet passenger cars were quad headlights, an anodized aluminum grille, hidden fuel filler, and a central raised crown over the bumpers. The crown served not only to protect the front bumper, but also the grille. Inside the crown was horizontally ribbed sheet metal painted silver. A very similar arrangement was applied to the rear bumper. Bel Airs and

The Nomad name was used for the top-of-the-line Chevrolet six-passenger station wagon starting with the 1958 model year. It was now a four-door sedan rather than a two-door as had been the case from 1955 to1957. Sales were much higher for the four-door. Station wagon models had a wider tail and lift gate for an increased loading area. (Photo Courtesy Brian Earwest)

For 1958, Chevrolet introduced its most luxurious model to date in the Bel Air series dubbed "Impala." It was offered in just two body styles, a two-door hardtop and a convertible. This convertible is powered by the 315-hp 348 Special Super Turbo-Thrust V-8 bolted to a close-ratio 3-speed transmission driving a Posi-Traction axle. It is also heavily accessorized with a spotlight, twin rear-mounted antennas, fender skirts, spinner wheel covers, rocker panel molding, and more.

The fuel filler was not hidden in the driver's side taillight this time but was instead virtually hidden with this filler door located underneath the trunk lid toward the driver's side of the car. Shown is an Impala as indicated by the lighting arrangement that included standard backup lights. (Photo Courtesy GM Media Archive)

The frontal design of the 1958 Chevrolet passenger cars featured quad headlights, fender-top ornaments, and an anodized aluminum grille. The parking lamp shape was inspired by the engine nacelles of two of the U.S. Air Force's bombers, the B-47 and the B-52, which had recently entered service. A central raised crown was placed over the bumper. Inside the crown was a horizontally ribbed sheet metal painted silver.

Biscaynes had twin pod, conical taillights, though the inner taillights could be replaced with optional backup lights.

Other exterior trim details included four simulated vents on the front fenders as well as the windsplit on the lower quarter panels of all Bel Air models and the Nomad. All sedan models, except station wagons, had "thin pillar styling" which combined "the beauty of sport models with the structural safety of the regular sedan." For the Bel Air and Biscayne series, window frames were trimmed in bright metal while those of the Delray had painted frames. With the windows raised, these cars had the appearance of a hardtop. Station wagons had a conventional pillar design.

Interior Features

As in the past, each series was defined by its list of standard features, including the amount of bright work, grade of interior, and the body styles offered within each series. Even though the Impala was listed as a member of the Bel Air series, it received its own unique interior, detailed later in this chapter. As for the Bel Air and Nomad station wagon, interiors were offered in six color combinations with the seats covered in a pattern-cloth diamond design and leather-grain vinyl. A ribbed, oblong

Styling for the 1958 Bel Air two-door hardtop was very much like that of the Impala, though sheet metal aft of the cowl was unique to the latter. This Bel Air is painted Anniversary Gold and Arctic White. The year was celebrated as the 50th anniversary of the founding of General Motors, which transpired on September 16, 1958.

Instrument panels were completely redesigned for 1958. Major instruments were housed in separate housings and a textured metal insert surrounded the instrumentation on all models. The new foot-operated parking brake was suspended at the left side cowl kick panel. Its release handle, placed within easy reach of the driver, was activated with a light upward push. This 1958 Bel Air Sport Coupe is equipped with a 283 and 3-speed with overdrive as well as the Wonderbar radio. Bel Air series cars had a full horn ring while the Delray had a horn button. The interior on this car is original.

The interior of the Bel Air was not as lavish as that of the Impala, but it certainly was not second rate. It was two-toned with vinyl and pattern-cloth for the seats and full carpeting. (Photo Courtesy Collectible Automobile)

design covered a large area of the backrest. This pattern was repeated on the seat side facings. Door panels were of three colors of leather-grain vinyl with bright metal inserts dividing the colors. Deep-pile carpeting covered the floor front and rear. The steering wheel had a bright metal horn ring integral with the wide bar covering the center portion of the wheel spokes.

While the interior appointments for the Biscayne were not quite as lavish as those of the Bel Air, they would just about have been appropriate for earlier renditions of the Bel Air. The interior of the Biscayne and Brookwood station wagon included basket weave–pattern cloth covering much of the lower seat cushions and the lower seat backrest. Leather-grain vinyl covered the sides, forward edge of the seat cushions, and the lower area as well as the upper portion of the

The Yeoman station wagon was a member of the Delray series and was offered in both two- and four-door body styles. This wagon was available for fleet orders, such as for law enforcement agencies. (Photo Courtesy GM Media Archive)

backrest along with two bolster inserts sewn into a modified V-design. Two-tone vinyl-covered door panels with simulated stitching were molded with an attractive rocket-fin pattern. The steering wheel had less bright metal trim than that of the Bel Air and Nomad. Vinyl-coated rubber mats covered the floor front and rear.

The Delray and Yeoman station wagon series' upholstery was a patterned cloth with a rectangular design covering the seat cushions and lower portion of the seat backrest. The upper portions of the backrests were covered in a contrasting leather-grain vinyl featuring four large embossed rectangles. Door panel design, also of leather-grain vinyl, matched the seats. The Yeoman differed in that vinyl substituted for the cloth. The steering wheel had little bright work; the horn ring was not included, but instead a horn button was placed at the center. Rubber mats covered the passenger compartment floor. All station wagons had leather-grained vinyl covering the wheel houses and a load platform of ribbed linoleum.

A More Elegant Chevrolet

The purpose of the Impala was to break out of the low-priced market to enter the lower end of the medium-priced market. It met this goal successfully, as indicated by the number of Impalas built for 1958: 125,480 hardtops and 55,989 convertibles. These figures accounted for 15 percent of Chevrolet's total output of cars. Overall sales figures vary depending upon the source, but *Automotive News* reported a total of 1,249,485 Chevrolets (including the Corvette) were built for the model year, giving the division a market share of nearly 29.6 percent, a figure representing the division's zenith for the decade of the 1950s. This outcome was especially significant because it happened in a year of economic recession. Sales would have been even better without the recession. While Chevrolet's sales were not as high as they could have been, those of competitors Ford and Plymouth were lower than the prior model year.

This photograph taken inside Chevrolet's Van Nuys, California, assembly plant shows the front sheet metal for a 348-powered 1958 Impala being installed by assembly line personnel. Note the car was moving over a pit occupied by another employee. (Photo Courtesy GM Media Archive)

Centered at the rear of the Impala hardtop roof was a Mercedes 300SL–inspired simulated air extractor vent. Ahead of the rear wheels on the quarter panels was a "pitchfork" molding simulating yet another vent. Wheel covers featuring crossed flags at their center and three radial fins were standard issue.

The Impala lived up to the image suggested by its name in part by having some of the styling attributes of a Cadillac, including a lavish interior with tri-tone upholstery and plenty of bright trim. The Impala's interior featured a competition-style two-spoke steering wheel with a graceful Impala figure over a set of crossed flags on its hub and a full-circle chromed horn ring. Its unique interior decor was comprised of vinyl upholstery with tri-tone, horizontal-striped pattern-cloth inserts, bright front seat end panels, and a perforated vinyl headliner. Color-keyed, leather-grained vinyl-covered door panels were adorned with tinted anodized aluminum, and armrests with a wide, concave red reflector at the back end to warn oncoming traffic at night of an open door when the car was parked. (Parallel curb-side parking was quite common even well into the latter part of the 20th century.) In between the back-seat cushions was a pop-up armrest, another unique feature of the Impala. Color-coordinated carpeting covered the floor.

This model had more exclusivity than just its extra trim and special upholstery. Sheet metal from the cowl back was unique to the Impala. Its overall height was 1 inch lower than the Bel Air and its rear deck was longer. The Impala's rear lights consisted of a pair of taillights with a standard backup lamp between them. The idea behind the increased number of taillights for the Impala was to take advantage of the public's perception that more lights implied a more expensive car.

While the Impala was a hit with the public, it would not be quite as popular for 1959. Though the car was still equipped essentially the same, its styling was off-putting to some buyers.

Upholstery for the Impala was vinyl with tri-tone, horizontal-striped pattern-cloth inserts, bright front seat end panels, leather-grained vinyl-covered door panels adorned with tinted anodized aluminum, and armrests with a wide, concave red reflector at the back end to warn oncoming traffic at night of an open door when the car was parked. Also standard was a unique two-tone steering wheel. Note the dealer-installed accessory compass mounted on the top side of the dash.

This Roman Red and Artic White Impala Sport Coupe is one of 164,901 of the model built for the 1959 model year. The 6-cylinder and V-8 powered passenger cars were broken into separate series with the 6 being model 1737 and the 8 being 1837. The pictured car is the latter and is denoted as such with the V hood emblem. A total redesign that year resulted in the new Chevrolets being about 200 pounds heavier and with a wheelbase 1.5 inches longer than the 1958s. Furthermore, roofs sat 3 inches lower and bodies measured more than 2 inches wider overall.

The 1959 Chevrolet's "Vista-Panoramic Windshield" compound curved windshield cut into the upper roof a bit and was angled back sharply. On the Sport Coupe, it was said to offer 61 percent greater forward visibility than the comparable 1958 model.

1959: A Radical Look

The 1959 Chevrolet passenger car design that ultimately emerged from GM Design and Chevrolet Engineering was a bit controversial when new. Most people liked it at the time, though some hated it. Today, the Impala is a serious collectible for some while others hate it. There seems to be no attitude of indifference to the radical look of the car. Earlier design proposals for 1959, though, were far more radical.

In addition to the new styling, several mechanical modifications were made to the 1959 Chevrolets. Among them were optional 348s offering even higher performance, changes to the chassis, and attempts to improve the reliability of the Level-Air suspension.

Designing the 1959 Chevrolets

At first, the designs for 1959 were based on the 1958 models, but not long after the first proposals were rendered, GM management decided to drop the 1958 A-body used exclusively for Chevrolet and Pontiac and merge it into the yet-to-be designed 1959 B- and C-bodies. The move saved General Motors millions of dollars, but it forced a redesign of everything. Harley Earl supervised some of the early revisions and then made his annual trek to view the automobiles on exhibit at the European auto shows. While he was away, major changes in the direction of the styling for 1959 took place.

This change in direction had its roots in a sneak peek had by GM designer Chuck Jordan of the not-yet-released 1957 Chrysler products. The cars were in a storage area behind Chrysler's Mound Road plant. Jordan made a point of checking out the competition ahead of the new model year release date and on this visit he was in for a shock. As he explained to author Michael Lamm for the September-October 1991 issue of *Special Interest Autos*, "They looked so clean and lean with that thin roof and the nice proportions of glass; just the opposite of what we were doing at GM at that time." Jordan immediately told Bill Mitchell about the all-new cars from Chrysler; he, too, was stunned by the cars. Others began the trek over to the plant to get a look and had the same reaction. They all knew in an instant that Harley Earl's preferred beefy, massive look (massive bumpers, domed hoods, arched roofs, and heavy applications of bright trim) would not be competitive with the "clean and lean" Chrysler products. To make the adjustments needed to the designs for the 1959 models, a crash program was instituted, resulting in a couple of months of seven-day work weeks and many hours of overtime each day.

Even before Chuck Jordan got his early look at Chrysler's cars, Harley Earl was getting pressured by GM president Harlow Curtice as well as from some divisional managers to get away from the 1958 styling. That advance look by Jordan and his fellow designers, though, was the catalyst leading to dramatic changes for 1959 model year planning. When Earl returned from his trip, he was taken to the GM Design courtyard where he was shown a 1957 Plymouth two-door hardtop rented by GM Design engineer Ken Pickering. According to Pickering, Earl was not impressed with the car. Earl candidly voiced an opinion that was completely opposite the majority. He went on to add, "There really was a 'palace revolt' in redesigning these 1959 cars and when HJE returned from Europe, there was great uncertainty as to how he would react. Frankly, we had seen the 1957 Plymouth and sisters and were deeply worried that we were losing our design leadership. HJE could have fired on the spot most of the instigators, but instead he accepted the new direction. Maybe he was relieved that he had been 'saved' by his design people."

Even with the major rethink under way, there were some rather odd styling proposals across the board and Chevrolet was no exception. There was a strong push to think in terms of nothing being too weird to at least consider. Most of the far-out proposals, such as centrally placed stacked headlights, were ultimately rejected, but some, such as the gullwing fins for Chevrolet, were used. Other features, though, were not so far-out, such as the thin roof pillars applied to all body styles and the "flying wing" roof for the Sport Sedan.

Model Lineup

The Impala was separated from the Bel Air series for 1959, making it a stand-alone model. Furthermore, body style offerings were expanded from just the two-door hardtop and convertible to also include a four-door sedan and hardtop, the latter of which was still labeled a Sport Sedan. A top-of-the-line four-door station wagon, the Nomad, was included as part of the Impala series, but "Impala" script did not appear on it; instead, "Nomad" was spelled out within the side molding in the same manner and location in which "Impala" was spelled out on those models.

The Sport Sedan featured a flattened roof with thin A- and C-pillar posts with wraparound windshields in back and front. With the large expanse of glass area, excellent all-around visibility was provided. Its rear overhang also helped shield rear-seat occupants from direct sunlight, at least when the sun was well above the horizon. This design was called the "flying wing" roof, and it was also used for all GM passenger car divisions.

The Bel Air series, now displaced to second-tier status, was comprised of the two- and four-door sedans, a four-door Sport Sedan, and two station wagon models, Parkwood and Kingswood. The latter was approximately $100 more expensive than the Parkwood and featured a rear-facing third seat that no longer had to be removed to obtain additional cargo space; instead it could be folded down into the cargo floor.

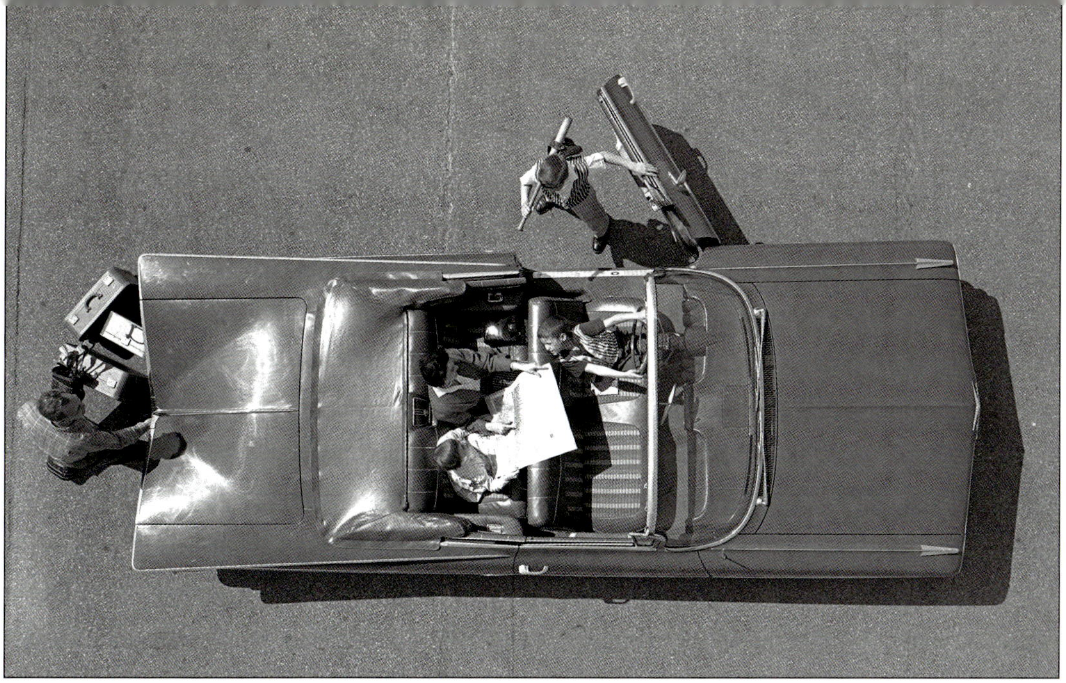

The flaring rear quarter panels are quite evident in this overhead view of a 1959 Impala convertible. An all-new body design, the second in two years, with distinctive styling makes the 1959 Impala one of the more appreciated or hated cars by enthusiasts today. There seems to be no one today who has no opinion one way or the other in regard to its styling. It was a bit controversial when new, too, but it helped get Chevrolet its second most profitable year in its history. (Photo Courtesy GM Media Archive)

The top-of-the-line station wagon for 1959 again carried the name "Nomad." This six-passenger model offered 52 cubic feet of cargo space and came standard with such features as deep-pile color-coordinated carpeting, vinyl headliner, and the same competition-style steering wheel as the Impala. With the 6-cylinder engine (model 1735) it had a base price of $2,891 and with the base V-8 (model 1835), $3,009. (Photo Courtesy GM Media Archive)

Despite being a low-production car each year, Chevrolet continued to offer the Utility Sedan for 1959. As in the past it lacked a back seat. The Utility Sedan was often purchased as a fleet order by businesses or by traveling salespeople who could carry their inventory and samples in the rear compartment and did not need the cargo capacity of the more costly station wagon. It offered flexibility for hauling these items as well as providing easy loading and unloading. (Photo Courtesy GM Media Archive)

At the bottom of the hierarchy was the Biscayne series. The Delray, which had previously been Chevrolet's lowest priced series, was dropped. Biscayne body styles included two- and four-door sedans, a two-door utility sedan (no back seat), and two station wagon types in two- and four-door sedan form, both labeled as the Brookwood.

The Distinctive 1959 Chevrolet

A road test report in the January 1959 issue of *Motor Trend* concluded that "all in all the Chevrolet stands out as the most unashamed proponent of the 'bigger and wider styling school' in its field." The new Chevrolets were about 200 pounds heavier and had a wheelbase 1.5 inches longer than the 1958s. Roofs sat 3 inches lower and bodies measured more than 2 inches wider overall.

The most dominant styling characteristic of the 1959 Chevrolet was its deeply sculpted fins. An early report in *Popular Mechanics* about the 1959 Chevrolet said of the car, "Styling is the thing with the new Chevrolet . . . Its low, flaring rear end is as expansive as the deck of an aircraft carrier and looks almost as wide from the driver's seat. Horizontal taillights squint, like giant cat's eyes, from under chrome eyebrows." Fisher Body tried to persuade against their use due to the large number of spot welds required, but once the decision was made final a stainless molding was used to cover the weld seams.

Somewhere along the way the claim was made that the fin design caused lift at high speed, something that was not true. The cars were raced in NASCAR and did not fly. In fact, Junior Johnson won the 1960 Daytona 500 in a 1959 Impala driving an average speed of 125 mph; the fins did not lift his car off the track.

As for the front view of the car, *Popular Mechanics* said the paired headlamps "are set as low as the law allows to accentuate the road-hugging design." The headlights were lowered several inches and sat at each end of the convex grille composed of horizontal and vertical bars. The Chevrolet's low, wide hood added to the lower, wider look of the car. All but the Buick Division used the basic design. Doors were also shared among all the passenger car divisions.

Another new styling feature for the 1959 Chevrolets was the "Vista-Panoramic Windshield." The compound curved windshield cut into the upper roof much like the one on the 1955 Chevrolet Biscayne dream car, though not quite as far. On the Sport Coupe, it was said to offer 61 percent greater forward visibility than the comparable 1958 model.

The hidden fuel filler was retained for 1959 and was placed behind the license plate mount positioned between the taillights. It swung down for access to the filler.

Various changes to the chassis resulted in lowering the overall height of the 1959s by 1.3 inches.

A Stronger Body

The body of the 1959 Chevrolet passenger cars was designed to be stronger and more rigid through more beam strength in important areas and improved underbody stiffness for a quieter ride. Heavier gauge steel was used for the shallow roof panel to ensure proper stiffness. Fully enclosed box section windshield and back window header rails offered greater rigidity than the channel type previously used. Roof side rails were similar to those for 1958, but the new styling allowed them to be more effectively tied into the body structure in the area of the wheelhouses. The truss-like structure resulting from this design better supported the top and added stiffness to the rear quarter body area. Another structural enhancement to the rear quarter area was an added reinforcement at the lock pillar, which improved attachment to the body sill and strengthened the forward portion of the wheelhouse section.

Increased underbody stiffness came through new ribbing,

This cut-away 1959 Impala Sport Sedan created for the auto show circuit showed off a number of features of the car, including the 348 Super Turbo-Thrust, Turboglide transmission, the X-frame, Posi-Traction rear axle, and the Level-Air system. (Photo Courtesy GM Media Archive)

both longitudinal and transverse, in the luggage compartment area and a wider rear cross sill. The underbody cross sill was extended full width, which contributed to increased stiffness in the body rear quarter area.

Engine Choices

Chevrolet's standard engine remained the inline 6-cylinder, even for its top-level Impala. It was modified with a new camshaft with decreased lift and a smaller amount of valve overlap along with new valve lifters to provide improved fuel economy. Buyers could still opt for any one of several optional V-8s at extra-cost, including all of those from the 1958 model year. Also, the 290-hp Ram Jet Special returned to the list of optional engines for any model of the big Chevrolets except the Sedan Delivery, which was considered a truck. (The Ram Jet Special was largely identical to the 1957 version, which was officially rated at 283 hp but was now advertised with the more accurate rating.) The fuel-injected engine was further refined for 1959 and these upgrades are covered in chapter 4. The full-size

The fuel-injected 283 for passenger cars returned for 1959. It was very rarely ordered and was ultra-rare in the convertible. Among the unique parts for the fuel-injection setup for 1959 were the script (GM PN 3759114 for both the left and right side) and ornaments (PN 3759115, left side and 3759116, right) mounted on the front fenders. Considering the waning number of Chevrolet passenger cars being ordered with the fuel-injected 283, spending money for unique tooling to produce these parts seems quite unusual.

Both the 250- and 290-hp fuel-injected 283s were offered for the 1959 Chevrolet passenger cars. This Impala convertible is equipped with the 290-hp version. Some changes were made to the setup for greater reliability. The air intake was unique to the 1959s. Power steering is yet another option on this Impala. (Photo Courtesy Angelo Van Bogart)

Door panel design and the tri-tone upholstery pattern were freshened for the 1959 Impala, but were again exclusive to what was now a separate model. This highly documented and accurately restored car is not only equipped with the 290-hp fuel-injected engine and 4-speed transmission but also power brakes, power steering, Autronic Eye, Flame-Out Ashtray, and Speed-Minder that flashes a light when a preset speed is reached. (Photo Courtesy Angelo Van Bogart)

Chevrolets equipped with the Rochester fuel-injection setup had the fact noted with a unique fender-mounted ornamentation and "Fuel Injection" script.

Notable differences defined each version of the fuel-injection engines. The 250-hp Ram Jet came with cast alloy aluminum pistons with notched heads while the 290-horse Ram Jet Special received pistons with slipper skirts and domed heads. Compression ratios in the respective engines were 9.5:1 and 10.5:1. The Ram Jet had hydraulic lifters while the Ram Jet Special had solid lifters. Valve size was 1.72 inches for the intake and 1.5 inches for the exhaust on both engines, but the tolerances differed. For the Ram Jet engine a tolerance of +/- 0.005 inch was specified, but on the Ram Jet Special the allowed tolerance was zero. Rod and main bearings were different between the two engines, too.

The 250-, 280-, and 315-hp 348s remained available at the start of the model year. Also offered at the start of production was an additional 348 4-barrel rated at 305 hp at 5,600 rpm. Torque was listed at 350 ft-lbs at 3,600 rpm. Labeled as the Special Turbo-Thrust, it had the same 11.0:1 compression ratio as the 315-hp Special Super Turbo-Thrust engine. However, later in the model year, the 315-hp engine was dropped while two more 348s offering even higher performance became available. They were needed because the 1959 models were heavier than the 1958s.

Higher-Performance 348s

During January 1959, a pair of even stronger 348s was added to the list of available engines. Both featured 11.25:1 compression ratios, dual valve springs, centrifugal distributor, and scavenger exhaust headers. The 4-barrel version had an output rating of 320 hp at 5,600 rpm while the other with its three 2-barrel carburetors pumped out 335 hp at 5,800 rpm. Peak torque was stated to be 358 ft-lbs at 3,600 rpm for the 320-hp engine and 362 ft-lbs at the same rpm for the 335-hp 348.

Tom McCahill reported in the November 1958 issue of *Mechanix Illustrated* that his 280-hp 348-powered Sport Sedan test car managed a 0–60 mph time of 13.1 seconds and 40–60 mph in 6.2 seconds. His 0–60 time was considerably slower than the 10.3 seconds he achieved testing a 1958 model.

Even though Chevrolet was officially out of factory-backed support for racing teams, Ed Cole continued to push for greater

The 348 returned for 1959, though with more variants, as did Level-Air as shown in this underhood photograph. Note the pulley-driven compressor for the air suspension. Despite improvements, it was not reliable enough, few of the systems were sold, and the option was dropped by the end of the model year. The 348 hung around, though, through 1961. (Photo Courtesy GM Media Archive)

performance from Chevrolet's 348. According to author Michael Lamm's interview of Zora Arkus-Duntov for the book *Corvette: An American Classic*, Duntov was quoted as saying, "Cole told me that we were going to do some work on a new 348 cubic inch V-8 engine that had initially been designed for trucks. My assignment was to make a good racer out of this engine. In 1959 at Daytona, at the new track, we had five Chevrolets running, and they either won their races or placed second or third. We didn't win the main event [the Daytona 500] because of timing chain problems. The next year we won the Daytona 500 and were the NASCAR champion. Our efforts were considerable with the 348 cubic inch engine. We got everything out of it that we could in spite of everything. It was, however, a very inefficient engine—nothing like the 283."

Transmissions

Transmission choices remained about the same. However, a 4-speed with a floor-mounted shifter was finally advertised as available. It was in great demand, but the strike by employees of BorgWarner, the company that supplied the units to Chevrolet, made getting a 4-speed rather difficult, so much so that Chevrolet had to give preference to the Corvette when the 4-speed gearbox was ordered. Many customers who ordered the 4-speed on their full-size Chevrolet finally settled for a 3-speed unit to speed delivery of the car.

The Powerglide was available with the 6-cylinder, any of the 283s (though the 250-hp fuel-injected engine could be had with the Corvette version of the transmission) and the 250-, 280-, and 300-hp 348s.

The Turboglide automatic transmission was again offered as an option, but still could not be had with the very-high-output engines. Engineers further modified it and among the changes was a five-spoke-hub second turbine to replace the three-spoke design, a six-active-face multiple-disc reverse clutch, an eight-active-face multiple-disc forward clutch in place of the former cone designs, and three additional pinions in the front planetary gearset. Furthermore, the second turbine shaft came with new support bearings for increased durability. It had become much better, but its reputation was damaged with most consumers.

Chassis

Both the frame and suspension maintained their basic architecture from 1958, but changes were made to adapt to the wider 1959 body as well as improve ride characteristics. The steering ratio was decreased, tread widths and wheelbase measurements were increased, tires were improved, brakes were larger, a new Z-crossmember was added to the rear frame, and the four-link rear suspension was refined.

The steering was modified to decrease steering effort under all conditions, to further minimize damping of road shocks, and make adjustments for the new geometry imposed by the longer wheelbase. Steering ratio for regular production cars was changed to 24.0:1 from 20.0:1. With the new steering gear and altered linkage, the overall steering ratio went from 23.0:1 to approximately 28:1. This gave the driver a 21-percent increase in mechanical advantage. The same ratio was used with the optional power steering. Furthermore, vibration from road shocks was reduced through a new flexible coupling of fabric-rubber composition in the steering shaft just above the steering gear.

Front tread width was increased by 1.5 inches and rear tread width by 0.5 inch. This was said to improve handling, but it also was a styling consideration. The wheelbase was increased to 119 inches, a 1.5-inch increase over that for 1958. Those 1.5 inches of extra length were all ahead of the center of the car's frame.

More durable tires for 1959 were the result of improved Rayon tire cord. They offered up to 7-percent longer tread life and could withstand up to 10 mph greater speed with relative safety. A softer ride and less rolling resistance were additional benefits of the new tires.

Brake drums retained their 11-inch diameter, but were widened, as were the brake shoes. Front drums and shoes were widened by 0.75 inch and the rear ones by 0.25 inch, thus providing a 17-percent greater effective braking area, which went from 157 square inches to 183.8. The larger brakes gave better resistance to fade and increased brake shoe life because of the spreading of pressure applied to a larger surface area. A new low-pedal power brake unit was offered as a regular production option or as a dealer-installed option. It utilized many of the same components as the standard manual braking system and was more easily serviced than past units.

A new crossmember of modified Z-section was added to the frame to maintain dimensional stability between the side members. It interconnected the side members at the point where the rear suspension lateral control bar bracket attached to the frame.

The 1958-type rear suspension was modified to improve stability and roll-steer characteristics and to eliminate undesirable side reactions to the frame. New rear suspension bushings gave better durability and lessened the harshness of road shocks. For 1959, the rear control arms were relieved of lateral loads by a new independent lateral control bar. A new single upper control arm worked in combination with the two lower control arms to resist lift during stopping and squat during acceleration. The single upper control arm improved overall ride geometry by causing the suspension roll center to nearly correspond with the rear axle roll center, significantly reducing the tendency of the rear suspension to cause a lateral thrust on the frame when

The Radical Corvair

The compact car market began to emerge in the latter part of the 1950s. For the most part, only foreign manufacturers offered a compact car. AMC jumped into the compact car market with its Rambler in 1958. The "Big Three" began design work on their own compact car models in 1957 and all had an entry ready for introduction as 1960 models. For Chevrolet it was the innovative, but ultimately controversial, Corvair, a six-passenger model. It was released at the start of the 1960 model year in October of 1959 in three trim levels, the Series 500 Standard, Series 700 Deluxe, and the Series 900 Monza. The Standard and Deluxe were both offered in two- and four-door sedan body styles while the Monza was available only as a two-door sedan. *Motor Trend* magazine bestowed its "Car of the Year" award to Chevrolet's new compact car.

The Corvair's lightweight aluminum air-cooled horizontally opposed 6-cylinder engine, unique suspension system, and rear-mounted transaxle were considered radical for the time. Ed Cole recognized the need for a small car was nearing. Early design studies commenced in July 1956 and initial styling got under way a little more than one year later. He wanted a small car to compete with the imports that were just then starting to come to the United States in meaningful numbers. By early 1958, Cole was able to persuade GM president Harlow Curtice that a compact car was needed in the Chevrolet lineup; with even greater numbers of imports being sold by then, there probably was not much persuading that Cole needed to do, and Curtice gave the project official approval. While the Corvair project was moving forward, General Motors began selling its Vauxhall Victor and Opel Rekord in the United States. Vauxhall and Opel were GM-owned manufacturers based in Britain

The compact car market began to emerge in the latter part of the 1950s. Chevrolet responded with the innovative, but ultimately controversial, Corvair, a six-passenger sedan with a rear-mounted aluminum, air-cooled, horizontally opposed 6-cylinder engine. It was released at the start of the 1960 model year in October of 1959.* Motor Trend *magazine bestowed its "Car of the Year" award to the new model. Shown is the Deluxe 700 four-door sedan, the midlevel model. (Photo Courtesy GM Media Archive)

and West Germany, respectively.

Several foreign small cars were studied, and, of them, the Volkswagen appeared to be the best. It was judged to offer easier steering as a result of light weight over the front wheels, a lower center of gravity, and less need for air-conditioning since the engine heat trailed the passenger compartment. In addition, its flat floor helped in comfortably seating three passengers abreast front and rear.

Designated the "Y-body," the Corvair was developed as a unit body with a 108-inch-wheelbase chassis and was designed around its engine. The Y-body shared very little with other Chevrolets, and because of this, it required its own assembly plants. Though very different, the original four-door sedan had a family resemblance with Chevrolet's full-size four-door hardtops, as they shared the flying-wing roof styling.

The 1960 Corvair's engine was sized at 140 ci and developed 80 hp at 4,400 rpm on an 8.0:1 compression ratio. Unfortunately, it weighed more than originally envisioned, 366 pounds, a 78-pound overshoot. Because of this, weight had to be shaved, leading to the use of thin bumpers and an austere interior.

Cost-cutting led to the removal of the anti-roll bar from the front suspension at the last moment. Conventional unequal-length upper and lower A-arms with coil springs were in front. However, the rear suspension was not quite as conventional and Corvair's simple and cheap swing axle eventually became a source of controversy. Though the swing axle was not at all new (Volkswagen, Mercedes, and other European models employed the swing axle), American drivers were not familiar with the handling characteristics specific to this setup despite the rather large presence of Volkswagen Beetles in this country. This feature, combined with the rear-mounted engine and no anti-roll bar in back either, led to some bad publicity for General Motors. However, owners of Corvair were expected to drive properly for the conditions of the road, obey the posted speed limit, and keep the low-profile tires inflated to the correct pressure. Those who did not generally were the ones who had the controversial accidents. By 1964, Chevrolet engineers made changes to the rear suspension to mitigate handling issues in hard cornering.

Ed Cole recognized the need was nearing for Chevrolet to offer a small car to compete with the imports that were just then starting to come into the United States in meaningful numbers. By early 1958, Cole was able to persuade GM president Harlow Curtice that a compact car was needed in the Chevrolet lineup. (Photo Courtesy GM Media Archive)

Over the decade, the Corvair lineup was greatly expanded and included a convertible, a station wagon, and even van and pickup versions. It stayed in the Chevrolet lineup until about the middle of the 1969 model year when it was canceled after the sale of 1.8 million of the cars over its 10 years of production. Competition from Ford with its Mustang and even Chevrolet's Camaro resulted in diminishing sales of the car. In 1972, a government report cleared General Motors of wrongdoing regarding its 1960–1963 Corvairs.

one wheel was subjected to a bump. Directional stability was improved through a change to the rear suspension geometry to increase understeer. The frame-mounted pivots for the lower control arms were lowered nearly 1.5 inches, which increased the angle of the arms relative to the ground. Even softer rubber bushings for the three control arms enhanced the quality of the ride and gave even greater durability than the previous type.

Offered at extra-cost was a handling package consisting of metallic brake linings, stiffer springs, larger shocks, and stronger wheel bearings and ball joints. Police cars were typically the ones ordered with this heavy-duty equipment, though anyone with high performance in mind could have purchased this option package. Another suspension option was, again, Level-Air.

Level-Air

The Level-Air system received several improvements, some of which originated during 1958. Among the changes were those to reduce the noise level of operating systems (such as the air compressor pistons and the outside air intake), increase reliability and durability, and facilitate easier servicing.

The outside air intake got a modified check valve meant to eliminate failures of this component. Low- and high-pressure relief valves in the junction block of the air supply system were modified for more reliable and durable performance. The low-pressure relief valve pressure was reduced by 10 psi to 15, which reduced the compressor supercharging pressure as well as reduced operating loads. To reduce the chance of the high-pressure relief valve poppet becoming misaligned in the valve bore, its length was increased. In mid-1958, leveling valves in the air spring assemblies were modified with quieter check valves and all-rubber poppet valves that were more durable than the previously used rubber-faced rivet type. The left, front leveling valve had an external adjustment slot added to permit quick servicing for vehicles that were out of plane. A change was made in the anti-freeze used in the vaporizer jar. Testing with various types of Methanol anti-freeze revealed they contained additives that could be damaging to the Level-Air system. Denatured alcohol, wood alcohol, or GM windshield washer anti-freeze was now strongly recommended for filling the vaporizer jar.

Despite all the research put into Level-Air, it simply did not work well enough and was abandoned with the end of 1959 production.

Air-Conditioning Revised

An extensively revised air-conditioning system for 1959 included a new temperature-modulated viscous drive for the five-bladed fan of the factory-installed unit. It was quieter and required less power. The evaporator was moved to the right-side cowl plenum chamber, which improved the efficiency of the air conditioner and relieved congestion within the engine compartment. Its core was enlarged by about one-third to 125 square inches of area. Greater condenser and receiver capacity minimized the likelihood of excessive compressor pressure from an overcharge of the system.

The factory-installed "All Weather Air Conditioner" was available with any 1959 Chevrolet passenger car with a V-8 and automatic transmission except the fuel-injected 283 and the Impala convertible. A requirement when air-conditioning was ordered for the Impala Sport Coupe was the purchase of one of the tinted glass options, all-tinted glass or a tinted *rear* window. The rear window extended far up into the roof panel, and rear seat passengers were significantly exposed to direct sunlight.

Another air-conditioning system, the "Cool Pack" unit, was dealer installed and was offered for 6-cylinder and V-8-powered cars except those with the Ram Jet V-8 and any of the 348s with the special camshaft. Temperature regulation for it was by an electromagnetic cycling clutch and a thermostatic switch located in the evaporator. The system operated only on recirculated air and was completely impendent of the heater.

Additional Changes

Station wagon models had a retractable rear window, eliminating the need for a liftgate. The rear window had to be fully lowered, though, before opening the tailgate. A power-operated rear window, a feature showcased on the 1954 Nomad concept car, finally became an option.

The optional power steering featured better returnability and smoother transition of power application. These improvements were achieved mostly through decreased friction at key points and reduced hydraulic reaction on the control valve spool. A new lip-type seal at the steering gear housing replaced the garter-spring seal, and in the power cylinder, a synthetic rubber piston ring replaced the cast-iron rings formerly used. In the control valve, the hydraulic reaction area was reduced on the assistance-proportioning spool valve. Altogether, the changes reduced steering effort and provided better sealing of the components.

Electrical systems also received attention from the engineers. The ignition switch for 1958 had a three-wire connector along with three individual wires in back; this was simplified with a single four-wire connector. It also received its own light bulb for illumination at night. The switch had been illuminated by the general lighting of the instrument panel. An improved, larger rheostat in the main light switch was designed to provide greater durability. Other electrical system modifications simplified the wiring for the luggage compartment and battery charging systems.

Chevrolet's air-conditioning system received improvements each year and 1959 was no exception. It was extensively revised and included a new temperature-modulated viscous drive for the five-bladed fan of the factory-installed unit. It was quieter and required less power. Also, a set of vents was placed under the center of the dash for the first time in addition to vents at each end of the dash. (Photo Courtesy GM Media Archive)

A new six-way power seat was an option this model year. It offered the driver an infinite range of possible seat positions within the limits of its horizontal and vertical travel. The new power seat incorporated three reversible electric motors capable of moving the seat in six different directions.

The new cowl section of the body, though similar to that of the 1958 Chevrolet passenger cars, provided up to 18 percent more airflow through the ventilation system.

Single-speed electric windshield wipers were now standard on all 1959 passenger cars. The wipers operated at a speed of 55 cycles per minute.

Conclusion

As it had for the 1958 model year, Chevrolet again finished narrowly ahead of Ford for the 1959 model year despite the 1959 Fords being awarded the gold medal of the Comité Français De L'élégance at the Brussels World's Fair "for exceptional proportioning and elegance of line." Ford's heavily re-skinned lineup of big cars was quite conservative in comparison to the radically changed Chevrolets. Despite ad writers claiming the new Chevrolets had "slim-line design" and were "fresh and fine," some Chevrolet loyalists were not persuaded; many of them switched to Ford this year, though not in enough numbers to help Ford out-sell Chevrolet, which out-produced its archrival by more than 42,000 units. Sales of more than 1.481 million units put Chevrolet close to pre-recession (1957) production. However, this was accomplished by offering buyers special incentives throughout the model year.

While GM's lineup of its flamboyant 1959 models had mixed results, its cost-cutting and higher prices earned the second highest profit year in the history of the company. Market share, though, had dropped from a fraction above 50 percent to 48 for 1959. Competition coming from American Motors, with its smaller cars, as well as from the smaller offerings of foreign automakers, such as Volkswagen, began to erode sales. That year more cars were imported to the United States than exported from the country. Foreign car market share reached 8 percent. Some were evidently beginning to get tired of the big, finny, chrome-laden cars offered by General Motors.

For all its problems, General Motors was not alone. The competition was having its share of difficulties finding its way, too. Chrysler was especially hit hard later in the 1957 model year; its new cars, while beautiful, were prone to early corrosion. Chrysler's reputation quickly suffered as a result and quite some time passed before the company recovered. Mercury's Turnpike Cruiser had been a flop going against Oldsmobile and Buick, while the new 1958–1960 Lincolns and Continentals failed to compete with Cadillac. Ford's 1958–1960 Edsel proved to be a sales disaster as well. Evidently, no one was quite ready for the fast-approaching new decade of the 1960s.

For 1960, Chevrolet's designs of 1959, like the rest of the GM lineup, were toned down; then for 1961 all-new styling appeared for all GM passenger car divisions. Chevrolet led the way throughout the decade under the leadership of Bill Mitchell, Harley Earl's handpicked replacement to head GM Design. Profits were higher than ever with Chevrolet accounting for a major portion of them. After a bit of a stumble at the end of the 1950s, Chevrolet offered exciting new designs again, and as a result the division soared to a market share of 35 percent during the decade! (General Motors enjoyed a stratospheric 63 percent market share.) All of it was built upon the overall successes of the 1950s.

CHAPTER 7

CHEVROLET'S OPTIONS AND ACCESSORIES

1950–1959

Options and accessories offered by Chevrolet changed about as much as the cars did throughout the 1950s. In the early part of the decade items such as self-canceling directional signals and two backup lights cost extra, but later in the decade these and other features became standard equipment on many Chevrolets.

This 1956 Bel Air convertible is accessorized with the grille and fender guards as well as the seldom-seen front fender moldings.

While the major options offered by Chevrolet have been detailed in the previous chapters of this book, several other options, as well as dealer-installed accessories, were offered to add to Chevrolet and dealer profits as well as offer conveniences to drivers and passengers. It seems that Chevrolet offered everything possible in its extensive list of accessories. Even an electric shaver was offered! An exhaustive listing of every one of the options and accessories throughout the 1950s is not practical here, so presented are what in my opinion are among the most interesting. Some of them are simply presented in captioned photographs. You may find an accessory or two you did not even know existed.

The trunk guard and rear fender shields were extra-cost accessories for this 1950 Bel Air. It is also equipped with a grille guard attached between the bumper guards as well as front fender shields and an outside sun visor.

This 1950 Chevrolet Deluxe convertible is fitted with many extra-cost options and accessories, including wide white sidewall tires, radio, spotlight, front and rear fender shields, front fender stone shield, and wheel trim rings. Chevrolet, incidentally, sponsored the All-American Soap Box Derby from 1935 to 1972. Myron Scott, the same man who gave Chevrolet's Corvette its name, was a photographer for the Dayton Daily News. *In 1933, he photographed six boys racing their homemade cars built from discarded wooden crates and got the idea to organize an annual event. In 1935, Chevrolet agreed to sponsor the event, and in 1937 Scott went to work for Chevrolet Public Relations. (Photo Courtesy GM Media Archive)*

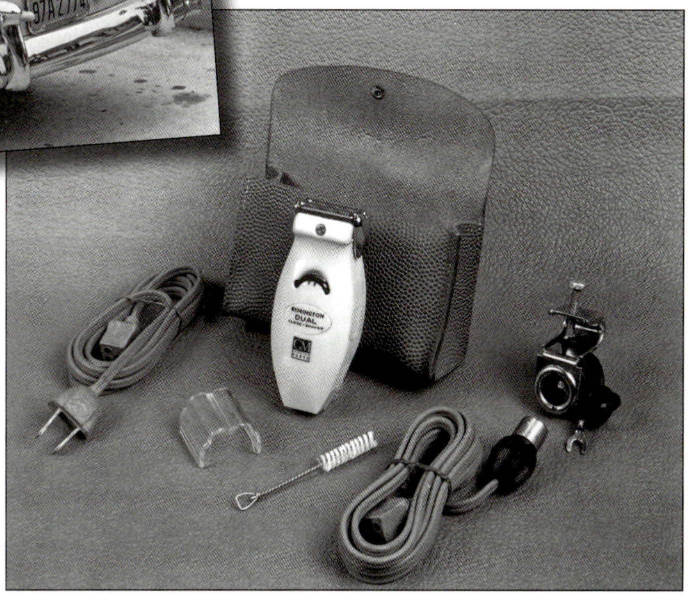

A Remington electric shaver was a dealer accessory. This kit from 1942 is representative. It could be used in the car by plugging it into the cigarette lighter. (Photo Courtesy GM Media Archive)

Protection — where you need it

Grille Guard Safety Bumper

Front Fender Guards

Part of grille guard unit safety bumper to give additional protection to fenders and front end.

Front Fender Shields

Gasoline Tank Filler Guard

A stainless steel guard that adds to the appearance and prevents the paint from being chipped around the filler door

Door Handle Shield

A gleaming, stainless steel guard; protects the paint around the door handles

Rear Fender Guards

Massive, heavily chromed bumper guards that protect fenders and help to prevent bumper locking.

Door Edge Guards

For your lighting needs

Underhood Lamp

A useful service lamp when inspections are required under the hood at night.

Automatic Headlight Control Unit

Automatically lowers head lamp beams and automatically returns to high beam after passing the approaching car.

Safetylight and Mirror

A handy combination of a remote controlled, powerful light and rearview mirror.

Luggage Compartment Lamp

Floods trunk with light, operating automatically with the raising and lowering of trunk lid.

Courtesy Lights

Automatically flood floor with light when either front door is opened to give increased convenience and safety.

Portable Spotlight

A powerful, chrome plated, sealed beam light with a 12-foot cord. Useful as a trouble lamp all around the car; for reading signs and tire changing.

Electric Brake Signal Light

Saves wear on emergency brake linings; prevents stalling and driving with the brakes on. A red warning light flashes until emergency brake is released.

Back Up Lamps

Useful in assisting driver in backing safely in dark areas or driveways, give warning to others. Integral part of tail lamps; light automatically when car is shifted into reverse.

For the look of distinction

Wheel Trim Rings

Extra wide rings of highly polished stainless steel to give a luxury appearance to the wheels.

Rear Wheel Fender Panels

Gives your car that low, sleek appearance and protects … from mud splashes. … "Two-Ten" and "One-…

Exhaust Pipe Extension

A heavy stainless steel extension. Protects bumper from discoloration and …

Wiring Junction Block Assembly

Places all accessories fuses in one convenient location. Reduces possibility of … accessories turned on after …

License Frames

High grade stainless steel telescope tubing to fit all sizes of license plates. Clips firmly over edges of license plates

Wire Wheels

Add a distinctive, sport car appearance to the wheels.

Wheel Discs

These bright, full wheel, stainless steel covers add smartness and beauty to your wheels.

Accessories for every need were listed in Chevrolet's sales literature, including this 1954 catalog. Among the extra-cost items were a fuel filler door guard, door handle shields to protect the paint from scratches from a person's fingernails, door edge guards, underhood lamp, luggage compartment lamp, spotlight, exhaust pipe extension, wire wheels, wiring junction block assembly to bring all fuses together in one place, license plate frames, and more.

Below: This low-mileage 1955 Bel Air Sport Coupe has the accessory fuel filler door guard, the "Electric Brake Signal Light" to remind the driver when the emergency brake was engaged, and the rare accessory tool kit.

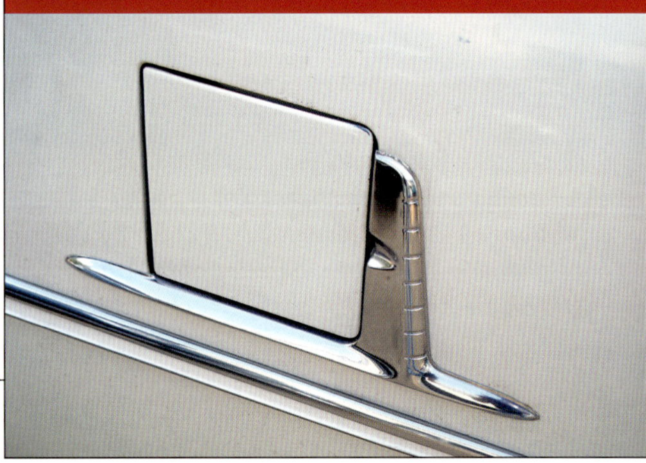

A foot-operated windshield washer and a traffic light viewer were among the accessories offered by Chevrolet dealers for 1955. The latter was a prism that allowed a driver to see the color of the traffic light in the event the car's body blocked a direct view of the traffic light. The traffic light viewer is a popular item with enthusiasts today.

The 1956 Bel Air four-door sedan for display at an auto show was loaded with accessories and options such as the wire wheels, stone shields, fender-mounted ornaments, radio, "Continental Wheel Carrier," two-tone paint, and the 205-hp 265 V-8. The Continental Wheel Carrier was introduced the prior model year. (Photo Courtesy GM Media Archive)

The "Continental Wheel Carrier" was offered as a dealer-installed accessory and is shown on a 1956 Bel Air four-door sedan in this photograph. It offered extra trunk storage by removing the spare tire from the compartment to outside the car. The spare tire carrier could be pivoted to one side to help in the loading or removing of cargo from the trunk. Though rather common on restored Bel Airs today, it was not nearly as common when these cars were new. (Photo Courtesy GM Media Archive)

Chevrolet's full line of accessories was heavily promoted at auto shows, as seen in this photo of displays surrounding a 1957 Bel Air four-door sedan. The display in the foreground includes all three types of radios, spotlights, power antenna, window-mounted sun shades, and other items. (Photo Courtesy GM Media Archive)

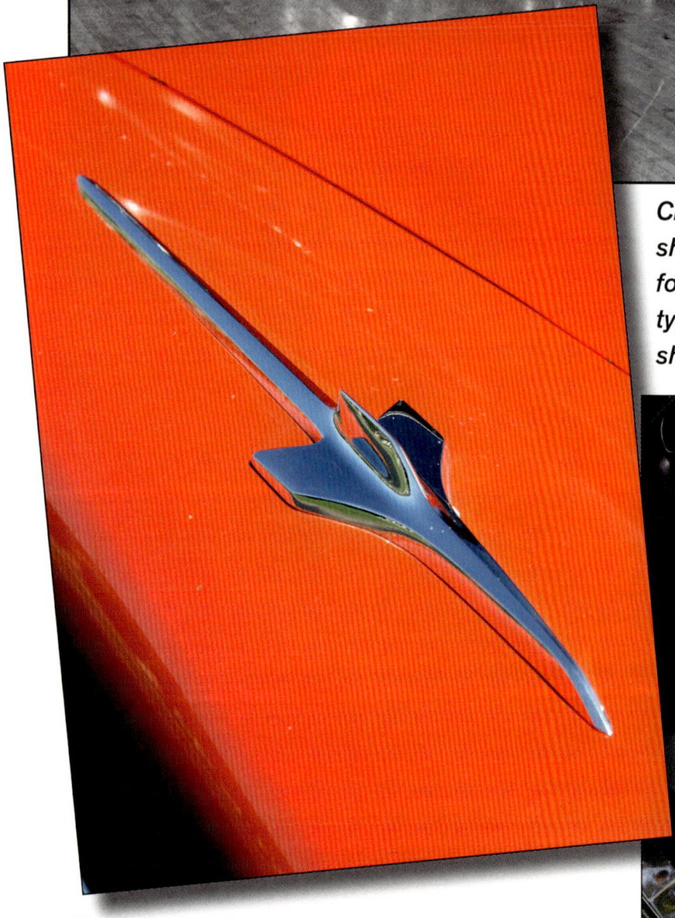

The front fender moldings were dealer-installed accessories. They were die-cast metal and chrome-plated with a shape clearly inspired by modern fighter jets and their condensation trails, or contrails.

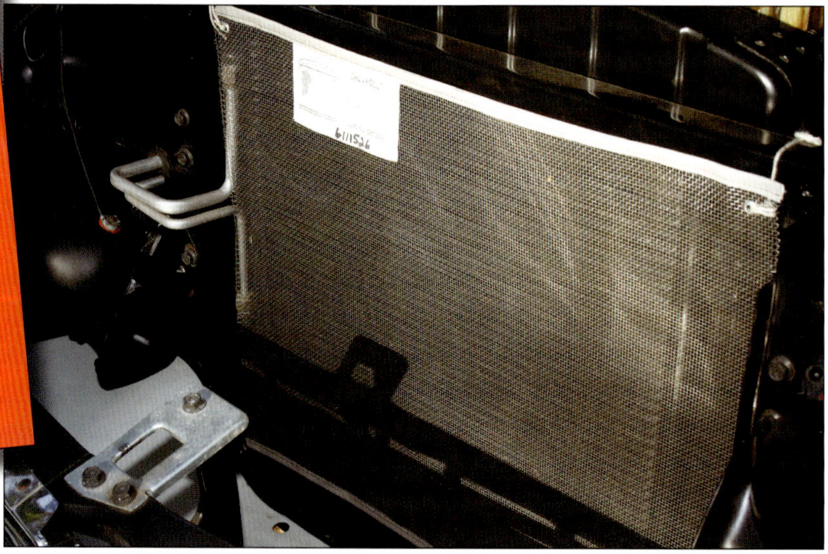

A bug screen for the radiator was available as a dealer-installed accessory. It was easier to clean than the radiator because it could readily be removed, cleaned, then quickly reinstalled. The one shown on this 1956 Bel Air convertible, though, is a reproduction piece.

The chrome-plated steel exhaust extension was yet another dealer-installed accessory. The genuine dealer item had the Chevrolet bowtie emblem embossed upon it. This one is on a 1956 Bel Air convertible.

This 1957 Bel Air Sport Sedan is equipped with a 283, Powerglide, air-conditioning, and two-tone paint. It is also fitted with an outside rearview mirror and the rare dash-mounted inside rearview mirror.

The dash-mounted inside rearview mirror was offered for the Sport Sedan in the Two-Ten and Bel Air (shown) series. The Sport Sedan had a lower overall height than the four-door sedan. It was made available perhaps because it offered the driver a somewhat better view to the rear than the standard placement on the windshield header.

Door handle shields, such as on this 1957 Bel Air Sport Sedan, protected against fingernail scratches around the door handle.

This 1958 Impala convertible is loaded with accessories, including fender skirts, spinner wheel covers, rocker panel molding, twin rear-mounted antennas, door handle shields, spot-light, and dash-mounted compass. It is powered by the optional 315-hp 348 coupled to the 3-speed transmission and Posi-traction rear axle.

Wheel covers were standard for Bel Air models, but could be had with a three-bar spinner that gave the appearance of knock-off hubs like those of sports cars. Knock-off spinners held the wheels in place on most sports cars rather than the lug and lug nut arrangement since they offered the advantage of being able to quickly remove and re-install the wheels for tire changes during racing. They also had the secondary advantage of an attractive appearance.

A tissue dispenser was a popular dealer add-on. It mounted underneath the dash and was designed to accept commonly sized boxes of tissues, which slide in from behind. The unit pivoted out for easy access.

Autronic Eye

General Motors first introduced the automatic headlight dimmer, dubbed the "Autronic Eye," for use on Cadillacs and Oldsmobiles in 1952. The following year it became available for all passenger car lines. Advertising for the Autronic Eye said it was the "biggest advance in night-driving safety in 30 years," and could "save you 200 steps an hour," which made reference to the number of times drivers had to manually depress the floor-mounted dimmer switch with their foot. The option's purpose was a simple one: to allow a driver to travel with their high-beam headlights on and rely on the Autronic Eye to automatically dim them for approaching drivers then switch on the high beams again once the oncoming traffic had passed. Making it work reliably, though, was not so simple.

The system was composed of a "black box" housing the vacuum tube amplifier, a heavy-duty relay, wiring harness, an auxiliary foot-operated switch near the standard dimmer switch, and a dashboard-mounted phototube, or "eye." Placement of the phototube was on the far left side of the dash just inside the windshield. The amplifier unit served as the power supply for the relay and the phototube, which was a light-sensitive electronic device that created electrical current when exposed to light. When the lens of the phototube received light from an approaching car, it focused it through a filter and mask to the phototube. The phototube converted the light into an electrical impulse conducted by wiring to the amplifier unit mounted under the hood. In turn, the amplifier unit operated the power relay installed near the amplifier in response to a signal from the phototube unit. Upon receipt of a signal from the phototube unit through the amplifier unit, the power relay switched the headlamps between the upper and lower beams. The auxiliary switch allowed the driver to either deactivate the system or select the automatic setting to activate it.

The Autronic Eye, an automatic headlight dimmer, was first offered for the Cadillac and Oldsmobile lines starting in 1952; it was made available for all GM passenger car lines by the following model year. Made by GM's Guide Lamp Division, it was intended to ease driver effort by automatically dimming the car's brights for oncoming drivers. In practice, though, it proved troublesome.

The units varied a bit depending on the model years, car line, and whether it was factory-installed or dealer-installed. The phototube initially came with a square lens. While all divisions switched to a round lens in mid-1954, Chevrolet kept the square lens until mid-1955 before switching to the round lenses for the remainder of the 1950s. Chevrolet also had to adapt the 12-V system to its 6-V electrical system until the division went to a 12-V setup in 1955. It accomplished this with a 12-to-6 reducing resistor, but it placed a larger load on the charging system.

The Autronic Eye did not always work as intended. It was susceptible to erratic operation due to various light sources other than headlights, such as street lamps, low-angle sunlight at sunset, etc. Dealers' service garage technicians spent a lot of time making adjustments to the setup using special equipment in an attempt to get the Autronic Eye to work correctly for customers. Many times, the system was just disconnected. An attempt was made to improve the Autronic Eye for 1958 with adjustable sensitivity for rain, snow, bright city lights, and low-angle sunlight. Eventually, Chevrolet gave up on the device.

Today, the "Intellibeam" automatically dims the headlights on Cadillacs. Using modern electronics capable of detecting light similar to the way the human eye does, the system will turn off the high beam headlamps as oncoming traffic approaches, though instead of just switching the high-beam off, the Intellibeam system gradually dims these lights as approaching vehicles get closer.

Automatic Top Raiser

An automatic convertible-top raiser was offered as an accessory for 1955. This accessory was evidently inspired by the system included on Harley Earl's 1951 GM LeSabre, a one-off "idea car" featuring a multitude of styling and mechanical innovations. In the event of rain beginning to fall on the parked car with its convertible top in the down position, the rain sensor located on the console of the LeSabre raised the top as well as the power-operated windows. It even secured the top to the windshield header. The system for the LeSabre was fully automatic; thus, Harley Earl could leave his convertible parked with the top down and not be the least bit concerned about the car's fancy interior getting soaked. The one offered as a 1955 Chevrolet accessory was not nearly as sophisticated. How it got released as an accessory as it was designed is a mystery. It must have been done simply as a gimmick, but it was one very few people even knew existed.

A most impractical dealer-installed accessory was the automatic top raiser for the 1955 Bel Air convertible. The concept was proven practical on the experimental 1951 GM LeSabre, but the Bel Air was no LeSabre! The idea behind it was for the system's rain sensor to trigger the activation of the convertible top in the event of rain if it were left down while the owner was away. There were problems with it on the Bel Air convertible that simply did not exist with the experimental car. The accessory was dropped after 1955.

The automatic top raiser accessory offered for 1955 consisted of a set of relays and a moisture-sensitive grid that when struck by moisture raised the convertible top, but only when the ignition switch was off. Harley Earl's LeSabre did not have a convertible top boot, but instead its top was fully concealed underneath an electrically operated, pivoting, flush-fitting lid. The 1955 Chevrolet Bel Air convertible had no such feature; its folded top could be covered with a snap-on boot, and the owner had to remember to leave the boot off at times when rain was in the forecast. The alert owner also had to raise the windows even if the car was equipped with the power window option since the accessory did not raise the windows. Even if the owner left off the convertible top boot and raised the windows, the top would not automatically lock itself to the windshield header, leaving quite a gap for rain to enter. One other problem with the setup: If the top was lowered as per the instructions the plastic rear window would be unzipped and the accessory did not zip the window in place either. Incidentally, Ford also offered the accessory (it may have been from the same vendor) and had the same drawbacks. Both Ford and Chevrolet dropped this accessory after 1955.

Seat Belts

Safety promotion did not do much for selling cars, but Ford Motor Company did it anyway while Chevrolet made seat belts and a padded dash available as optional equipment, but without particularly heavy promotion of the fact. Indeed, many executives at the time felt offering seat belts suggested to the public the company's cars and trucks were not safe. Some were not convinced of seat belts' value in protecting occupants of automobiles. They noted the device could be the source of injuries and that an unconscious person in a vehicle that caught fire after an accident could be more difficult to extract by rescue personnel. There was also the belief that seat belts in convertibles were dangerous, that an occupant had a better chance if thrown clear of the car. Even European auto manufacturers supported that view. There were instances of people surviving accidents because they were thrown clear of a tumbling car. However, the opposition pointed to relatively minor accidents where the front seat occupants were killed because they struck the dash and windshield, as well as cases in which the doors popped open in a crash, causing passengers to be thrown out of the vehicle and resulting in fatalities. A research group at Cornell University found that passengers thrown from an automobile were, indeed, more likely to receive greater injury or be killed than those who stayed inside. In the end, the conclusion from all the discussion and research was that seat belts, when properly designed and used, mitigate or even prevent significant injuries and prevent deaths in some types of accidents, but were absolutely useless in other accidents. Some experts estimated that seat belts would save somewhere between 62 and 84 of every 100 motorists who would otherwise be killed.

The seat belt was no simple device. To do what it was intended to do, it had to be designed properly. Everything involved had to be carefully considered; the belt material, the

Chevrolet offered seat belts with or without shoulder harnesses starting in 1956. This 1956 Bel Air Sport Coupe is shown with both shoulder harnesses and the lap belts. Note that the shoulder harnesses, like the lap belts, are bolted to the floor. They were offered for the front and rear seat. Seat belts were not a major seller. (Photo Courtesy GM Media Archive)

anchoring bracket, anchoring points, and buckles had to be developed. The anchoring bracket through which the seat belt webbing was laced, for example, had to have slots free of sharp edges and burrs to prevent cutting of the webbing under high load conditions. Belts attached to the vehicle flooring required at least 5/16-inch heat-treated mounting bolts along with 2½ –inch washers to spread the load over a large area to prevent the mounting bolts from pulling through the flooring. Furthermore, the seat belt release had to be easily operated with a light pull from one hand even with the occupant suspended upside down.

For 1956, Ford offered its "Lifeguard" option comprised of a padded dash and seat belts. A dished steering wheel was standard issue. Ford heavily promoted the safety equipment. However, Ford was not the first with seat belts. Nash began offering them in 1950. Seat belts were introduced as extra-cost equipment for 1956 not only by Ford, but also Chrysler and General Motors as a whole. General Motors spent two years developing seat belts before releasing them as an option. At the time, automobile safety was quickly becoming a subject of interest of the federal government. In fact, the U.S. House of Representatives introduced a bill in mid-1955 that would have required that seat belts be mandatory in vehicles used for interstate commerce, but it failed to pass. California passed a law requiring seat belts to conform to aircraft standards set by the Civil Aeronautics Authority. However, most car buyers gave seat belts little attention and few cars were so equipped until they became mandatory equipment in the mid-1960s. Even then, car owners were not especially likely to use them.

Chevrolet not only offered lap belts, but also shoulder harnesses front and rear. At least one 1956 Chevrolet, a Bel Air two-door hardtop, also equipped with a special-order dual-quad Corvette engine, had the extra-cost shoulder harnesses. Even though few people ordered them, seat belts remained a factory option until they eventually became mandatory equipment. Numerous aftermarket seat belts were available through a variety of sources.

Signal-Seeking Wonderbar Radio

The Wonderbar radio was developed by Delco Radio and released in 1947. It was the first automatic station-seeking radio tuner. The Wonderbar first became available for a Chevrolet automobile in 1953 with the introduction of the Corvette and became an option on Chevrolet passenger cars for 1956. Drivers only had to set the minimum desired signal strength with a knob and the device would scan through the radio frequencies until the first suitably strong station was detected. The signal-seeking unit could be turned off when desired via a foot-operated switch attached to the floor near the dimmer switch.

The need to set the desired signal strength was simply due to the fact radio waves lose their strength and fidelity over distance. The weaker the signal, the more static noise becomes a problem. Since there are differing levels of tolerance for static among drivers, the Wonderbar radio was designed with a means to set the minimum acceptable signal strength into which the radio would tune. A driver who was tolerant of a higher level of static could set the minimum differently than a driver who wanted only the clearest of signals. Of course, the more tolerant of static the driver was the more stations the Wonderbar would detect. With the signal strength set, the driver simply pushed the Wonderbar button on the radio, released it, and could continue to do so until a radio station of interest was found.

The Wonderbar button was attached to a push-to-make switch that allowed electricity to flow between two contacts when held. A quick push and release of the switch briefly completed an electrical circuit long enough to initiate a separate scanner circuit consisting of an electrical motor, power source, amplifier, and heterodyne or frequency mixer joined to the antenna.

The so-called "Tri-Five" Chevrolets could be had with any one of three types of radios: manual tuning, push-button tuning, and the Signal-Seeking type. This dealer display has survived and belongs to a collector of Chevrolet memorabilia. (Photo Courtesy David McGee)

This is the deluxe push-button radio as it appears mounted in the dash of a 1956 Chevrolet Bel Air Sport Sedan.

The setup worked well and it looked even better than Chevrolet's less expensive push-button radio. Their appearance alone makes them a desirable feature for today's enthusiasts who are restoring a 1956 or 1957 Chevrolet. However, owners of vintage cars equipped with the optional radio are faced with repairing their Wonderbar unit because it does not work, will not stop seeking stations, or will not scan at all. Like all radios of the era, they were fitted with old-style paper and wax capacitors that have long since failed as well as vacuum tubes that may or may not function. Today there are a few qualified repair shops offering a rebuild of Wonderbar radios.

The Wonderbar radio, such as the one on this 1958 Bel Air, offered the driver the convenience of finding a preferred radio station simply by pressing the bar at top. Setting the minimum desired signal strength with a knob let it scan through the radio frequencies until the first suitably strong station was detected. The signal-seeking unit could be turned off when desired via a foot-operated switch.

Vacuum-Operated Ashtray

This dealer-installed accessory, dubbed the "Flame-Out Ashtray," became available for Chevrolet passenger cars in mid-1957 and remained available through 1958 (though one source claimed 1960). It was a simple device for evacuating the ashtray of ashes, cigarette butts, or other small-size litter. A spring-loaded valve was mounted near the ashtray and the vacuum was sourced from the engine. With a push of a button, the debris was pulled away and deposited into a glass jar with a screw-on cap mounted on the driver's side underneath the dash. If the cigarette butt was still lit, the vacuum would extinguish it; hence the marketing name for this accessory. The jar could be removed from its mount and the contents could easily be emptied by unscrewing the cap and dumping the contents into the trash. The accessory was also available as an aftermarket item.

INDEX

Additional books that may interest you...

MOTORAMA: GM's Legendary Show & Concept Cars *by David Temple* Motorama expert and experienced author David Temple has comprehensively researched the show, the cars, and the personalities to create a fascinating story with new photos of these magnificent cars. Temple goes into detail on the body, frame, engine, drivetrain, and special features of each showcase model. He has also retraced the ownership histories of some of these cars. This book features fascinating period photography of Motorama cars at the show, in development, and at different locales. No other automotive show rivaled the extravagant and elaborate Motorama for stunning productions and awe-inspiring cars. Hardbound, 8.5 x 11 inches, 192 pages, 400 color and b/w photos. ***Item # CT533***

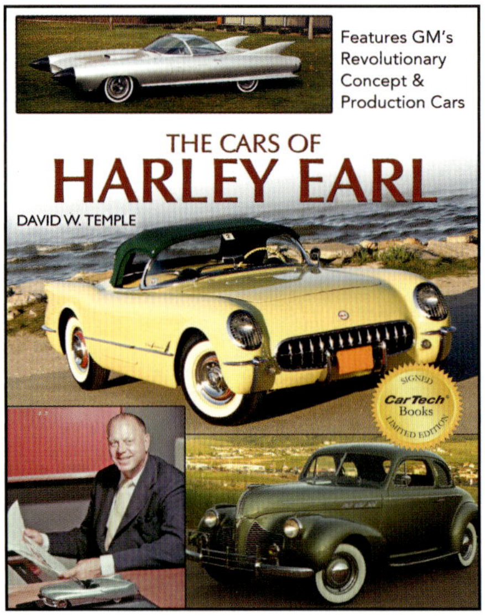

THE CARS OF HARLEY EARL *by David Temple* Harley Earl's drive toward bold and innovative design spurred American car design during the mid-twentieth century. His distinctive designs defined the 1950s finned cars and set American automotive design on the path it has followed into the modern era. With this in-depth examination, you learn the inside story of these remarkable cars and the man behind them. It's an essential addition to any automotive library. Hardbound, 8.5 x 11 inches, 192 pages, 400 color and b/w photos. ***Item # CT556***

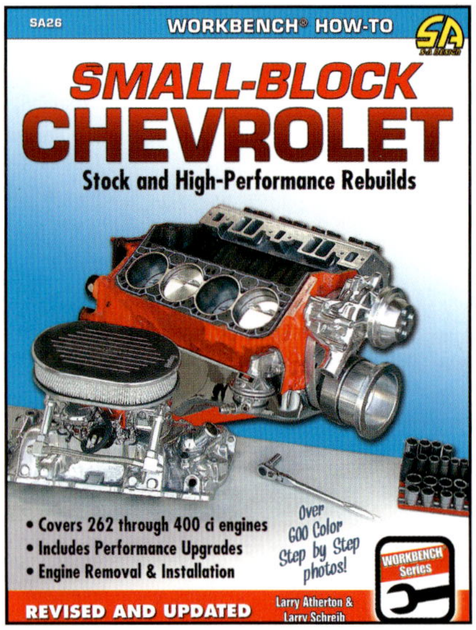

SMALL-BLOCK CHEVROLET: Stock and High-Performance Rebuilds *by Larry Atherton and Larry Schreib* In this newly updated edition, this step-by-step Workbench® Book shows you how to rebuild a stock or performance-oriented small-block Chevy in your own garage. The book includes more than 600 color photos and easy-to-read text that explains every procedure for disassembling a used engine, inspecting for signs of damage, selecting replacement parts, buying machine work, checking critical component fit, and more. Performance mods and upgrades are discussed to meet the needs of all enthusiasts, from restorers to hot rodders. Softbound, 8.5 x 11 inches, 144 pages, 637 color photos. ***Item # SA26***

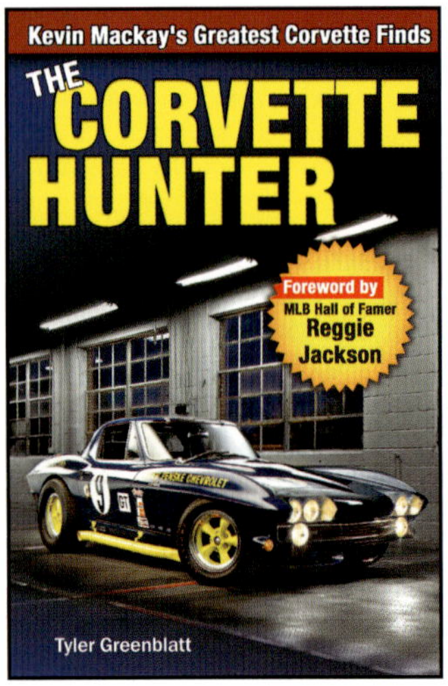

THE CORVETTE HUNTER: Kevin Mackay's Greatest Corvette Finds *by Tyler Greenblatt* Kevin Mackay tells story after story of finding and restoring valuable Corvettes such as the 1960 Briggs Cunningham Le Mans racer that took 1st in class. He also tells stories of Steve McQueen's 1966 Corvette, the 1967 Bounty Hunter racer, 1968 Sunray DX #2 and #3, and chassis #003 from 1953. Few authorities in the hobby could be counted on to provide this much entertainment in a single volume. Hardbound, 6 x 9 inches, 240 pages, 110 photos. ***Item # CT599***

Check out our website:

CarTechBooks.com

✓ Find our newest books before anyone else

✓ Get weekly tech tips from our experts

✓ Get your ride or project featured on our homepage!

Exclusive Promotions and Giveaways on Facebook
Like us to WIN! Facebook.com/CarTechBooks

www.cartechbooks.com or 1-800-551-4754